Other Titles in the Smart

D1545576

An Unauthorized Look at One Humongous Ape

King Kong's interest in nubile females remair

IT REALLY BEAU

King Kong is often
ful moment, the

KING KONG IS BACK!

EDITED BY

David Brin

WITH Leah Wilson

ILLUSTRATIONS BY BOB EGGLETON

BENBELLA BOOKS, INC. • *Dallas, Texas*

"Over the River and a World Away" © 2005
  by Nick Mamatas
"The Big Ape on the Small Screen" © 2005
  by Paul Levinson
"Not the Movie: *King Kong* '76" © 2005
  by Steven Rubio
"*King Kong* 2005" © 2005 by Bruce Bethke
"Three Acts of the Beast" © 2005
  by Don DeBrandt
"Thirty-Three" © 2005 by Rick Klaw
"*King Kong* and 1930s Science Fiction" © 2005
  by James Gunn
"The Making of *King Kong*" © 2005
  by Bob Eggleton
"Improbable Antics" © 2005
  by Dario Maestripieri
"Darwin, Freud and King Kong" © 2005
  by Joseph D. Miller, Ph.D.
"Dragon's Teeth and Hobbits" © 2005
  by Robert A. Metzger

"*King Kong* Behind the Scenes" © 2005
  by David Gerrold
"Of Gorillas and Gods" © 2005
  by Charlie W. Starr
"Why Does My Daughter Love King Kong So Much?" © 2005 by Adam Roberts
"'Twas Stupidity Killed the Beast" © 2005
  by Keith R. A. DeCandido
"Ann, Abandoned" © 2005
  by Adam-Troy Castro
"Scream for Your Life" © 2005 by James Lowder
"Divided Kingdom" © 2005 by Robert Hood
"Queer Eye for the Ape Guy?" © 2005
  by Natasha Giardina
"'Twas Beauty Killed the Beast" © 2005
  by John C. Wright
Illustrations © 2005 by Bob Eggleton
Additional Materials © 2005 by David Brin

BenBella Books, Inc.
6440 N. Central Expressway, Suite 617
Dallas, TX 75206
www.benbellabooks.com
Send feedback to feedback@benbellabooks.com

Printed in the United States of America
10 9 8 7 6 5 4 3 2 1

Library of Congress Cataloging-in-Publication Data

King Kong is back! : an unauthorized look at one humongous ape / edited by David Brin with Leah Wilson ; illustrations by Bob Eggleton.
    p. cm.
  ISBN 1-932100-64-4
  1. King Kong films—History and criticism. 2. King Kong (Motion picture : 1933) 3. King Kong (Fictitious character) I. Brin, David. II. Wilson, Leah.

  PN1995.9.K55K56 2005
  791.43'75—dc22

                                                                                2005024157

Proofreading by Jessica Keet and Stacia Seaman
Cover design by Todd Michael Bushman
Text design and composition by John Reinhardt Book Design
Printed by Victor Graphics, Inc.

Distributed by Independent Publishers Group
To order call (800) 888-4741 • www.ipgbook.com

For media inquiries and special sales contact Yara Abuata at yara@benbellabooks.com

Acknowledgments

A grateful "thank you!" to Raymond A. Dowaliby, Jr., and Jay Lamantia, webmasters of King Kong's Stomping Grounds (www.kkstomp.com), John Michlig of Fully Articulated Productions (www.fullyarticulated.com) and Bob Eggleton for their assistance in reviewing the manuscript for this book.

Contents

III. THE PHILOSOPHY OF KING KONG: THINKING ABOUT THE GREAT APE

Introduction
The Ape in the Mirror

David Brin

LONG BEFORE THERE WERE TWIN TOWERS in New York, destined to rise and then crash down upon beleaguered Manhattan Island, two other great wonders loomed over that storied skyline—behemoths that were uneven in mass but appeared as equals in our hearts, and to our watching eyes.

One was real, a building named after imperial ambition, erected in a fever of zealous optimism that defied even the depths of the Great Depression. Propelled by the renowned American appetite for commerce, technological achievement and hubristic accomplishment, the Empire State Building symbolized—far better than the later, doomed, World Trade Center towers—a brash Modernist Agenda.

The other titan was mythical, a fabled embodiment of all that contrasted with modernism. King Kong. An ape, but so much more. A proto-man, primitive, solitary and fiercely proud, representing everything about us that the architects and builders aimed to ignore, or leave behind.

But we *cannot* simply leave it all behind. The legacy follows us everywhere, even into our prim urban landscapes—the pure-but-dangerous innocent that we find both attractive and terrifying, especially when we look in a mirror and realize how few generations separate us from the jungle, from the cave.

Movies last an hour or two, but legends need time to grow. Though *King Kong* was a commercial success in 1933, the giant gorilla flickered only briefly on a few hundred screens before giving way to other stirring tales, or real-life concerns. As some of the contributors to this book relate, Kong's story had to be repeated on television's smaller screen for new generations of youth and adults to embrace it fully as their own, making it a core fable of our culture, recognized by all.

At the surface, there is little to this simple story that cannot be described in a single paragraph. A movie impresario, modeled after *Kong*'s own adventurer-producers, Merian C. Cooper and Ernest Schoedsack, takes a brave crew and beautiful ingénue to a distant, uncharted isle. There, natives barely stave off prehistoric beasts through liberal use of sacrificial virgins—the stuff of pulp adventure fiction at its lowest ebb. (Even Edgar Rice Burroughs and H. Rider Haggard gave their distressed-but-plucky damsels more to do than simply scream and writhe enticingly, the pathetically simple role assigned to poor Ann Darrow, as played by Fay Wray in the original *King Kong*.) When natives kidnap our blonde temptress as an offering to their ape-god, the impresario sends a hunky hero-type, who leads movie-expendable crewmates into the jungle to battle a mélange of exaggerated Mesozoic and Cenozoic monsters in order to rescue her. Meanwhile, Beast has a few bonding moments with Beauty…including a bit of titillating, involuntary disrobing amid several desperate battles to protect his newfound treasure.…

All right, make it two paragraphs. When Hunk steals Beauty away from Kong's pinnacle lair, Kong makes his fatal error and follows. Leaving his domain, crossing the threshold "into town," he becomes vulnerable to urban humanity's power, a power made manifest by the impresario's marvelous sleep-gas bombs. Whereupon—through the wonder of cinematic cutaway—Kong swiftly finds himself put on humiliated display in a different kind of jungle entirely. And it is here that *King Kong* becomes more than just another early talky adventure film, or a notably clever experiment in stop-action photography. For here, at his humiliating nadir, Kong wins the movie audience over, forcing them to abandon all ambivalence. It seems, at that crucial moment, as if he draws as much strength from our sympathy as from primal rage. Shattering his bonds and reclaiming his ingénue prize, he scales the highest pinnacle that he can find. Seeking refuge? Or a sacred height to make his last stand?

Kong's hopeless struggle, against a swarm of machine-gun-equipped biplanes, has to be one of the great moments of heroic imagery, not just in cinema, but on a par with Hector confronting Achilles on the Plains of Illium, or the Old Guard standing hopelessly erect at Waterloo. Equal to Crockett at the Alamo, or Balin's futile defense of Moria.

No, it is better than all of those. At least I think so. I will argue that it's so.

But that is the point of this book. To argue joyfully about the meaning of something mythical—an event that never really happened at all! You have seen the original motion picture, possibly the 1976 sequel starring Jessica Lange and probably (by now) Peter Jackson's much-anticipated 2005 remake. If you were the sort of person who believed that "a story is just a story," you would not have picked up a book like this one, in which twenty-one insightful and richly varied thinkers try to show how much more depth and meaning reside in this legend than even its original makers consciously knew.

Surveying this collection of wit and insight has reminded me of another legend about a huge and marvelous beast. *The Blind Men and the Elephant* is a familiar fable about a dozen sightless philosophers, each of whom tries to appraise and describe a pachyderm by touch alone. One, stroking a huge leg, likens the elephant to a tree. Another, fondling the trunk, declares that it is very much like a snake. So it is here, as an eclectic and brainy bunch analyze Kong in the light of their own obsessions and concerns.

Essays range from nostalgic ruminations about young boys and their love of movie monsters all the way to entrancing, alternate-world fantasies like the one by David Gerrold. (Picture Kong, the fifty-foot-tall *actor*, who tragically only managed to make this one film before his untimely death.)

Some contributors chose to be tough-minded and grownup. Dario Maestripieri, Robert Metzger and Joseph D. Miller bring in science to tell us how much (or little) of the story is plausible, while Bruce Bethke supplies yet another reality check, showing why Peter Jackson had to go back in time, setting his *Kong* in the same Depression era as the original.

> *King Kong*, on the other hand, is a period piece and must always remain so. Dino De Laurentiis' 1976 remake failed, not especially because of the lousy acting or poor direction, but because it took Kong out of *when* he belonged and tried to put him into a then-contemporary setting. The story of Kong requires innocence; it requires *terra incognita*. . . .

Other writers went to the opposite extreme of wallowing joyfully in ungrounded fantasy. For example, Robert Hood enthusiastically compares Kong to the ever-popular Godzilla, while Adam-Troy Castro dives into a provocative thought experiment pondering how the story *might* have gone, if Ann Darrow had been left with Kong in his domain on Skull Island.

Paul Levinson, Robert Hood and Nick Mamatas relate, in their essays, how the images and lessons of *King Kong* impacted both their own lives and the society around them.

Film buffs aren't neglected. Rick Klaw relates the real-life adventures of Schoedsack and Cooper, whose hair-raising personal tales rival those of any movie hero. Renowned painter Bob Eggleton covers Kong as a marvel of cinematic art and special effects, a tradition largely invented by the legendary Willis O'Brien and carrying forward through his disciple, the great Ray Harryhausen, all the way to the brilliantly creative effects wizards in today's industry (arguably the *only* consistently original and creative element in modern cinema). While Steven Rubio disdains the 1976 remake, James Lowder ponders the tradition of classic horror stories, and Keith R. A. DeCandido repudiates *all* deep explanations in favor of what-you-see-is-what-you-get; an adventure tale of beast vs. hunters and anthropological stupidity, with "beauty" having very little to do with it.

Offering a genuine "Aha!" moment, Adam Roberts argues—persuasively—that *Kong* is essentially a *children's story,* appealing to us in much the same way that size differences—at both ends of the spectrum—fascinate kids, who both stomp and chew on their toys like a gorilla and warily avoid being stomped on by grownups.

(See more on this issue of *scale* below.)

Of course, there are essays for the sober intellectual. We haven't neglected literary criticism and textual analysis.

Yet, here is where comparison to *The Blind Men and the Elephant* becomes especially apt, with each savant zooming in upon a particular perspective, almost certainly excluding other interpretations. For example, John C. Wright examines Kong in terms of American hubris in a technological age that challenges our love of the underdog. And James Gunn gives us the context of contemporary science fiction in the 1930s, when SF became the most unabashedly American of all literary genres.

Can Kong be viewed as a metaphor representing the quandary of urbanization? Like millions who were at the same time pouring into cities from the countryside, Kong was faced with the problem of adapting. A hapless rube in Metropolis, did he speak for thousands of farm boys and girls who were finding strength to be a poor match for sophisticated city ways?

It gets deeper. For example, Charlie W. Starr argues that we should reverse the usual notion, that the giant ape represents primitive man. Starr contends instead that Kong symbolizes a new, rebellious individualism—the Nietzschean *Über*man, elevated by Darwinism to a position of Godhood, only to be brought down when the limits of his own animal nature are exploited by lesser men.

Starr adroitly points out some of the historical roots to this fable: "*In* King Kong *we're presented with an archetype as old as Enkidu and the Sumerian harlot in the* Epic of Gilgamesh...." (Still, I always thought that Enkidu was the retro figure in that tale, sent by gods to enforce old ways, not to open up the new.) In contrast, Don DeBrandt roots for Beauty, seeing her less as destroyer and more as preserver or creator. In all three King Kong films, according to DeBrandt, Beauty represents civilization. Though each film shows her changed by evolving values, and at first sight she seems vulnerable to beastly ravishment, the constant theme is that she endures, triumphant in the end.

4

Even more imaginative and focused, Natasha Giardina offers a post-modernist/feminist perspective that portrays the mighty ape as a towering monument to masculine insecurity, and perhaps misogyny. *King Kong* is a pure howl, according to Giardina, relentlessly expressing fear of obsolescence and emasculation by autonomous femininity. All sides in the classic confrontation—both Kong *and* his persecutors—represent pathetically terrified and libido-obsessed maledom. With back hair, yet.

But then, does this apply to *all* movie monsters, even those who aren't beauty-transfixed or spinally hirsute? And what of women who avow different, more complex feelings toward Kong?

Almost in direct refutation, Rick Klaw tells us about the marvelous Ruth Rose, who married Schoedsack, but only after proving her independent mettle with stirring, scientific adventures around the world, in jungles and at sea. In a league with Amelia Earhart and Anne Morrow Lindbergh, Rose later became lead scriptwriter for *King Kong,* a fact that raises a myriad of questions in modern minds. Like: *Why did so little of that "spunk" get translated into the role of Ann Darrow, as portrayed by Fay Wray?* Many aspects of that character were clearly modeled after Rose herself. And yet, clearly, *she* would have been more assertive in the same situation. Pursued by a giant ape, Ruth Rose would have done a lot more than just scream.

(Is that, perhaps, one of the messages? Throughout the film, there are countless opportunities for viewers—both men and women—to say *I'd do things differently, maybe a whole lot better.*)

What fun! Clearly, all of these authors and thinkers enjoyed writing their contributions, getting a bit extravagant on the topic of... well... the most extravagant fellow ever portrayed on celluloid.

My own role appears to be a bit more sober (alas!): to offer a range of perspective tools that the reader can take along on this adventure.

Let's start with a little humility. After all, at one level it *is* "just a movie," made to earn money through the simple delivery of entertaining diversion. Let me quote from one of the better books about *King Kong* written in the last century, *The Making of King Kong: The Story behind a Film Classic* (1975), by Orville Goldner and George Turner.

Many writers have tried to justify the public's love affair with a gigantic, ugly ape by reading into the film a great deal more significance than was intended by its creators. European Communists insist that when Kong smashes the gates of the native village he symbolizes Karl Marx. A French critic, apparently confusing Ruth Rose with Rose La Rose or Gypsy Rose Lee, attributed the picture's erotic aspects to the "fact" that it was partly written by "a former strip-teaser." Others insist Kong was black in order

5

to represent the plight of the Negro in America, who also was brought to these shores in chains and exploited by the white man. Freudians point with glee to the irony of Kong retreating to the top of "the most elaborate phallic symbol in the world"—the Empire State Building. For Freudians, too, are the "mock crucifixion" of Kong, the "proxy gratification" of depression-angry audiences via Kong's destructive rampage in New York, a Brontosaurus that reminds them of Leda's swan, and so on, ad nauseam. Such notions are firmly denied by the persons behind the film, who view them variously with disgust or amusement.

We earnestly suggest that simple explanations are best: Kong was not darker in hue than any other gorilla, he smashed the gates solely because he wanted to recapture Fay Wray, his atrocious behavior in the city had nothing to do with politics or economic conditions, and he climbed the Empire State Building because it was the highest point in the city, corresponding to his mountain-top lair in his homeland. *King Kong* is exactly what it was meant to be: a highly entertaining, shrewdly conceived work of pure cinema.

Well...as I said, the elephant can be viewed from many angles. Those who take their erudite symbolism seriously (and many of our contributors do) consider it to be quite irrelevant that the film's creators denied having underlying agendas. A favorite trick of pedants and scholars (as opposed to scientists) has always been to dismiss contrary evidence as "denial" and to claim that *they* can see all the real psychological motivations. Seldom is it even acknowledged that the symbols in question (in this case a great ape) are being interpreted in a mirror of their own obsession. The scholar winds up being exposed, far more tellingly than the original creator of the work.

On the other hand...aren't the "realists" also spoilsports? I mean, what could be more absurd and churlish than to try denying us some fun...the pleasure of using our prefrontal lobes to analyze and analyze and analyze! Isn't that even more essentially human than all our vaunted technology?

Sure, King Kong himself would snort at the very idea of diagnosing his motives through nonsense like *deconstruction* and textual *semiotics*. But Kong would already have hurled this book across the river—or eaten it.

Whereas *you*...

...well, by now, you've already paid for it. So what do I care?

Hmm. In fact, I do care a bit.

Moreover, having described the topic, this book and its contents, I can safely say that it's *my* turn, now, to talk about this wonderful film and what

King Kong says to me. So let's go back to one aspect that I commented on at the very beginning—the notion of *scale*.

Is it intentional that individual human beings appear, next to Kong, just as dwarfed as *he* will wind up appearing, beside the mighty Empire State Building? Vastly overpowering any single person, he nevertheless finds himself overmatched by our joined power, symbolized by the great tower that he attempts—in vain—to conquer.

None of the essayists mention what I consider to be the most critical lesson...that we are vastly stronger working together than we are apart.

One could interpret this darkly, by making a dismal comparison to the *fascist* preaching of united will, directed by a single leader, party and goal. That vile dogma was making inroads around the world at the very time that this film was made. Certainly the fate of individualist Kong presaged the doom of millions, including many who dared resist a rising tide of ideological mania. A madness that was exacerbated, horribly, by misused technology.

On the other hand, shall we dismiss the symbols of cooperative civilization, simply because mad over-simplifiers—like Hitler and Stalin and Mussolini—were too stupid and evil to get what it is really all about? *Not* monolithic subversion of the individual, but the creative building, step by step and brick by brick, of new things by a complex process of collaboration. Universities and laws. Cities and farms. Science and ethics. Plus all the new technologies and diversions that can be used—or misused—for well or ill.

What we're talking about is a topic that was very hot in 1933...the very notion of eclectic human improvability, which underlay every modernist ambition from schools to skyscrapers. A self-critical process, constantly re-evaluating old ways, from racism to gender roles, from music to mythology. A process based upon *confidence* in our ability to guide change...or at least to cope.

(No wonder it has lately come under intense battering, by cynics of every stripe.)

The Empire State Building is very much like the *film* that viewers are watching, in a theater or at home. Somehow, a legion of financiers, craft workers, artists, actors, writers, impresarios and countless others—each of them equipped with plenty of individual ego and spirit—combined their efforts to make something marvelous that is still used and loved and discussed seven decades later. None of those who created either the building or the movie still live today. But they endure, and not only in the classic biological way, through their progeny. They also continue, cheating death, through the fine things they built together.

7

Within the film, Kong is portrayed as a mighty but sterile being, denied *both* kinds of immortality. Even if he had been left alone on his island, Kong would have become dust by the year 2000, forgotten by the forest he once dominated. Even had he won and kept his Beauty, she could never have given him children or posterity. Speechless, he cannot persuade or move us, except to the basic emotion of sympathy.

Ultimately, it is not the gas bombs or biplanes that thwart Kong, but his inability to negotiate, argue and do all the other complex things that transform an old-style solipsist ape into one of the new-style, world-changing, cooperative individualists.

His inarticulate rage allows him only to see his fellow island beasts as rivals, never as potential allies—even when dangerous new interlopers invade their shared realm.

Likewise, he is unable to appeal to social rules (and maybe even hire a lawyer) when they have him trussed and humiliated onstage.

Or to woo his love in a manner that may heed *her* needs...

...or else to accept her rejection with the balm of philosophy.

Or to adapt and adopt the technologies that are used against him.

Or to (perhaps) even *join* in the adventures and ambitions of midget-anthropoid cousins who have taken on new ambitions, new pathways of evolution that render his strength useless, leaving him far behind...

...as many of us sometimes fear that *we* are about to be left behind.

Isn't that another primal dread, reflected and diffracted by this multifaceted movie? Each of us has had to deal with obstinate, retro types who cannot deal with change. And each of us has *been* the stubborn ape, who feels threatened and intimidated by change.

Yes, the power of collaborative endeavor is impressive, whether propelled by openly cooperative institutions or by competitive capitalism, combining the labor and skills of thousands of men and women to achieve what prior generations could barely have imagined. But during the Depression—as now—people had a right to their ambivalence. They had every reason to take *both* sides—pride in civilized accomplishments *and* worry over where it all might lead.

Again, I am attracted to those core symbols in the film's most powerful scene. More than any other skyscraper, the Empire State Building seems to reject the lesson of the Tower of Babel and its classic warning to mere mortals, that they had better leave the sky alone. Like a ship, it aims boldly at the stars.

But not everyone is welcome to climb aboard. Not the super-individualist, stomping and bellowing. No Nietzschean supermen or solipsists. Not if they tread on others. Even if they *are* poignant and passionate victims of a world transformed.

8

We sympathize during the movie's most stirring scene, while a vastly courageous and confused ape clutches at his throat, staggering in dim incomprehension as biplanes swoop to brutally enforce society's limits. Limits that even a permissive culture—one friendly to individual spirit—simply *has* to impose, lest we become the howling thing that each of us still carries around inside, that remnant left over from Cain, from the caves.

We may build new ziggurats to the stars. We may climb them, while bickering and competing, negotiating and telling grand tales. We may even take our inner beasts along with us, if they'll behave, and stay confined to art, where they belong.

But poor Kong. Good old Kong. Pure and simple Kong.

Our old *king* Kong...

...he does not understand, nor is he meant to.

On the temple steps, he is our sacrifice.

I

King Kong through Time: Nostalgia, Technology and the Twenty-First Century

Over the River
and a World Away
King Kong in Brooklyn

Nick Mamatas

W̶HEN YOU MENTION THANKSGIVING, some people ponder turkey, or pilgrims, or football. Nick Mamatas thinks of King Kong, for good reason.

Let's do a little word association, okay? Okay.
  Halloween?
  Jack-o-lantern
  Christmas?
  Santa Claus
  Valentine's Day?
  Cupid
  Thanksgiving?
  King Kong

If you're from New York, you know what I mean. For nine glorious years, between 1976 and 1985, *King Kong* was a Thanksgiving Day tradition. Gather round, kids, and I'll tell you a story of a time when television sets had knobs and local TV stations had personality, of a time when WOR (not a typo; the station was so old it only had three call letters) was home to the king of all monsters.

Before the proliferation of networks and the rise of cable, lots of television was local. Most cities had at least one station with their own kiddie

13

clown programming and a late-night, groovy ghouly of some sort hosting midnight showings of B-movies. Even big cities had kooky programming: one local Bay Area station had an owner who promised his mother that as long as she was alive, he'd always run *The Streets of San Francisco*. (She lived to be an extremely old woman, apparently. While Michael Douglas is likely okay, I always wondered what happened to his old TV sidekick once the lady died and his residual checks vanished.)

It was New York that had the best local programming, too. Not only did our UHF channels (remember UHF? Likely not, as cable has sealed most households off from their weak signals) show all sorts of great stuff, like the parodic and self-parodic kiddie TV program *The Uncle Floyd Show* (the Ramones appeared on the show fifteen times!), so did our VHF independents. WPIX was not only chock-full of *Star Trek* and *Twilight Zone* marathons and 3-D showings of *The Creature from the Black Lagoon*: they had an interactive video game system. Every day, a few lucky kids would call in and repeatedly shout "Pix!" into the phone to shoot video football passes or spaceships, while us unlucky kids watched the Intellivision-style graphics and bragged that we could do better than the moron who made it through the busy signals.

WOR, which had started as an AM radio station transmitting from the L. Bamberger & Co. department store in Newark, New Jersey in 1922, had the best of the local programming. They had a *Romper Room* franchise, of course, along with *Bowling For Dollars* and the infamous *Joe Franklin Show*, the latter a schmaltzy, late-night chat show which ran from 1950 to 1990 and was helmed by one of the worst celebrity interviewers ever. (Until recently, Franklin continued to host a show on the still extant WOR-AM.) And on Thanksgiving, they had *Kong*.

I was only four when *King Kong* first aired on WOR's Thanksgiving slot so of course do not remember it. By the time I became aware of the movie and was able to anticipate the next year's showing, it seemed to me that *King Kong* had simply always aired on Thanksgiving, since the day television was invented. Back then I thought the movie must have seemed, to its 1933 audience, like a documentary about a wild ape trashing a Manhattan filled with smartly blocked hats and automats. I didn't know anything about local TV; the whole world stopped on Thanksgiving to watch *King Kong*, which was assuredly the most important movie ever made—that's why they aired it on a holiday! Thanksgiving pageants, I was convinced, should not only feature third-grade Pilgrims and Indians in paper headdresses with feathers drawn by Magic Marker; they needed to have King Kong show up, too, to overturn the Thanksgiving feast and climb Plymouth Rock.

If it sounds silly, I should note that all my little friends at school agreed with me.

King Kong wasn't the only movie they showed; *The Son of Kong* and the forgettable *Mighty Joe Young* were also on the schedule, and the day after Thanksgiving featured *Godzilla vs. King Kong*, the version with the America-friendly, Kong-triumphant ending that I always found a little dubious given the tactical advantage of Godzilla's radioactive flame breath. Though the oldest movie, it was agreed that the original *Kong* was still the best. The other flicks were ape movies or monster movies; *King Kong* was a film that had a monstrous ape in it.

Though the animation was herky-jerky and the accents and idiom already archaic, the narrative dream was so compelling. The movie just seemed real, because it made no attempts to wink at the audience, to apologize for its narrative conceit, to break the tension with child characters or comic relief. When Kong turned to the camera and thumped his chest, you *knew* he meant business, even though there was no "he" there at all. The only moment in the other films in WOR's Thanksgiving programming that seared itself into my memory is obscure: in *Godzilla vs. the Smog Monster* there is a shot, lasting less than a second, of an infant trapped and crying in the grayish sludge left behind by the titular villain. All of *King Kong* felt like that weeping baby to me; watching the movie demanded so much sympathy of a young viewer. Kong was an animal, and the victim of a kidnapping and what he saw as a romantic betrayal; *King Kong* was an action film with no "bad guys." Pretty heady stuff for a kid already steeped in the genre of simplistically moral spectacles like *Star Wars*.

There's another reason why I think *King Kong* meant so much to my friends and me in those years. We were all the sons of immigrants living in a city famous for them, and as such we knew absolutely nothing of pro football. The connection may not be obvious at first, but it's there. Kids, especially sons, adopt the interests of their parents, and sports fandom runs in the family. A game like football isn't something that Brooklyn kids will even have much of an opportunity to play, either—the streets are much more hospitable to fast-moving games like soccer and, of course, good ol' stickball. That, combined with the fact that our OTB (off the boat) fathers had no interest in the game, meant that the movie was it. I didn't even realize that Americans were supposed to undo their belts, waddle to the living room couch and watch football after Thanksgiving dinner until my family moved to Long Island during my high school years.

I still wonder if the high ratings of the annual airing were based on the heavy immigrant presence in the city. Not only did it effectively counter-program the football on the other channels, but *King Kong* is an immigrant movie. Kong himself is an immigrant, after all, and his struggles to understand the new world around him, his attempt to become king of the city amidst the phalanx of opportunists looking to profit off him, is the struggle of every immigrant. And a black-and-white movie fit right in with a demographic that still had black-and-white TVs even into the 1980s.

King Kong wasn't killed by biplanes—the Empire State Building helped do him in. As the 1970s became the 1980s, VCRs and cable television proliferated, but they were late in coming to Brooklyn. Back when I was ten, my mother called for cable for the very first time only to be told to climb to the roof of the apartment building in which she lived and look over to the Manhattan skyline. "If you can see the Empire State Building," she was told, "you get cable."

We didn't get cable. We did get a weird movie channel called Wometco Home Theater. WHT involved a decoder box that allowed locals to tune to U-68 (yes, home of the aforementioned *The Uncle Floyd Show*) and see movies, including soft-core porn after midnight. WHT didn't have any monster movies, though, and as we couldn't see the Empire State Building from the roof of the apartment building, I wouldn't even have been able to see if King Kong had escaped his chains and decided to storm the building.

Cable finally came to Brooklyn, but by then *King Kong* was just another rarely seen old movie, put on some channel or other on the whim of the programmers. WOR had moved from New York to Secaucus, New Jersey, a fate widely considered to be significantly worse than death to New Yorkers. RKO, embroiled in a scandal over secret contracts with their advertisers, was forced by the FCC to sell the station, and it took *King Kong* and the rest of its movie holdings to cable. WOR tried to recover from the loss of *Kong* with a Thanksgiving marathon of the George Reeves Superman movies, but it didn't capture the imagination like *Kong* had. The Superman movies were visually superior, but the old series had concentrated on Clark Kent as a white-bread newsman, not on Kal-El as a lost son and new immigrant. Nothing to see here, move along.

Finally, the station became WWOR, Joe Franklin retired, and the channel dropped the rest of its local programming in order to compete as a cable-friendly "superstation," à la TBS. Now it's a UPN station, and its old competitors in the monster and kung-fu movie race, WPIX and WNEW (now WNYW), are the WB and Fox stations, respectively. Poor U-68 suffered the worst fate. It became a music video channel and then surrendered to the Home Shopping Network. Of course, nobody watches UHF channels anymore, so it hardly matters. The unused sections of the UHF band are now set aside for HDTV, forever ending the possibility of a return to good local television. The New York of the 1970s is as far from the experiences of kids today as the New York of the 1930s was to me.

The roar of Kong can still be found, if you know where to look. In May 2004, I went to the famed Loews Jersey movie palace in Jersey City (where you can see the Empire State Building from the roofs of most houses!) to hear Ray Harryhausen talk and screen a newly cleaned-up print of *Jason and the Argonauts*. Harryhausen, for all his decades in the film business, fielded most of the questions he was asked and happily spoke extemporaneously about the one famous animated movie he had never even worked on: *King Kong*. Yes, he still had the decades-old stop-motion equipment he gathered back when *Kong* first inspired him. Yes, he did manage to visit Fay Wray (who died soon after the lecture) in the city and, yes, she did do the scream for him. Yes, CGI, with its too-real descents into what psychologists and cyberneticists call "the uncanny valley," disrupts the narrative dream of modern animated films. Yes, *King Kong* will never be matched, not even by the army of skeletons in the climactic scene of his own *Jason*.

Kong is still percolating through New York's pop culture, both indirectly through folks like Harryhausen and directly from those Thanksgiving airings. Go to the Chiller Theater conventions in New Jersey, walk up the long snaking lines of autograph-seekers and ask loudly about Thanksgiving. Hell, find any New York–area writer, comic creator, game designer, science fiction and fantasy artist or fan, and ask them. Read their work, and underneath it all, I bet you'll find some kid who quickly hurried through a meal of dry turkey and powdered mashed potatoes to run to the TV and marvel at the king of the beasts!

NICK MAMATAS is the author of the Lovecraftian Beat road novel *Move Under Ground* (Night Shade Books, 2004) and the Marxist Civil War ghost story *Northern Gothic* (Soft Skull Press, 2001), both of which were nominated for the Bram Stoker Award for dark fiction. He's published over 200 articles and essays in the *Village Voice*, the men's magazine *Razor*, *In These Times*, *Clamor*, *Poets & Writers*, *Silicon Alley Reporter*, *Artbytes*, the *UK Guardian*, five Disinformation Books anthologies and many other venues, and over forty short stories and comic strips in magazines including *Razor*, *Strange Horizons*, *ChiZine*, *Polyphony* and others. Some of his short pieces were collected in *3000MPH In Every Direction At Once: Stories and Essays* (Prime Books, 2003). A native New Yorker, Nick now splits his time between NYC and Vermont.

The Big Ape
on the Small Screen
King Kong at Large
in the 1950s in the Bronx

Paul Levinson

NEW YORK WAS WHERE IT WAS at for King Kong, and not just atop the Empire State Building. This metropolis was also where the myth really grew, in the minds of viewers who got a chance to watch it—not just once—but over and over again. On millions of television screens, all across New York City, *King Kong* was broadcast repeatedly, every Thanksgiving. A tradition that locked in the fable as effectively as any bard chanting a favorite tale by the campfire. Homer, eat your heart out.

It was an age before DVDs and VCRs. There was no cable to speak of, except in a few rural areas, where cable piped in the networks. Sitcoms, Westerns, soaps, news programs and variety shows were all the rage on the air. Few if any movies made it to the little black-and-white screens.

Hollywood moguls had earlier scoffed at television and its power. Who would sit home and watch a flicker on the screen when you could walk a couple of blocks to a local theater, and see a big double-feature for a quarter? Sometimes these movie houses even brought back great old movies from earlier decades. That was the only way a kid in the 1950s could enjoy the media past.

But we heard tales. From friends with older siblings. From hipper parents. For some reason, a film about a huge ape riven with love and bullets on the Empire State Building caught my attention.

Meanwhile, things were afoot in the corporate media world of that day. General Tire had acquired RKO Radio Pictures and its movie library in 1955. This meant that WOR-TV in New York City—the local Channel 9—had access to lots of movies from bygone years.

Channel 9 had little else going for it. It was not affiliated with any of the major networks. But soon it had the *Million Dollar Movie*. The station was so starved for programming that it played the same movie every night during the week, plus three times on each day of the weekend.

On Thanksgiving and the surrounding week, it played *King Kong*.

THE VIEW FROM THE GRAND CONCOURSE

You can see the Empire State Building from some parts of the Bronx. A tower of Oz at the end of the yellow brick road of Broadway—which in fact runs from the Bronx all the way downtown through Manhattan.

I used to wonder, when I was watching that fabulous heart-rending end of *King Kong*, if I would have been able to actually see the ape on a clear day if he had been on top of the Empire State Building—clutching on to Fay Wray, swatting those damned strafing biplanes—and I on the Grand Concourse or University Avenue up in the Bronx.

I settled for seeing him in my living room, on the small, blurry, black-and-white Motorola that my father had picked up "for a bargain" someplace in the early 1950s. It gave us plenty of aggravation—my father hated to pay the repairman, who was needed at least several times a year—but it also gave us miracles every night, and some nights more than others.

Television was the second medium to bring entertainment into the home electronically. Radio was the first, and therefore had to invent lots of programming—news and entertainment—as it went along. Television was able to swoop down on radio and pick up some of its stars and a lot of its programs. Jack Benny and *Gunsmoke* both made the jump into vision. And then TV turned to Hollywood and scooped up some of its movies, too.

There was and is a world of difference between seeing a movie on a big screen in a public theater and a small screen in the bosom of your home. It was more than not being hit by a Goober candy or Jujy Fruit thrown by some kid in the back row. It was more than not having to pay a quarter for the ticket. It had to do with intimacy and convenience.

Somehow, watching *King Kong* in my underclothes made me more vulnerable, more engaged, more agape at his power than if I had seen him on the screen in the Allerton Movie Theater near my apartment building. He and Fay Wray and Bruce Cabot were just a few feet away from me, for God's sake. Sometimes, when I stretched out on the scuffed parquet floor, my nose up to the screen, they were just inches from me. Skull Island and the Empire State Building both were in easy reach, as close as the pennies under the couch. When Carl Denham intoned, "'Twas Beauty killed the Beast," he was imparting that weighty lesson only to me.

MULTIPLE VISIONS

And then there was the repetition. When it's something you love, or are on your way to loving, repeat performances are a good thing. Movie theaters of course allowed people to come back and pay as often as they liked. But even if the money was no problem—and, in the 1950s, quarters added up, especially to kids on a quarter-a-week allowance—who had the time to walk the three blocks to the theater every day and/or evening? Some theaters allowed you to stay as long as you wanted and see a second or even a third showing, at no extra charge. For those that did not, you could try hiding out in the bathroom. But even in those cases, no seat in a movie theater was as comfortable as the floor of your home.

Few media in the 1950s offered satisfyingly multiple renditions, at home or at large. Rock 'n' roll radio played the same songs over and over again, but not so that you could count on hearing the specific song that you wanted. Books could be renewed from the library, but lugging them back and forth was no pleasure. No one I knew could afford to buy too many books for enjoyment—well, at least we had comic books. Most of television was as fleeting as lightning, but there was the *Million Dollar Movie*. When *Kong* was on that show, it was a comic book come to life.

Repeated viewing allows attention to detail. *King Kong* on television rewarded it. I was struck, even as a kid, that this was not just an ape-gone-wild or horror movie, but a show about show business. The expedition to Skull Island is led by showman Carl Denham. Kong is brought back to New York to make money. It's not just beauty that killed the beast, but the exploitation of venal stardom and untamed nature.

Denham's schemes may have gone awry but, I found out later, the 1933 movie that told his fantastic story grossed almost two million at the box office. And Channel 9 did okay with the ad revenue it generated from the movie. A cash register rang every time Denham spoke Kong's epitaph.

There were other provocative aspects of the story which struck me later, in retrospect. King Kong is a big, *black* ape. His attraction to Ann Darrow

(Fay Wray) plays right into Southern racist stereotypes about the lust of black men for white women—and a knockout blonde, at that. The ever-pithy Denham observes on Skull Island, as a native chief takes notice of Ann: "Blondes are scarce around here." And later, when Jack Driscoll objects that getting Kong off the island won't be easy, Denham regards Ann and replies, "But we've got something he wants."

How many children or even adults got all of this in a single viewing of *King Kong* in a movie theater back in the 1930s? Television, often criticized for diluting profundity and reducing complexity in story-telling—for going for the lowest common denominator in its programs—turned out to be the best friend the creators of *King Kong* ever had. Writers Merian C. Cooper and Edgar Wallace (and James Ashmore Creelman and Ruth Rose) couldn't have asked for more. The subtleties and depth and overtones of the plot—as well as the nuances of the direction and cinematography—all rose to the gleaming surface on the small screen's multiple showings in the living room.

The *Million Dollar Movie* thus presaged some of the advantages of videotapes and DVDs. In fact, I watched *King Kong* more frequently during most Thanksgiving weeks than I see a movie I rent from Blockbuster or cable TV's Movies-on-Demand today. The main advantage of watching movies on current TV screens—other than the size and color—is that you can pause and rewind. Kong could neither be stopped nor reversed once he began his gloriously ill-fated journey on the *Million Dollar Movie*. But you could count on him coming back for a series of return engagements every single year.

VERTICAL VS. HORIZONTAL MYTHS

The nature of the *Million Dollar Movie* audience was also different from movie-theater audiences before and after the 1950s—and DVD audiences today—and worked to the advantage of *King Kong*. People usually see movies in theaters with just one or two friends and relations. They might talk about the movie for a few minutes or maybe a few hours on and off after leaving the theater, but the next day they are not likely to discuss the movie with anyone else, unless they too have very recently seen the movie, or the subject comes up for another reason (such as an upcoming Academy Awards). DVD rentals engender even more fragmented audiences—the likelihood that someone outside of your immediate family will want to talk about a DVD you just saw is slim.

In contrast, *King Kong* was a hot subject of discussion for me and my pals for a good week or more. Thanksgiving helped us out. We were off from school for a few days and had less than the usual amount of homework (not that it would have mattered if we had had a ton of homework). We could not only watch the movie repeatedly, but talk about it in between, go over particular scenes and dialogue and details, and be primed to look out for them in the next viewing. We each had favorite scenes. Jordie loved the jungle. Ray and Phil went for the scene in which Kong broke free of his chains. We all hissed the biplanes. (What was my favorite part? Well, I liked Fay in Kong's arms—I'm a hopeless romantic, what can I tell you....) Our group mind was brought to bear in appreciation and analysis of the movie before such a phrase became common in sociological parlance. Our hyper-scrutiny left no stone unturned.

The application of many minds to an idea, theme or story is an engine of myth-making. In the old days—in classic times or, actually, all times up until the electronic age—the only way a story could be embroidered by many minds was over time. An oral account, a handwritten manuscript, even a printed book, other than an immediate bestseller, just took too long to disseminate and percolate to become a myth any time soon. In order for the critical mass of mind power to be reached, the theme or story had to be passed down and commented upon by generations of people. I call this process "vertical" myth-making.

With the arrival of the electronic age—actually, not telegraph or telephone in the nineteenth century, but radio in the twentieth—a new way of generating myths was at hand. Huge numbers of minds could imbibe a radio show at the same time. Radio was the first instantaneous simultaneous mass medium. With the advent of national networks in the 1920s, radio could reach the mass of minds needed to make a story into a myth in a heartbeat. I call this "horizontal" myth-making.

Motion pictures in movie theaters never quite had this capacity. The theater offers pockets of simultaneity, not a single wave that pulls in everyone listening at that moment. Although the requisite number of minds to make a myth could be reached in motion picture houses a lot faster than in bookstores and libraries, it was still hit or miss in comparison to first radio and then television broadcasts. Indeed, anything less than a huge hit movie with a very long run at the box office was unlikely to have any long-range impact upon our popular culture.

King Kong was of course a pretty big hit in 1933. Had it not made a strong and continuing impression, it would not have been picked up by the *Million Dollar Movie* in the 1950s in the first place. But once on television, *King Kong* played to a very different audience: a world of kids unencumbered by jobs, free to stoke their imagination and cultivate their craving to watch and talk about the big ape fighting for love atop the Empire State Building, again and again.

The "kids" part of this equation is crucial. Only children (of all ages, but usually not yet fully adult) have that unquenchable desire, the intensity, to want what they enjoy over and over. Only local, low-budget television was in a position to satisfy that need back in the 1950s.

King Kong was there for us on the *Million Dollar Movie* in New York City year after year as we grew up. The brave, doomed ape and his enduring lessons remained the same on the screen as we got older; just like a Passover seder, in which the ancient story of how the Jews broke out of their bondage is re-told around the table once a year. Except Kong's story had no happy ending, and yet was much more fun. Even a sad movie beats an upbeat religious tradition.

REPEAT PERFORMANCES

In the movie, King Kong moves both horizontally and vertically—across the expanse of the globe, as Kong is brought from Skull Island to New York City, and up (and down) the Empire State Building, as the ape makes his last stand for love.

The pattern was also played out in the way Kong built his myth in America. Horizontally, as people first saw the movie in theaters across the country in 1933. Vertically, as word of the movie and occasional return engagements simmered in ensuing years. Horizontally again, in a big way, when kids in New York City saw it over and over again at the same time on the *Million Dollar Movie*. And it was topped off with a vertical thrust, as kids saw the movie year after year on the *Million Dollar Movie* at Thanksgiving time.

The broadcasting of the exact same program on a yearly basis was something unique for media in general and television in particular. Movie theaters of course had return engagements, but not a guaranteed yearly schedule. Specific television programs were rebroadcast as reruns, series and sitcoms continued for years, but none with the metronomic rhythm of the *Million Dollar Movie* and its holiday presentations, which you could count on like clockwork.

This wasn't limited to just *King Kong* on Thanksgiving. *Yankee Doodle Dandy* was shown every year for a week around July 4th. *March of the Wooden Soldiers* with Laurel and Hardy was shown on a rival NYC TV station—WPIX (Channel 11)—as great counterprogramming to *King Kong* every Thanksgiving Day. But *King Kong* made the longest lasting impression. There are no remakes that I know of scheduled for *Yankee Doodle* or *Wooden Soldiers*.

Patriotic musicals and Christmas comedies no doubt strike chords in our popular culture very different from the spine-tingling chimes of horror-adventure movies. Frankenstein, Dracula and the Wolfman have enjoyed sequels and remakes almost every decade. But *King Kong* did it the hard way—the same movie, the same ape, the same nearly forgotten actors on little screens in living rooms year after year. The more you consider *King Kong* on the *Million Dollar Movie* in New York City, the more it all fits into place. Kong goes down fighting from the top of the Empire State Building—which, by the 1950s, was not just the tallest building in the world, but the very tower from which television transmitters were broadcasting their programs to the city. Kong came from a prehistoric island—not only was the 1933 movie prehistoric by filmmaking standards in the 1950s, it was black and white at a time when film and TV were both set to make the leap into living color. This synchrony between the story of *King Kong* and the circumstances of its presentation on the *Million Dollar Movie* helped make it unforgettable.

Indeed, I doubt that Peter Jackson would even have remade *King Kong* in 2005 had it not been for the ape's extraordinary sojourn on television in the 1950s. That small screen was a time capsule, with a window that carried Kong first into our living rooms in the dawn of television and then into our psyches and permanent popular culture the half-century after. Kong stayed reassuringly the same on the small screen for a few years, and then grew into mythic proportions in our recollections and imaginations.

So enduring was King Kong's impression on the small screen, that when the 1933 movie was released in black-and-white VHS in 1998, a typical review on Amazon.com began: "As a young child in the 1950s, I used to watch this film whenever it appeared on TV on *Million Dollar Movie*. I loved it then. I love it now. Time has not diminished the capacity of this film to mesmerize and hold the viewer in its thrall." The review was signed by "Lawyeraau." It could have been written by me, but it was not. (I don't believe in pseudonyms. Denham taught me the value of fame.)

POSTAGE STAMP RESURGENT

Television has grown enormously since the 1950s. Where once there were three or four national networks and a smattering of small local stations, today there are hundreds of stations on cable and satellite. Where once what you saw on TV was gone the instant after you saw it, and repeat performances of something you loved were a gift from on high, today we have TiVo and movies-on-demand and VCRs and DVD players and any number of ways to see something as often as we please. Where once the screen was small and black and white and blurry, today our screens are clear and colorful walls.

But the small has survived and has even mounted something of an amazing comeback. Cell phones have come in on little cat's feet—or people's little fingers—and they're not just for phone calls anymore. "Mobisodes" and "V-casts" are offering new kinds of television for cell-phonic viewing, with episodes just a few minutes long. Beyond that, pretty much anything available on the Web is becoming accessible on the cell phone.

So I'm looking forward to Peter Jackson's *King Kong*. But in an ideal world, I'd hop into my Mini Cooper after the movie and drive to a nice, quiet spot on the Grand Concourse in the Bronx. I'd make sure I could see the Empire State Building. Then I'd call up the 1933 movie on my little cell phone screen....

I know I'd watch that last scene a few times—hey, I'm not so enamored of the past that I don't take advantage of modern perks. And as I drove down to the highway afterward to get back to wherever I was going, I'd put the phone to my ear, so I could hear Denham say, "'Twas Beauty killed the Beast," one more time, just to me.

Then I'd call up some of my friends from the 1950s—Ray, Jordie; yeah, I'm still in touch with a few of them—and we'd talk about it.

What part of that is more fantasy than reality for me these days? Only the Mini Cooper—but, hey, you never know....

PAUL LEVINSON'S *The Silk Code* won the 2000 Locus Award for Best First Novel. He has since published *Borrowed Tides* (2001), *The Consciousness Plague* (2002) and *The Pixel Eye* (2003). His science fiction and mystery short stories have been nominated for Nebula, Hugo, Edgar and Sturgeon Awards. His eight nonfiction books, including *The Soft Edge* (1997), *Digital McLuhan* (1999), *Realspace* (2003) and *Cellphone* (2004), have been the subject of major articles in the *New York Times*, WIRED, the *Christian Science Monitor* and have been translated into eight languages. He appears on *The O'Reilly Factor*, *The CBS Evening News*, *Scarborough Country* and numerous national and international TV and radio programs. He is professor and chair of Communication and Media Studies at Fordham University in New York City.

Not the Movie: *King Kong* '76

Steven Rubio

THERE WERE MANY THINGS that went wrong with the 1976 remake of *King Kong,* at least according to the movie-going audiences of the time. But it wasn't the filmmakers' fault. As Steven Rubio points out, an audience nostalgic for the 1933 original wouldn't have been happy no matter what they did.

"THE MOVIE"

A sculptor friend of mine once told me the following tale. It was apocryphal, perhaps even entirely made up; my friend was a raconteur who never let the truth get in the way of a good story. As he told it, a band of anthropologists found a primitive tribe somewhere beyond civilization as we know it and began to study it. One day (and here the story starts to lose whatever remnants of truth it might once have held) the scientists decided to introduce the natives to motion pictures. And so they set up a movie screen (my friend told me the story long before the days of VCRs, much less DVD players), cranked up a projector and proceeded to show the natives the original movie version of *King Kong.* The tribespeople were enthralled at this amazing, magical feat; they loved the movie. They loved it so much that they asked to watch it again, and the anthropologists said Okay, they could watch it again the next week. And the next week arrived, and they set up the screen and the projector, and they showed another movie. This time it was…and my memory fails me, as I can no longer re-member the title of the second film. In any event, they showed this new movie, and after a couple of minutes, the tribe grew restless. After a few more, their distress became vocal. And after a few more, they started yell-ing at the screen. "Where is the movie?" they asked. "This isn't the mov-ie!" The scientists were puzzled, for they were indeed showing a movie. But the audience soon made their opinion clear: whatever that thing was on the screen, it wasn't the movie. "The movie" was *King Kong*; *King Kong* wasn't being projected; therefore, they weren't watching "the movie."

So it was that every week forever after, they would set up the screen, crank up the projector and show *King Kong*. Because it was the movie.

In 1976, Dino De Laurentiis produced a remake of *King Kong*. It seemed like a good idea at the time: the original film had long been a part of Ameri-can pop folklore, and the era of the blockbuster was upon us. Surely a new version of the old classic, spiced up with the latest special effects, would be a success. The film was made, the fans flocked to the theaters…and when it was over? "Where is the movie?" they asked. "This isn't the mov-ie!" The producers were puzzled, for they had indeed made a movie about King Kong. But the audience soon made their opinion clear: whatever that thing was on the screen, it wasn't the movie. "The movie" was *King Kong*; *King Kong* wasn't being projected; therefore, they weren't watching "the movie."

A RETURN TO CHILDHOOD

Pauline Kael's first *New Yorker* review for 1977 was of *King Kong*. Kael was the scribe of the American film renaissance of the late '60s/early '70s, a re-naissance that was already over, although few recognized it at the time. Only two months before, Kael had published her thoughts on *Jaws*, the movie that began the blockbuster era (she liked it, which is more than can be said for most of the big films that followed); before the year was out, she would review *Star Wars*, which she didn't much like. In a telling com-ment, Kael noted of the latter that "the excitement of those who call it the film of the year goes way past nostalgia to the feeling that now is the time to return to childhood" (Kael 291).

King Kong, on the other hand, was "a good time," "a romantic adventure fantasy" and "a pop classic that can stand in our affections right next to the original version" (Kael 234, 239). Obviously, Kael misused the inclusive "our" in this case, for few films have been as reviled as the remake of *King Kong*, for reasons Kael herself suggested.

28

Her review analyzed the ways the remake differs from the original. She began by arguing that the remake had to be different, "since we know what's coming" (234). She praised newcomer Jessica Lange ("you like her, the way people liked Lombard") and identified the "central enjoyment of the film" to be the relationship between Lange's character, Dwan, and the great ape (236). Kael had her own ideas about why the original film still resonated with the public decades after its release. "Kong has become a pop deity," she recognized, adding that the film has "magical primeval imagery" (234). But she also placed the 1933 version in its historical context, stating "the original *King Kong* wasn't made innocently: it was an ingeniously made exploitation picture, and camp elements are integral to it"

(237). Kael watched the remake as another movie in a long line of movies; she wasn't romanticizing the original, nor was she seeing the new film through glasses tinted with nostalgia for the old. Therefore, she assumed the differences are necessary, and her enjoyment of the remake was intertwined with her appreciation of that difference.

Which puts her in direct contrast with an awful lot of people who wanted to see "the movie"—the original 1933 film.

Jeffrey Blair Latta's invaluable Web site, Kingdom Kong, details the response of critics to the remake. "It wasn't the airplanes Dino De Laurentiis' Kong needed to fear," the Web site states, "it was the ghost of the original.... [B]y 1976, just about every critic had grown up on that version, and could imagine no other interpretation. It was the film of their childhood, seen through the worshipful eyes of children, even if those eyes now belonged to supposedly staid, learned critics." Jessica Lange was panned; *King Kong* was her first film, her two acting Oscars were still ahead of her and she wasn't Fay Wray. Vincent Canby in the *New York Times*, at least, blamed the writers rather than the actress: "The filmmakers have turned a conventional heroine into a pseudo–Marilyn Monroe character who seems less dizzy than certifiably daft, aggressively unpleasant and out of place in this sort of movie." Canby is right about one thing, the nostalgic desire for a "conventional heroine." Fay Wray was "the heroine"; Jessica Lange wasn't Fay Wray; therefore, viewers of the remake weren't watching "the heroine."

One assumes the audiences of 1933 understood the "joke" about Kong and his great love. Kong may have lacked a penis (although he did have the Empire State Building), but it was always clear that even if he did have an appendage, it wasn't going to do him a whole lot of good with Fay Wray. What wasn't a joke was the effect the pre-Code Wray had on many young boys who saw the film on television in the 1960s (even though the version shown in those days was missing the scene where Kong peels off Wray's clothes). Wray was indeed sexier than pretty much anything else on television at the time, but it was already a nostalgic sexiness, something that had taken place long ago, before most of those boys were born. It would be impossible for Jessica Lange to equal such a fantasy; even before screenwriter Lorenzo Semple Jr. inserted his 1970s sensibilities into the script, Lange was competing with nostalgia, a competition she would lose by definition. She couldn't be "the heroine." And those boys, now grown, were in fact, as Kael claimed about *Star Wars* fans, "past nostalgia to the feeling that now is the time to return to childhood." Semple's screenplay, simultaneously loving and ironic, and thus in both cases consciously distanced from the original, assumed an adult audience that could differentiate between youthful memories of Fay Wray and a modern appreciation of Jessica Lange. But the audience wanted to return to childhood.

JESSICA'S LEGS

I worked with a friend at the time the remake of *King Kong* was released who was a huge fan of the original. He had a book which detailed the making of the 1933 film, and during free moments on the job he would pore over its pages, calling me over to show me the finer points of Willis O'Brien's stop-motion techniques. My friend was looking forward to the new film; whatever disagreements he would eventually have with the production were unrecognized in advance. Jeffrey Blair Latta argues that the film's pre-release publicity helped to doom it amongst critics, who were put off by the campaign's extravagances ("The most exciting original motion picture event of all time" is a bit much, even for Hollywood), and there is no question that in the case of the film's hot-and-cold special effects, the publicity blitz likely set up expectations that couldn't be met. But I doubt my friend was the only person whose anticipation was raised by that blitz. He imagined an updated, higher-tech version of an old favorite, but what he and many others didn't realize was that they didn't want a new version of an old favorite; they wanted the old favorite. They wanted to return to childhood.

When the movie came out, the disappointment was immense. Looking for somewhere to place the blame, viewers like my friend derided the special effects, the performance of Jessica Lange or even minor issues like the World Trade Center replacing the Empire State Building. They couldn't see the movie in front of them, because it wasn't "the movie."

Take the special effects. O'Brien's work was impressive for 1933, but in the twenty-first century world of computer-generated imagery, Kong looks more quaint than anything else. The 1976 version of Kong, mostly Rick Baker in an "ape suit" (a belittling phrase for a performance Latta argues is "comparable to Boris Karloff's Frankenstein"), isn't quaint, but neither is it ever allowed by the film's detractors to be impressive. The focus is on the special effects (which Scott Weinberg, writing many years after the fact, calls "side-splittingly hilarious"), as if the problem is merely that the effects are no match for the original's. Which is true, of course—they are no match. It was forty-three years later; to utilize the same effects techniques in 1976 that worked in 1933 would have been ludicrous. But when a film has worked its way so deeply into the collective psyche, change is nearly impossible. O'Brien's were the special effects; these weren't O'Brien's; there-fore these effects weren't special. The effects draw attention to themselves because they are different from the original, and that attention snaps the viewer out of the reverie that constitutes a return to childhood fantasies.

Jessica Lange's Dwan is problematic for similar reasons. As suggested earlier, Fay Wray's sexuality is safely in the past. Dwan, though, is a sex-ual creature of the present, too "present" in fact to be of much use for childhood fantasies. Lange's gams are a special effect in their own right, and they aren't covered by an ape suit, either. But there's a more serious problem for fans wanting a nostalgic trip to the past: Dwan, and Dwan's relationship to Kong, is presented not just as an updated version of the original, but as something new and particular to the time in which it was made. (This specificity of time makes certain scenes look silly to a twen-ty-first-century viewer, but no sillier than what transpires in the 1933 ver-sion.) As Charles Taylor argued in *Salon*, "This 'Kong' is a comic book recapitulation of the war between the sexes that takes feminine coquet-ry and masculine aggression to absurd extremes, a comedy of epic sexu-al frustration." The recapitulation to which Taylor refers is informed by a 1970s pop-feminist mentality. It assumes that "feminine" and "masculine" are absurd. When Dwan calls Kong a "chauvinist," the writers are having fun with the notion of male chauvinism, but they are also acknowledging a world where male chauvinism is recognized. For men who pine for a time when the Fay Wrays of their imagination merely screamed at the sight of a big ape, such a recognition is startling and unpleasant, placing Dwan, Lange and the movie itself in the present, when what these men desire is a return to the past.

Taylor was even more on target when he stated that people "often get huffy when the ridiculous aspects of the pop myths they take seriously are pointed out to them." The remake loves those myths, but also thinks they are silly. Taylor continued:

> The movie's detractors seemed most upset that this *Kong* was a come-dy. How could a love story between a starlet and a gigantic gorilla not be?...Semple isn't out to debunk the original. There's no cynicism in his approach. Bringing the silliness inherent in this story out in the open—not just the ape-girl angle but all the portentous foreshadowing—doesn't diminish it; just the opposite. Being free to laugh makes it more involv-ing, and ultimately more affecting, than ever.

While the film has an ironic attitude that passes for comedy, that com-edy is largely self-reflexive. (As Kael noted, Semple, knowing that the audience has already heard the story, "turns our knowledge to advantage by giving the characters lines that are jokes on them" (234).) The most memorable scenes, though, have a different tone. When Kong blows dry the wet Dwan, it's a moment much lovelier and touching than anything in the original film. (Scott Weinberg, perhaps speaking for all the film's detractors, found this scene so hilarious it might induce viewers "to catapult popcorn out of your nostrils," which demonstrates the chasm between the reactions of those who like or hate the movie.) And, in perhaps the single biggest difference between the two versions of the story, the remake shows us the trip from Skull Island to Manhattan. The original jumped from Kong's capture to his introduction in New York City, but here we see Kong jailed in the bottom of the ship, a more explicit and disturbing connection between the story of Kong and the story of slavery. The film's general tone of irony would seem to make such a connection trite, but the irony is missing from these scenes, which acknowledge the racial undertones of the story in ways at which the original only hints.

P. T. BARNUM AND THE SONS OF KONG

It would be a mistake to exaggerate the qualities of the 1976 version of *King Kong*. It is a far more interesting picture than its reputation would suggest, but much of that interest comes from the ways this remake illuminates the original and its fans. I told a young acquaintance that I was writing this paper, and he told me that the remake had been on television many times when he was growing up, much as the original was for my generation. When I noted that he must have liked it to have watched it so many times, he explained that actually, he'd never been able to watch the whole thing—it was on late at night, and he always had to go to bed before the movie ended. That doesn't sound like a childhood memory that will inspire the kind of fanaticism which grew out of the original.

Meanwhile, in 1986, De Laurentiis finally "proved" what his detractors had "known" all along: that he was never interested in Kong as anything but a moneymaker. In that year, De Laurentiis produced *King Kong Lives*, a sequel to his remake. This was a movie every bit as bad as the remake's reputation. Kong, it turns out, didn't die when he fell off the World Trade Center. For the last ten years he'd been kept on life-support, awaiting an artificial heart. When the heart is ready, Kong needs a blood transfusion, but of course, there are no other giant apes in the vicinity, so what to do? Luckily, an adventurer finds a female Kong in the jungle; "Lady Kong" is used for her blood, Kong is saved and Kong and his Lady fall in love. The

usual hijinks ensue, including the lovely pair cavorting in scenes of domestic bliss. You can guess the rest, including the ending, which features
the birth of a new Baby Kong.

Here's all you need to know about *King Kong Lives* in one easy scene:
Kong, a fifty-foot ape, is wandering around in Tennessee or Georgia or
some such place down South, looking for the pregnant Lady Kong. Some
guys are playing golf and, despite the fact that Kong is fifty feet tall, the
golfers don't seem to notice that the big lug has walked onto their golf
course. So one of the golfers takes a swing, hits the ball...

...and the ball hits Kong in the face.

Surely it's impossible to rescue the reputation of Dino De Laurentiis and
his Kong oeuvre after this.

But there's more. Because in 1933, encouraged by the apparent success
of *King Kong*, Cooper and Schoedsack rushed a new film that made it to
theaters before 1933 had run its course. This film was *The Son of Kong*.
Seems the original filmmakers had money on their minds, as well.

Perhaps the problem in the 1970s was that we knew in advance that the
remake was a crass piece of commercialism, and we treated it accordingly. Kael disagreed that this was a problem: "The most meritoriously inten-
tioned movies are often stinkers, and this epitome of commercialism turns
out to be wonderful entertainment" (239). But Kael's fond review of the
film was always out of touch with the more fanatical element within the
audience. As suggested earlier, many of those fans came to the film from
re-releases and television showings. For them, the movie was always part
of the past, and nostalgia made that past seem far more pure than it was
in reality. Robert Armstrong's huckster was close to the spirit of those who
made the original movie, but later fans attached themselves to the simultaneously virginal and sexy image of Fay Wray, losing the huckster in the
process. Commenting on that supposed purity, Taylor described the movie as "what P. T. Barnum might have come up with if he'd had access to a
movie studio and lucked on to some amazing visual effects." Yet Dino De
Laurentiis gets attacked for what Merian C. Cooper and Ernest B. Schoedsack were able to take for granted. Because no one wants to be told that
their childhood fantasies are silly.

The reaction to Peter Jackson's twenty-first-century remake will be interesting. Jackson has proven himself equally at home with splatter and
big-budget mythology; his film looks, in advance, to be much better than
the '70s version. More importantly, the childhood fantasies he'll be up
against are rooted in that version, and lack the resonance with which the
original enthralled so many.

This generation is ready at last for a different "movie."

Works Cited

Canby, Vincent. "'King Kong' Bigger, Not Better, In a Return to Screen of Crime." *New York Times*. 18 Dec. 1976.
http://movies2.nytimes.com/mem/movies/review.html?title1=&title2=King%20Kong%20%28Movie%29&reviewer=VINCENT%20CANBY&v_id=27392.

Kael, Pauline. *When the Lights Go Down*. New York: Holt, Rinehart and Winston, 1980.

Latta, Jeffrey Blair. Kingdom Kong.
http://www.pulpanddagger.com/canuck/kongpage.html.

Taylor, Charles. "Fool For Love." *Salon*, 18 Jan. 1999.
http://www.salon.com/ent/movies/tayl/1999/01/18tayl.html.

Weinberg, Scott. Movie review.
http://efilmcritic.com/review.php?movie=2311&reviewer=128.

STEVEN RUBIO teaches critical thinking at American River College. His primary interest is contemporary American popular culture, and he has taught courses on *Buffy the Vampire Slayer*, teenage culture and literature and film. His writing has ranged from a computer program that simulated a therapy session to three years writing for the *Baseball Prospectus*. More recently, he has contributed essays to several books, including *The Aesthetics of Cultural Studies*, *What Would Sipowicz Do?: Race, Rights and Redemption in NYPD Blue* and *New Punk Cinema*.

King Kong 2005

Bruce Bethke

FOR HIS 2005 REMAKE, Peter Jackson chose to set the film back in its original time period, the Depression-plagued 1930s. Bruce Bethke explains why.

A bear wandered into town last week. There was nothing terribly remarkable about him. He was just another typical specimen of the common black bear, *Ursus americanus*: 300 pounds of curiosity and appetite, with impressively large canine teeth and a set of steak knives for five on each paw. At 6:30 A.M. he was spotted rummaging through the dumpster behind my favorite restaurant. An hour later he was seen crossing the K-Mart parking lot, following his nose to the drive-up window at Burger King.

Another half hour after that and he was the top-of-the-hour urgent breaking news story on all the local network affiliates. *Live Team Coverage! Bear on the prowl!*

The immediate reaction was amazing to behold. For miles around, schools went into panic-stricken lockdown and people brought their dogs indoors. In the skies above, TV chopper pilots dueled for good camera angles, like flying aces in Fokkers and Sopwith Camels. The police threw a cordon around the area and allegedly sealed it off, while officers from three neighboring jurisdictions were called in to assist. Emergency vehicles raced up and down the streets, sirens blaring, lights flashing.

The bear, realizing the jig was up, cut across my dentist's backyard, ducked through a nearby marsh and followed a drainage ditch south into an office park.

That's where he made his fatal mistake. If he'd just kept going south, he would have crossed into a heavily wooded 500-acre park, where he could have spent the next few weeks having fun, scaring joggers and mountain bikers, before finally reaching the river flats and finding his way out of town again. If he'd turned east, the authorities would have announced that he was circling back the way he'd come and let him go, all the while congratulating themselves on a situation well managed.

Instead, the bear turned west, into a densely populated residential neighborhood, and the animal control officers felt they had no choice but to dart and sedate him. By noon, the TV stations were announcing that the bear crisis was over, and showing their aerial footage of the officers dragging the sedated beast back to their truck. By 5 P.M., the TV stations were announcing that both the local zoo and the state's Department of Natural Resources had refused to accept custody of the bear, and so the city animal control authorities had been forced to euthanize him.

By 6 P.M., the animal rights protesters were out in force, demanding an inquest into the bear's death, reminding everyone that bears were here first and harshly criticizing the animal control officers for dragging the sedated 300-pound bear back to their truck instead of gently and respectfully hand-carrying it.

I am not making this up.

As I write about King Kong, I can't help but think of that poor, unlucky bear. Kong will always occupy an especially affectionate place in my mind. When I think of King Kong, I think of childhood afternoons spent with Vern, Gerry and Bobby, poring over *Famous Monsters of Filmland*, putting together Aurora monster model kits and inhaling way more Testor's airplane cement and enamel fumes than was probably good for any of us. Back in those ancient days, long before DVDs or even VCRs, it was a strangely golden time to be a fan of monster movies. All our knowledge of our monstrous heroes was based on what we'd read, what we'd heard from other kids and the occasional rare glimpse of an actual movie on late-night black-and-white TV. Yet we knew all the classic movie monsters like modern kids know Pokémon. We knew their histories, their special powers, their secret weaknesses. We could spend hours debating such enormously important topics as, who would win: Frankenstein or Wolfman?

There was another world out there, one of first-run movies, of which we were only dimly aware. In the U.K., Hammer Films was busy pounding out horror movies that were considered far too risqué for children our age, as the monster invariably stripped some lovely British lass down to her brassiere before he was vanquished. In California, Roger Corman and the rest of the American International Pictures crew were busy producing miles of grainy, low-budget footage that went straight to the drive-in movie circuit, which was my generation's equivalent of straight-to-video. In Japan, stunt men in rubber suits were busy stomping HO scale cities flat all over the Toho Studios soundstage, and when these movies occasionally crossed the Pacific, it was usually with awful overdubbing and the part of the token Caucasian played by Nick Adams.

We were dimly aware of all those movies, the ones we weren't seeing, and yet, it didn't matter. For we all knew that the best monster movies were the *old* monster movies, and they were made in *America*, and of them all, Kong was king. Yes, the Japanese could call Godzilla the "King of Monsters" if it made them feel better, but we knew that if they ever really met, Kong would kick Godzilla's scaly butt. When the 1962 Toho production *King Kong vs. Godzilla* finally made it to American television, it only confirmed what we'd known all along. Kong—even Kong as played by veteran samurai film actor Shoichi Hirose, and played as if he were an all-star wrestler in one of the most moth-eaten gorilla suits ever captured on film—was the greatest. He was the mightiest monster ever to walk the Earth.

He was the king.

Forty-some years later, I still get a thrill from watching the original 1933 version of *King Kong*. Partly it's from simple nostalgia. Partly it's because it's just such a gosh-darn swell adventure story. But in large part it's because I did a little stop-motion animation work, before I wisely realized that film school was not for me, and to this day I remain in awe of the pioneering work of both Willis O'Brien and his disciple, Ray Harryhausen. It's hard to watch *King Kong* with my ten-year-old son, as he's grown up with CGI animation and is quick to point out every continuity error and sloppy matte shot, but I continue to be amazed by the expressiveness and genuine emotion that O'Brien managed to wring out of an eighteen-inch tall puppet, one frame at a time, more than seventy years ago. O'Brien's animated Kong is so vastly superior to the full-sized head, hand and foot models RKO built for close-up shots that it's almost embarrassing when the latter appear on-camera.

Beyond the technical brilliance, though, I've long felt there was a fundamental problem with *King Kong*, but until recently I had trouble putting my finger on it. Then, as I thought of that poor black bear wandering across the K-Mart parking lot, I began to grasp the issue. My current theory goes something like this:

Some monster stories are timeless. Vampire and werewolf movies, for example, appear to be remake-proof, and very nearly actor and director-proof. Even William Shatner could probably direct and star in a serviceable vampire or werewolf movie, given a modest effects budget and a decent co-star. Other monster tales are inherently flexible enough to permit regular reinvention; for example, every generation gets to remake its own version of *Frankenstein*, as our ethical perceptions change and our knowledge of medical technology increases.

King Kong, on the other hand, is a period piece, and must always remain so. Dino De Laurentiis' 1976 remake failed, not especially because of the lousy acting or poor direction, but because it took Kong out of *when* he belonged and tried to put him into a then-contemporary setting. The story of Kong requires innocence; it requires *terra incognita*; it requires a certain level of technology, but no more. Kong requires a world that existed no earlier than 1919 and no later than 1939 and, above all, it requires a heroine who needs to be rescued and screams her lungs out when she sees the beast, not one who says, as Jessica Lange does: "I'm a Libra. What sign are you?" When Fay Wray's Ann Darrow is kidnapped by the natives and offered up as a sacrifice to Kong, Captain Englehorn barks, "Serve out the rifles! Man the boats!" and without hesitation, fifteen brave men race into the jungle to rescue her.

When Jessica Lange's Dwan is taken, a crew of modern men might very well say, "Looks like we need a new blonde bimbo, sir."

To prove my theory that *King Kong* must be a period piece, then, I'd like you to join me and my two favorite sock puppets, Rolf and Gunter, in a little *gedanke experimentieren*. Starting with the original 1932 Creelman and Rose screenplay, we're going to rewrite the script while making just one teensy change; we're going to bring the big ape into the present day. Ready? Then here we go, with:

KING KONG 2005

ROLF: *FADE IN on a composite glass shot over the Hoboken docks—New York Skyline dimly seen in background. Snow. Sounds of tugboat whistles. DISSOLVE TO—*

GUNTER: Whoa, stop right there. Docks? Tugboats? Where are we?

ROLF: On a tramp steamer, about to leave New York.

GUNTER: On a boat? Why?

ROLF: Well, because that's how we get everyone to Skull Island.

GUNTER: Skull Island? What kind of name is—oh, never mind. Where is this island?

ROLF: You're getting way ahead of the story. But if you insist....

GUNTER: I do.

ROLF: Okay, it's off the southwest coast of Sumatra, in the Dutch East Indies.

GUNTER: Dutch East Indies? You mean Indonesia?

ROLF: Yeah, right, Indonesia. Real unknown territory.

GUNTER: Hardly. The Hindus and Malays fought over that area for ages. The Moslems colonized it in the thirteenth century, the Portuguese in the sixteenth, and the Dutch in the seventeenth. By the nineteenth century it was quite well known and charted. I mean, just look at all the scientific reports that were sent out by telegraph before Krakatoa exploded. Then think of all the recon photos the Navy took after the Battle of Sunda Strait or, for that matter, of all the satellite images you can download from TerraServer.com or DigitalGlobe.com.

But never mind that. I still want to know why we're on a boat.

ROLF: Because that's the only way to get the whole crew and all their gear to Skull Island.

GUNTER: Really? I just did a quick search on AirGorilla.com. On any given day of the week there are at least eight round-trip flights from Heathrow to Jakarta. We can do the trip in fifteen hours, with a layover in Singapore. Why not fly?

ROLF: Because we'll never get all the weapons through airport security, okay?

GUNTER: The boat's carrying *weapons*? Cool! What kind?

ROLF: Rifles. Explosives. Gas bombs. Enough ammunition to blow up the harbor.

GUNTER: Wow. Does Homeland Security know about this boat?

ROLF: Look, never mind the boat. In the next scene we introduce CARL DENHAM, the man behind this whole thing. See, he's this indie filmmaker, and he's arguing with this theatrical agent—

GUNTER: On the boat?

ROLF: Will you forget the boat already? Now, Denham—

GUNTER: Doesn't have a cell phone, apparently. Who doesn't have a cell phone?

ROLF: No, Denham has a *problem*. You see, he's going off to make this sort of half-documentary, half-improv film, and he doesn't have a lead actress.

GUNTER: Or a script either, it seems.

ROLF: Right. Okay. Skipping ahead. So Denham goes into town, looking for a hot babe he can talk into being his leading lady—

GUNTER: In *Hoboken*? "Hello, sailor! For fifty dollars I'll be your leading lady all night long!"

ROLF: —and he runs across ANN DARROW, who's beautiful but obviously broke and starving, just as she's getting busted for shoplifting some food. So he takes her into a diner, buys her a meal, learns that she's an out-of-work actress and pitches her on joining the project.

GUNTER: "Hmm, let me think about it. You say you're a filmmaker and you want me to be the only woman on a boat with forty men, while we go off somewhere for three months to make a movie you won't describe? Excuse me. Officer, you may continue arresting me for shoplifting now."

ROLF: No, she says *yes*, and they ship out in the morning. Now, the next thing we do is go through a montage, to indicate weeks passing and, more importantly, to show that Darrow is slowly developing a relationship with JACK DRISCOLL, the ship's tough-guy first mate, who should probably be played by Vin Diesel if we can get him. We end the montage with the ship creeping slowly through the fog, trying to find the only gap in the reef—

GUNTER: They don't have sonar? RADAR? GPS?

ROLF: —to reach the only good landing beach on Skull Island—

GUNTER: I'm still having trouble with that name, you know.

ROLF: We'll fix it in the rewrite, okay? Now, when the fog lifts, they go ashore and find the natives all gathered in the center of the village for this sort of dance and ceremony thing. There's drumming, and singing—

GUNTER: —and a big crowd of eco-tourists with camcorders—

ROLF: *What?*

GUNTER: —and these six women from Scarsdale wearing Birkenstocks, neon-blue hiking shorts and REI windbreakers, and they are just babbling on and on about how this compares to the native cultural shindig they saw last week on—say, do we at least know by now which island group we're in?

ROLF: The Nias. The ship's captain listens to the natives' language and says—

GUNTER: The *Nias*? Dude, the Nias have the *best* surfing in the entire Pacific! They have a major tournament there every year. Like, there's this right break there that is so righteous, it's like, *whoa*, and then it's like, *whoa*, and then—

ROLF: Are you done now?

GUNTER: I think so, yes. Aside from putting in a gratuitous plug for SurfingSumatra.com.

ROLF: Thank you. Now, like I said, the natives are doing some kind of very exciting ceremonial dance in front of this huge wall that separates the human-inhabited part of the island from the rest of it, and everybody gets to speculate out loud for a minute on who built the wall, and why.

GUNTER: *I* know.

ROLF: Then suddenly the native chief spots Ann Darrow, and he shouts out—

GUNTER: *"Look, it's Pamela Anderson!"*

ROLF: No.

GUNTER: I mean, let's face it. There is nowhere on this planet you can find people who don't have a satellite dish and haven't seen *Baywatch*. Outer Mongolia, maybe. So let's just skip over whatever bit of possibly racist and definitely neo-colonialist nonsense you were about to relate and cut to the chase. Darrow winds up on the bad side of the wall, doesn't she?

ROLF: Yes.

GUNTER: And this wall was built by, who? UNESCO? The IUCN? I mean, obviously, its purpose must be to protect the native wildlife from the humans. So what's on the other side? A UN Biosphere Preserve? A wildlife sanctuary for GRASP, the Great Ape Survival Project? Another Jurassic Park?

ROLF: Close. But you've got it backward. The wall was built to protect the humans.

GUNTER: From what? Something that isn't afraid of an AK-47? Show me a modern-day Third World country that isn't swimming in AK-47s.

ROLF: This one isn't. Anyway, Darrow winds up on the bad side of the wall—

GUNTER: And Driscoll and a bunch of redshirts have to go rescue her, I get the picture. Let's skip ahead. This Kong, he's a big gorilla, right? Just how big is he?

ROLF: Oh, twenty-five, maybe thirty feet tall.

GUNTER: And you're familiar with the square-cube law?

ROLF: Not really.

GUNTER: Okay, the square-cube law says that for any given shape, the surface area increases in proportion to the square of the linear dimensions, while the volume increases as the cube of the dimensions. It's basic geometry. This means the cross-sectional strength of something is proportionate to the square of its height, while the mass—the weight—is proportionate to the cube. The square-cube law is why we don't have hummingbirds the size of helicopters or ants the size of Buicks. Their bodies couldn't support their own weight. So a typical adult male gorilla is how big?

ROLF: About six feet tall and 500 pounds.

GUNTER: Which means our twenty-four-foot-tall Kong would weigh, oh, about sixteen *tons*. He's going to have to eat a lot and he's not going to be moving real fast.

ROLF: Trust me, he moves fast. Anyway, we get this exciting chase through the jungle—

GUNTER: Following a sixteen-ton, dim-witted vegetarian.

43

ROLF: And they run into—

GUNTER: Dian Fossey!

ROLF: *What?*

GUNTER: No, really, Dian Fossey. Y'know, *Gorillas in the Mist?* Sigourney Weaver? That could really make this movie, if we have a scene where Vin Diesel gets captured by Sigourney Weaver, tied up, stripped naked and whipped with nettles.

ROLF: No, no, no! Look, there is no Dian Fossey here. No anthropologists, no UNESCO research stations, no *National Geographic* photographers, no IMAX crews, no people camping in trees to save the rainforest. This place is crawling with dinosaurs, okay?

GUNTER: Aha! So we *are* doing another Jurassic Park! Just like Willis O'Brien made *King Kong* right after he did Sir Arthur Conan Doyle's *The Lost World.*

ROLF: Noooo. . . .

GUNTER: And now we're back to the natives and that wall again. I'm telling you, it's to protect the animals from the humans. If people can hunt rhinos to the brink of extinction just to grind up their horns to make aphrodisiacs, think what a few ounces of genuine Triceratops horn would sell for. It'd be bigger than Viagra.

ROLF: Right. Skipping ahead again. Okay, so they've rescued Darrow and captured Kong, and they're taking Kong back to New York—*on the boat,* okay?

GUNTER: Oh, that's going to upset the Indonesian government. And the World Wildlife Fund. And the Fund for Animals, the Gorilla Protection Project, the International Primate Protection League, the Humane Society of the United States, the Ape Alliance, the International Gorilla Conservation Program. . .the list goes on and on. The people at WildlifePimps.com will, pardon the expression, go ape over this. Ingrid Newkirk will no doubt issue one *very* nasty PETA press release about this atrocity, and Ted Koppel will wind up interviewing Koko on *Nightline.* You remember Koko? That gorilla who communicates in sign language?

ROLF: They get him to New York—

GUNTER: How? Have you ever traveled overseas with a dog or a cat? Or even tried going through Customs with a lousy tangerine in your carry-on bag? I mean, talk about your flagrant violation of the Trafficking in Endangered Species Act. . . .

ROLF: They get him into New York—I don't know how, they bribe someone somewhere—and the next thing we see is this Broadway marquee: *KING KONG, The 8th Wonder of the World!*

GUNTER: Just down the street from *Cats*. You can spot the theater right away. It's the one with all the animal rights protestors out in front, throwing fake blood on the people in the ticket queue.

ROLF: There's some business backstage with the reporters, and then: *The curtain rises to disclose a raised platform, on which is KONG, loaded with chains and so fastened that he can move nothing but his head.*

GUNTER: Oh lordy, he's crucified. I can see the pic on the NoMoreMonkey-Business.com Web site now: *King Kong died for your sins.*

ROLF: The reporters start shooting pictures. The popping flashbulbs enrage Kong—

GUNTER: Flashbulbs? What are these "flashbulbs" of which you speak?

ROLF: —and he breaks free! The audience flees in screaming terror! Driscoll and Darrow duck out the stage door, moments before Kong smashes down the loading dock door and follows! Kong grabs Darrow and charges off into the night—

GUNTER: Heading north, to Central Park, where he can hide out comfortably for a few days until things cool down?

ROLF: No, heading south, to the Empire State Building, which he climbs. C'mon, work with me here; we're setting up the money shot. So here's Kong, standing on top of the Empire State Building—

GUNTER: Messing up the radio, TV and cell phone reception for miles around.

ROLF: —holding Darrow in his hand and roaring his defiance at the world—

GUNTER: Waiting for the TV news choppers to show up so he can begin making his statements and issuing demands.

ROLF: The police sergeant calls up the Army—

GUNTER: A clear violation of the *Posse Comitatus* Act, and something that could never happen without a court order, an appeal, a judicial review, a *guardian ad litem* being appointed for Kong and a friend-of-the-court brief being filed by PETA.

ROLF: Okay, forget the Army. The NYPD sends up a SWAT team in their own NYPD choppers—

GUNTER: That's better.

ROLF: And we get this wonderful, heart-pounding scene of Kong fighting a desperate, doomed battle against the helicopters, before he finally catches that last fatal bullet in the neck. He reaches down to gently touch Darrow one last time, with a sort of big, dumb, I-don't-get-it hurt look in his eyes—

GUNTER: Just another country kid who came to the Big Apple, fell in love with a peroxide-blonde actress and discovered too late that she would ruin his life.

ROLF: —and then he turns, staggers and plunges to his death in the streets below.

Last shot: the cops pushing back the crowd of gawkers, while Denham and the NYPD lieutenant are looking at Kong's body. The lieutenant says, *"Well, Denham, the choppers got him."* And Denham answers, *"Oh, no. It wasn't the choppers. 'Twas Beauty killed the Beast."* Fade to black....

GUNTER: And let's stop right there. Now, think this through with me. Kong weighs about sixteen tons, right? And the Empire State Building is some 1,250 feet tall? So, assuming air resistance is negligible, it's going to take him roughly 8.8 seconds to fall the distance, and he's going to be traveling at around 282.8 feet per second when he makes contact with the pavement. Now, kinetic energy equals one-half mass times velocity squared, so he's going to impact with—oh, let's round it off to 40 million foot-pounds of energy and call it close enough.

So, depending on which side of the building Kong fell off of, Denham and the cop are either going to be looking down into a crater of collapsed sewer lines, ruptured water mains, squashed pedestrians and imploded subway tunnels, or they're going to be standing knee-deep in gorilla pâté.

ROLF: You're really sick, did you know that?

GUNTER: And instead of fading to black, we roll the credits, intercut with fake actualities of New Yorkers talking to reporters. Like, "I don't see why they had to kill him. He climbed up there by himself. He would have climbed down when he was good and ready." And, "Gorillas were here first, you know. We must learn to respect and live in harmony with all of nature's creatures." Or maybe, "I just don't understand why they couldn't tranquilize him and relocate him to somewhere uninhabited, like Iowa." And the final shot is of Darrow and Driscoll sitting side by side, nervously, while Jerry Springer asks, "Ann, is there something you want to tell Jack?" And she turns to him, smiles sadly, and says, "Jack, honey? Have you ever heard the expression, once you go-rilla, you never go back?"

And thus we come to the end of our little experiment in terror. When I heard the news that Peter Jackson was doing a remake of *King Kong*, I was happy, because if anyone can do it right, he will. I fully expect Jackson's version to have first-rate acting, better than the original dialogue and state-of-tomorrow's-art special effects. More importantly, Jackson has already announced that he's remaking *Kong* as a period piece, and shown that he knows how to treat original material with respect. Peter Jackson is one of the few directors working today who seems able to resist the urge to insert jarring modernisms and, more importantly, he's unafraid to make his men *real* men, his women *real* women and his large, furry creatures from mysterious islands *real* large, furry creatures from mysterious islands. Thus, I'm looking forward to the new *Kong*, if for no other reason than I expect that this will be the version of *King Kong* that both I and my son, the film critic, can finally enjoy together.

Now if someone would just reissue that old Aurora plastic model kit....

BRUCE BETHKE works, writes, and when time permits, lives in beautiful, mosquito-infested Minnesota. In some circles, he is best known for his 1980 short story "Cyberpunk." In others, he is better known for his Philip K. Dick Award–winning novel *Headcrash*. What very few people in either circle have known until recently is that he actually works for America's leading maker of supercomputers, and all his *best* science fiction gets repackaged as "futurism studies" and sold at stunningly inflated prices to various government agencies, where it is promptly stamped SECRET and filed away, never to be seen again.

Bethke can be contacted via his Web site at www.spedro.com.

Three Acts of the Beast

Don DeBrandt

D ON DeBRANDT BELIEVES in the strength of Beauty, no matter how powerful the Beast that threatens her. Ultimately, Beauty *doesn't* kill, DeBrandt says. No, Beauty does something much more insidious and marvelous.

ACT ONE

It was Hitler's favorite movie.

It's not hard to see why, really. On one level, *King Kong* is about the brutishness and primitive nature of an inferior species; those so inclined could argue that Kong himself is just an amplified version of the natives who worship him, a glorified archetype of a mongrel race. He is defeated by technology in a clearly military victory, shot down by biplanes much like the one flown by the Red Baron in World War I.

And—even when viewed from the perspective of someone who's *not* an insane would-be world conqueror—there is some truth to this point of view. Kong *does* represent raw, primitive power, but it's not an element limited to any one branch of humanity. It's the power of the Beast, the animal that lurks in the backbrain of each and every one of us.

The original *King Kong* was released in 1933. If all the world's a stage, then the performance about to unfold across Europe and elsewhere was a morality play with a clearly defined villain—the Nazis. Some conflicts seemed as black and white as the films of the time…and despite setting box office records and winning worldwide acclaim, *King Kong's* underlying theme boils down to an equally simple, sexist message: Man's strength comes from his killer instincts. Woman—represented by Beauty—saps that strength, inevitably leading to Man's destruction.

Simple messages have a power of their own. They distill the chaos of life into easy-to-understand slogans. They promise easy answers to hard questions; they offer stability, they offer order. They speak to the Beast inside us, bypassing all that messy, complicated thinking and appealing directly to what we really want. The Beast, ultimately, is a creature of simplicity...and one of the simplest of all messages is that of blame.

Hitler himself amassed a great deal of power through blame. He blamed all sorts of people: intellectuals, homosexuals, people of varying races. Jews bore the brunt of these attacks; treated like animals themselves, they were rounded up, shipped off in cattle cars and processed through slaughterhouses.

The Jewish people, though, are a religion as well as a race. Which raises the question: which were they killed for? Where did the so-called Aryans place the blame—on the Jews' genes or their beliefs?

The obvious answer is the racial one—after all, what does the Beast know of religion? It attacks as an animal attacks, out of rage or fear or hunger. It attacks those it identifies as Other, and it is far easier to spot a different genetic mix than a different philosophy. Complexities like the existence and nature of God don't matter to the Beast...do they?

No. But the existence of other species, other Beasts, does. And a religion, it can be argued, is also a creature. A multi-celled one, to be sure, but still a living organism, one with a sense of survival and the ability to reproduce.

As the first act of *King Kong* ends on the global stage, the Beast has lost. Kong lies dead at the foot of Beauty. A metaphor for seduction, the power that ultimately destroys Kong is female—but female power is at its heart creative, not destructive. As a consequence of this power, Kong will rise again.

In a few years Hitler will shoot himself in a bunker. But other Beasts are growing stronger....

ACT TWO

"And the Prophet said, 'And lo, the beast looked upon the face of beauty. And it stayed its hand from killing. And from that day it was as one dead.'"
—Old Arabian Proverb

50

This is the quote that opens the 1933 version of *King Kong*. The 1976 remake doesn't bother with it, though it does have Jeff Bridges quoting a few other ominous-sounding historical passages to set up the mythic aspect of the monster. Many people dismiss the '76 version as a B-movie remake, but it's much better written and acted than the original. The first *Kong* was a straightforward pulp adventure that clubbed you over the head with its theme; the remake has a little more depth. Whereas the original was simply about an adventurer who wanted to make a movie starring a giant ape, the '76 *Kong* is an eco-fable about Man's willingness to rape the environment for profit—or more specifically, for oil.

Oil. The lifeblood of twentieth-century civilization, more important than gold or frankincense or myrrh. A substance so powerful that it warps reality, bending politics around it like a black hole bends light, generating both wealth and war. It's what makes our entire consumer-driven culture possible; without it, we wouldn't have cars or plastic or mass production. In the next act of our drama, Beauty is played by Western Civilization itself—and oil is the blood that runs through her veins.

Fred Wilson is the man in charge of the '76 expedition, an oil company executive hunting for a new source. He's perfectly capable of mowing down any pesky jungle—or jungle creature—that might get in his way, the sort of arrogant, greedy, short-sighted entrepreneur that typifies a particular kind of thinking—a kind of thinking all too often identified with Western Civilization in general and America in particular.

Beauty in the original version is represented by Ann, a down-on-her-luck actress, reduced to stealing food to live. When first approached by Carl Denham, the organizer of the expedition, she misunderstands when he says he wants to hire her to put out to sea with a boatload of men. Her reaction is reluctance, not outrage—she doesn't really *want* to be the ship's entertainment, but if the money's good....So, right off the bat, we know that she's a thief—and if not an outright prostitute, at least willing to consider the idea.

In the remake we have Dwan, the survivor of a shipwrecked yacht, and, like Ann, she's an out-of-work actress of questionable morals. Why the yacht blew up is never explained, but the reason Dwan survives is because she's up on deck, while everyone else is below watching a pornographic movie with the sleazy producer that brought Dwan along.

When the ship gets to the island, Dwan insists on being included—she thinks she'd be perfect for some kind of corporate spokesmodel gig. "You know, the All-American girl who was saved from an exploding yacht by *Deep Throat?*" she says.

Beauty in the '76 remake—the year the U.S. celebrated their Bicentennial—is quintessentially American, so entwined with the idea of fame that the two are almost one concept. Ultimately, that concept is also the villain: Dwan's obsession with fame leads her to become the carnival barker for the spectacle of Kong's capture, a sideshow complete with huge banners, chains to keep the ape immobilized and a gigantic *faux* crown fastened on his head.

Dwan—who's changed the spelling of her name from Dawn to be more memorable—is an American archetype. She wants to see her name up in lights; she wants everyone to love her. She wants to be a *star*. After Kong dies, Dwan is surrounded by reporters, cameras going off like muzzle flashes, the crowd of paparazzi so thick it separates her from Jack, her lover. She's gotten what she wanted, and it has destroyed everything good in her life. Kong, representing the environment and the innocence of nature, is destroyed by the selfish values of a culture obsessed with wealth and fame.

In act two of our drama, it's still Kong versus Civilization—but now, the roles have been reversed. A vain, self-absorbed Beauty has killed a noble, simple Beast, an innocent creature of God's creation. The idea that America represents these sorts of arrogant, selfish ideals was becoming more and more prevalent in the world. The spark of pity felt when Kong died in the original film became, by the second, a flame of anger; in some places Beauty was viewed with outright hatred...and the popularity of other, less noble, Beasts grew in response.

Religions feed on belief and money, and the more they have the bigger they grow. Once a religion gets to Kong size, it's almost inevitable that a schism will occur, and a smaller, more extreme version will split off: a mutant offspring espousing either a twisted or more rigid interpretation of the faith's core beliefs. These offshoots, feral descendents of domesticated parents, are usually referred to by the term "fundamentalist."

In a biological sense, the fundamentalist Beast is a niche animal; it appeals to a narrow range of people, espouses a narrow philosophy and only thrives under specialized conditions. This Beast is by nature tenacious, and can be highly dangerous when provoked. It behaves much like a mob—in many ways a fundamentalist religion is simply a mob that has been given a direction.

Christianity, Judaism and Islam have all given birth to a wide variety of these Beasts, but the factor *all* these offshoots have in common is intolerance. God, it seems, is very specific about what He *doesn't* want. Depending on the breed of fanatic, almost anything can be labeled forbidden: sexual practices, the preparation of foods, even dancing in front of others. From a secular point of view, these rules range from the absurd to the inhumane.

For example, take the injunction against idolatry as stated in the Hadith, the second pillar of Islamic faith. Taken to its extreme, it forbids creating lifelike replicas of any living creature—no statuary of people or animals at all. Under this dictate, an entire branch of art is illegal; during the reign of the Taliban in Afghanistan, many priceless works of sculpture were destroyed. If Michaelangelo's David were within their reach, it surely would have been reduced to rubble as well.

In act two, the arrogance of Western Civilization's Beauty killed the Beast of God's creation. But there is more than one Beast in the jungle...and now, the others want revenge.

The curtain on our third act rises on the morning of September 11, 2001.

ACT THREE

Buildings are often symbols.

The Empire State Building, for many years the tallest structure in the world, certainly was. After *King Kong* it acquired a different sort of notoriety—who can envision it now without seeing Kong perched at the very top, angrily swatting at biplanes?

Things change, of course. In 1976, when *Kong* was remade, the biplanes were replaced by helicopters, and the title of world's tallest hadn't belonged to the Empire State Building in a long time.

That distinction belonged to the World Trade Center.

It makes sense, then, that they would relocate the site of Kong's final battle to the WTC. It was, after all, one of the most recognizable silhouettes of New York's skyline; in fact, it's the outline of the buildings that call to Kong in the first place.

Who could have guessed that twenty-five years later, that outline would call to another Beast?

One of the most powerful and enduring images from *King Kong*—both versions—is the wall built by the natives to keep Kong on his side of the island. In the middle of the wall is an immense gate. Since the wall was made to keep Kong out, why make a gate big enough for him to walk through in the first place?

Because the gate—and the wall—are more than they appear. They're symbols of the barrier between our animal and civilized natures; we all have a wall in our heads, with a great, red-eyed Beast lurking behind it. The gate is the size it is to acknowledge that, sometimes, the Beast breaks loose...and sometimes, we even open the gate ourselves.

Symbols, like simple messages, are powerful tools. The image of a giant, enraged ape, pounding at a sixty-foot gate until he finally hammers his way through, resonates so strongly because we recognize what the act represents. When the gate is destroyed, it symbolizes not just a victory for the Beast, but a loss for civilization.

The Beast is loose. Terror and death will follow....

Aircraft have always been Kong's downfall. A quarter-century after the last time they brought him crashing to the pavement, they returned...and brought down the towers themselves.

It has become the defining event of our generation. The sheer emotional weight of the tragedy overshadows anything in its immediate vicinity; no mention of the World Trade Center or the eleventh of September is possible now without invoking the shock of that day. When juxtaposed with an immense, enraged gorilla, images from the 1976 film take on a surreal intensity both tragic and absurd.

Kong, trapped on the roof of one of the towers, is attacked by soldiers with a flamethrower. His fur ablaze, he makes a desperate leap from one tower to the other. The camera suddenly shifts to a view from the street. Overhead, a fiery shape almost seems to drift from one tower to the next....

Both versions of the film end with Kong lying dead in the street. In the remake, the camera pulls slowly back from the crowd of onlookers filling the plaza at the base of the towers; the music is haunting, as befits a tragedy. A list of names slowly scrolls past. There's no way of knowing exactly how many people were in that crowd...but watching them mill around, people of every age and race and description, I was struck by the sudden certainty that the number of people I was looking at was just under three thousand....

It has been said, more than once, that since 9/11 we have been living in fictional times. It sometimes feels as if reality itself has been supplanted by some kind of cinematic universe; as if the supervillains and monsters have somehow come to life, as if the larger-than-life conflicts and apocalyptic disasters have broken free of their chains and are now menacing the real world. Viewed in that light, *King Kong* almost seems prophetic....

But it's *not*.

We created Kong. And by *we* I mean Western Civilization, Act three's Beauty, itself; I mean Hollywood and New York, pulp fiction and adventure serials, comic books and celebrities and radio and theater, a collective imagination too wild and free to let itself be wrapped in chains. Do we go too far? All the time. Do we indulge in bad taste, crude humor, gratuitous sex and violence? You know it.

Movies, television, magazines. Singers, actors, serial killers. Everybody wants their fifteen minutes of fame, and they'll do just about anything to get it. Reality shows, blogs, guesting on *Jerry Springer*. It doesn't matter *what* you do to inject yourself into the public consciousness, as long as you're there. Does this sound like a healthy culture to *anyone*?

But it *is* a culture, an artifact created by us. It's a human construct, one that embodies our strengths as well as our flaws. Like a mirror, it does more than reflect appearance—it's also a very useful tool. It's been argued that the use of tools is the dividing line between man and Beast, but I would have to disagree. It's not the tool; it's what you do with it.

The original Kong was killed by biplanes—human beings, using technology to end the rampage of a dangerous animal. At first glance, the attack on the WTC seems similar, in an inverted way: human beings using technology as a horribly effective weapon.

But that's an illusion. Ultimately, the weapons responsible for toppling the two towers weren't airplanes—they were *box cutters*. Knives, wielded by men who had become less than human by surrendering their own will to a larger organism, becoming no more than organic extensions of it. Living weapons, walking claws and fangs.

Teeth of the Beast.

What happened on September 11 wasn't a case of technology triumphing over the Beast; in fact, just the opposite. It was the Beast itself, fastening its fangs on the throat of Beauty.

Beauty bleeds as the third act ends.

And the Beast roars.

Usually, at the end of the third act the movie is over. But that's the nice thing about our crazy, media-obsessed, mile-a-minute culture; we always reserve the right to change the rules. It's one of the things that makes us unkillable.

The Beast knows the power of Beauty: the power to seduce. It hates and fears that power, because history has shown how successful it is. Beauty doesn't confront, it *co-opts*; eventually, its enemy becomes a version of itself.

And our arsenal is pretty goddamn powerful. We have every superhero on the planet. We have the Rolling Stones, the Beatles and Elvis. We have TV and movies and magazines and the Internet. We have *supermodels*. If that isn't enough, we can always import giant ninja robots from Japan...and then there's our *secret* weapon.

Puppets.

Kong was at least half-puppet himself. Though many actors over the years claimed to be "the man inside the ape suit," there *was* no ape suit—

not in the original, anyway. Full shots were all done using miniature models and stop-motion animation, while a gigantic, hairy hand and head were used when they needed Kong to interact with human beings. The hand and the head were essentially huge puppets; on the outside they appeared to be parts of a giant ape, but on the inside human beings were in control. No different, really, than anything we've seen in any of the Muppet movies or on TV.

Or on the Web. There's a wonderful, funny Web site called *Bert Is Evil*, which documents the hidden agenda and unsavory background of Ernie's long-suffering roommate. In the sort of deranged, blackly humorous, pop-culture-heavy ironic style that the Web seems made for, we are told that Bert has connections to the Jonestown massacre, the Ku Klux Klan, the JFK assassination and more. He's Photoshopped into a number of pictures, so that he appears to be hanging with all manner of nefarious figures—including Ayatollah Khomeini.

Following 9/11, fundamentalist fanatics in Muslim parts of the world held celebrations. They gathered in crowds, cheering and shouting and praising Allah. Many of them carried signs; it's a popular practice to brandish placards bearing the likenesses of martyrs, those who've demonstrated their faith by committing public suicide and taking as many infidels with them as they could.

But—strict Islamic law forbids the realistic depiction of humans or animals. Or at least it did...but over the many years since photography has been introduced, it's gotten harder and harder for even fundamentalists to resist the lure of technology. And so pictures of martyrs—on big, full-color signs—are allowed. They look a lot like movie posters.

Beauty *loves* technology.

It's so helpful, isn't it? Even if you're a crazed fanatic going out to celebrate a crushing blow delivered to the Great Satan, access to certain kinds of tech is just so *handy*. Need a picture of the top ten Al-Qaeda martyrs? Just Google it. Look, here's a whole montage! Download it, print it off on that spiffy inkjet, staple it to some cardboard and a stick, and you're good to go.

And, hey, someone takes *your* picture. It gets posted on the Net. And there, for the whole world to see, on the bottom corner of the montage you downloaded from that site with the strange name...is Bert.

This isn't conjecture. I've seen that picture...and when I did, I knew the Beast would never win.

You can't stop us. One of our operatives has already infiltrated your organization—and the very fact that he's there at all demonstrates you've already compromised your own principles. Just be thankful we didn't send Miss Piggy....

And it's not like we're going to stop. See, we understand what *real* tools are: things that let you create, not destroy; things that disseminate information and change the way people think. Knives and guns and bombs are pathetically limited when compared to a computer or a cell phone or even a video game. PSP game platforms now let people watch movies anywhere they want—and I'm sure a number of them have already found their way into your children's hands. Somewhere out there, deep in a fundamentalist neighborhood, some kid with less-than-strict parents has a crowd of wide-eyed friends clustered around him as he proudly lets them watch *Spiderman 2*. The number of movies available for the PSP isn't that big right now—monkey-sized, you might say—but it's going to get bigger.

They'll start with blockbusters. Peter Jackson's upcoming remake of *King Kong* promises to be a surefire hit—bigger than *Spiderman*, I'm thinking—and the PSP version is gonna be *huge* with the kids. Beauty's power is the ability to seduce...and it's finally come full circle. The new *Kong* isn't a Beast at all: it's Beauty.

Act four is about to begin.

And sooner or later, Beauty *always* finds a way to kill the Beast.

DON DeBRANDT has been accused of authoring *The Quicksilver Screen*, *Steeldriver*, *Timberjak*, *V.I.* and the *Angel* novel *Shakedown*, as well as writing two books under the pseudonym Donn Cortez: *The Closer*, a thriller, and *The Man Burns Tonight*, a mystery set at Burning Man. He does not deny these charges and is currently working on two *CSI: Miami* novels.

II

The World of King Kong: Science, Art and the Making of a Classic

Thirty-Three

Rick Klaw

SO YOU THINK MOVIEMAKERS use their films to act out things they'd never do in real life? Think again. *King Kong* only hints at the wild and adventurous personalities who gathered together to make this motion picture.

For my thirty-third birthday, my wife gave me a vintage *King Kong* movie poster. The gorgeous five-foot print is a replica of the poster used for the Italian release. I doubt she understood the significance. The original *King Kong* premiered on March 3, 1933, or 3/3/33.

Numerologically, thirty-three is an important number. Jesus Christ was crucified when he was thirty-three. There are thirty-three segments in the spinal column. Thirty-three is significant in Kabbalah. The name of God appears thirty-three times in an English translation of the first chapter of Genesis (and what was Kong but a god to the people of Skull Island?).

Thirty-three symbolizes the character traits of empathy, gentleness, kindness, loving service, nurturing instinct and selfless giving with no thought of return, along with unpretentiousness, carelessness, martyrdom and slovenliness. King Kong displays all these attributes.

There are thirty-three degrees of the Masonic order. The thirty-third is the highest. While I found no evidence that anyone involved with *King Kong* was a part of the order, it would not be shocking to learn that Merian C. Cooper was a Mason.

---

[1] She was a spy for the United States from 1917–1923 in the Soviet Union and Japan and authored several books and articles about her experiences in Russia and Asia.

By the time Cooper and co-director Ernest B. Schoedsack were thirty-three years old, they had already established names for themselves by creating popular "natural dramas." Their first such film, *Grass* (1925), followed journalist/spy Mrs. Marguerite Harrison[1] on her search for the people of the forgotten Asian tribe Bakhtiari. After an arduous journey, she found them on the shores of the Persian Gulf, their winter home. Mrs. Harrison accompanied the tribe on its forty-six-day trek across the fabled Zardeh Kuh range to the high mountain valleys at the edge of the central Persian plateau. She and the filmmakers were the first white people to ever make the trip. Cooper and Schoedsack caught the entire adventure on film.

Grass premiered to critical acclaim in New York on February 19, 1925. After a successful New York run,[2] *Grass* had a national release, though with no stars and no real "love interest" it was not a national box office success. However, Jesse L. Lasky, vice president of the Paramount-Famous Players-Lasky Corporation, was impressed sufficiently enough to finance another Cooper-Schoedsack adventure.

Neither Cooper nor Schoedsack was a stranger to adventure. Both served in World War I, where Cooper ended the war as a German P. O.W. After WWI, both men aided war-torn Poland (which had declared its independence on Armistice Day—November 11, 1918) in its struggle against Soviet Premier Vladimir Ilyich Lenin, who was determined to occupy the only physical barrier between the Soviet Union and Germany.

Schoedsack, as part of the Red Cross Relief Mission,[3] was smuggling Poles out of Russian-occupied territories when the Red Army attacked Poland in January 1919. On February 9, the Polish counteroffensive began. In an effort to protect the refugee Poles, Schoedsack arranged for a Swiss military guard to escort them out of hostile areas.

Schoedsack first met Merian C. Cooper in mid-February 1919, while in Italian-occupied Vienna. Cooper had traveled there tracking his Naval Academy Sword, which he had sold during a drunken night in Annapolis in 1914 and finally managed to reacquire previous to encountering Schoedsack. Cooper, recently expatriated from a German prison where he had been incarcerated after his biplane was shot down in the Argonne, wore mismatched boots, one German and the other French. The men became instant friends.

Cooper's past was as colorful as Schoedsack's, if not more so. After Annapolis, Cooper had been a sailor and then a journalist, and served in the

---

[2] Successful enough to repay the original $10,000 investment plus a modest profit.

[3] He left the U.S. Army Signal Corps in France near the end of the war.

[4] The first US offensive during the war.

Georgia National Guard during the Pancho Villa campaign. After "getting his wings," his plane was shot down by Germans during the Battle of St. Mihiel in September 1918.[4] Cooper was awarded the Distinguished Service Cross, though he refused it on the grounds that all of his fellow soldiers "took the same risks" (Goldner 24) and therefore no one should be singled out.

After the Vienna meeting, the men went their separate ways. On October 1, 1919, Cooper reported for duty as a pilot in the Polish Air Force. He was made Squadron Commander on July 3, 1920, getting shot down once again over Soviet territory just twelve days later.

When captured, Cooper only identified himself as an American working for the Poles, as the revelation of his status as a commander would have resulted in instant execution. While he languished in prison, the war raged on. An armistice was signed on October 12, 1920, but since the Soviets viewed Cooper as an American criminal rather than a Polish P.O.W., he remained a prisoner until April 21, 1921. That night, with two fellow prisoners (Polish officers), Cooper escaped.

The three men slept during the day and traveled by night, following railroad tracks since they had no compass. They eventually hopped freight trains, and on the third day Cooper found himself in a car full of Russians. Not able to speak Russian, he feigned being mute.

They only had enough money for two days' worth of bread. When that ran out, the men traded their clothes for food. Hunger was the least of their worries, however. To elude soldiers, they once hid in a chimney for thirty-six hours. After fourteen days and 500 miles, the group, dressed in tatters, arrived in neutral Latvia, where they were rescued. Cooper made his way to Warsaw, where he was awarded the *Virtuti Militari* (Cross of the Brave), the highest tribute Poland can bestow. A statue was even erected in his honor.

On Cooper's way out of Europe, he and Schoedsack met up once again in London. Schoedsack was working as a freelance newsreel cameraman and Cooper was on his way to New York as a reporter for *The Times*. While together, they discussed creating an epic film set in some exotic place, but both men were broke and so unable to make their plans a reality.

Schoedsack's skill with a camera would soon become big news in many parts of Europe. He was present during the Greco-Turkish War of 1919–1922 when the Greeks were forced out of Smyrna (now Izmir). Three-fifths of the city was destroyed and a large portion of the Greek population was slaughtered. Schoedsack captured the battle on film and his work was shown widely. The shy Schoedsack became a celebrity and was given the Distinguished Service Medal "for humanitarian work in Smyrna and the refugee camps of the Near East" as well as "[risking] his life in the performance of duty and [being] instrumental in the saving of many lives" (Goldner 26).

In September 1922, Cooper hooked up with Captain Edward A. Salisbury and his 83-ton two-masted schooner *Wisdom II*. On ethnological expeditions, the schooner's crew had toured the world. Now Salisbury and Cooper planned to film the continuing journeys for a motion picture. When the original cameraman quit, Cooper cabled Schoedsack, who joined the crew. The Pygmies of Murderer's Island and the mounted knights of the Abyssinian Empire[5] were among the incredible sights they witnessed. Later, Schoedsack shot the first movies of pilgrims journeying to Mecca, only to lose all of his film in a shipboard explosion—the first Cooper-Schoedsack production literally went up in flames.

Returning to New York, the men were determined to make a movie similar to Robert Flaherty's *Nanook of the North*. While there, they re-established ties with Mrs. Marguerite Harrison, a widow whom Cooper had first met at a ball in Warsaw during the early days of the Russo-Polish conflict. The flamboyant Cooper convinced her to finance their next project, but as part of the agreement, Mrs. Harrison insisted on accompanying the duo on the production of what was to become *Grass*.

When *Grass* premiered in New York, Schoedsack was in the midst of a six-month job as the cinematographer on the *Arcturus* for the New York Zoological Society's expedition to the Sargasso Sea and the Galapagos Islands. It was during this trip that he met his future wife and *King Kong* co-scripter Ruth Rose.

Daughter of theatrical producer and dramatist Edward Rose,[6] Ruth Rose was mentored by legendary actor and playwright William Gillette.[7] After appearing in numerous plays and a few films, the Actors Equity Strike of 1919 prematurely cut short the petite, beautiful Rose's acting career.

Although she lacked scientific expertise, Rose volunteered for the New York Zoological Society's Tropical Research Station at Kartabo, British Guiana (now Guyana). She was soon working alongside the six trained technicians capturing and studying a variety of creatures discovered in a vast, largely unexplored jungle. The only other humans nearby were Akawi Indians and the inmates of the infamous French penal colony Devil's Island.[8] During her time in Guiana, Rose overcame her fear of snakes by adopting a small whipsnake, and later helped to capture a giant boa constric-

---

[5] Some of the Cooper-Schoedsack pictures later appeared as a three-part series in *Asia Magazine*.

[6] Best known for writing *The Prisoner of Zenda*.

[7] In the first third of the twentieth century, Gillette was famous for his definitive stage portrayal of Sherlock Holmes, and in 1930 became the first man to perform Holmes on the radio.

[8] Scene of the book and movie *Papillon*.

tor. She also survived earthquakes, meetings with jaguars and encounters with innumerable other exotic snakes. Her writing skill was respected, and she was appointed the official historian of the expedition. Magazines published her reports, and she was often quoted in books about the Beebe.

Ruth Rose also served as the historian and research technician aboard the *Arcturus*. During the 12,000-mile trek, Rose and Schoedsack fell in love.

After Schoedsack's return to New York, he and Cooper immediately headed for Siam (now Thailand) to film their next movie, *Chang: A Drama of the Wilderness*. They filmed in a jungle that no white man had ever visited, capturing close-ups of tigers and an elephant stampede[9] in the days before zoom lenses, when the heavy cameras had to be hand-cranked. The Cooper-Schoedsack footage was used as stock footage for decades in Hollywood jungle features and was a key influence on the Tarzan series as well as many adventure-exploration films of the '20s and '30s.

Both men were thirty-three when *Chang*[10] premiered to critical praise on April 28, 1927.[11] Paramount further enhanced the dramatic film by using "Magnascope," a device which widened the screen during the elephant stampede. The film was nominated by the Academy of Motion Picture Arts and Sciences as "Most Artistic Production"[12] and was considered a financial success. Jesse Lasky asked for another movie.

Soon after the premiere of *Chang*, the duo (actually now a trio with the addition of Ruth Rose) set out for Africa. In an attempt to try something new, Cooper and Schoedsack decided to incorporate actors into their next "natural drama," the first film adaptation of A. E. W. Mason's *The Four Feathers*. In post-production, the film was heavily edited by others, and new scenes not supervised by the duo were added. Dismayed by the changes, the friends edited their future films personally. Released on June 12, 1929, months after the talkies began to dominate the movie industry, the silent film was a financial disaster.

Frustrated, Cooper and Schoedsack temporarily went their own ways. Schoedsack directed the 1931 hunting film *Rango*, which featured comedic sequences with monkeys and apes. He followed it up the next year with the

---

[9] To get this famous shot, Schoedsack sat in a five-foot-square, seven-foot-deep pit covered with heavy logs. A low turret of logs was built in the center to allow a camera to project above ground level. The natives drove the elephant herd toward and over the pit. One elephant stepped on and shattered the turret, showering Schoedsack with splinters. The beast pulled his foot free and continued on.

[10] The Laotian word for elephant.

[11] Mordaunt Hall remarked, "This new subject is an unusual piece of work, beside which all big game hunting films pale into insignificance, and through the clever arrangement of its sequences, excellent comedy follows closely on the exciting episodes."

[12] It lost to F. W. Murnau's *Sunrise: A Song of Two Humans*.

first movie treatment of Richard Connell's *The Most Dangerous Game*. Cooper flew to New York to join the fledgling Pan Am's board of directors.

Since distributors insisted that movies with love interests made more money, Cooper conceived an idea for a story about a giant gorilla and a beautiful woman while in New York, and teamed up with crime writer Edgar Wallace to produce a script. While they were working on the initial draft, Wallace contracted pneumonia and died. Cooper shelved his project until he saw scenes for Willis O'Brien's *Creation*.

Willis O'Brien (Obie to his friends) was best known for his special effects on the initial film version of Sir Arthur Conan Doyle's *The Lost World* (1925). The first movie in which actors shared the screen with stop-motion effects, *The Lost World* was a commercial success that impressed even the most cynical critics.[13]

Due to a series of mishaps and studio closings, it was another five years before O'Brien started on his next feature, *Creation* (1930–31). The movie was scrapped at RKO due to budget cuts by new studio head David O. Selznick, who later produced *Gone with the Wind*. Luckily for O'Brien, the finished dinosaur effects work on *Creation* caught the eye of Merian C. Cooper, the man Selznick charged with reviewing RKO's production schedule and determining which projects were worth keeping, who had convinced Selznick to produce his new idea. For *King Kong*, O'Brien devised the most stunning special effects ever seen. His techniques in both stop-motion and fight direction influenced every science fiction film that followed.

Cooper approached Schoedsack, who was filming *The Most Dangerous Game* for RKO at the time, to co-direct. The duo used many of the sets and actors from *The Most Dangerous Game*, including Fay Wray,[14] who plays the beauty that breaks the beast's heart.

When creating the story for Kong, Cooper used himself as the model for Carl Denham, Schoedsack for the hero Jack Driscoll and Schoedsack's wife, Ruth Rose, for the adventurous young Ann Darrow. Elements of their exciting lives permeate the film. Rose and James Ashmore Creelman[15] wrote the final screenplay.

The March 3, 1933, premiere of *King Kong* was the first film ever to play

---

[13] When addressing a meeting of The Society of American Magicians in New York City, Doyle shared some magic of his own. Without explanation, he showed the magicians Obie's test reel for *The Lost World*. The entertainers and press were amazed, wondering if Doyle had indeed viewed another world.

[14] She was actually the second choice for the role. Jean Harlow was initially offered the part, but she turned it down.

[15] The prolific scriptwriter also worked on *The Most Dangerous Game*. He was thirty-three soon after *King Kong* premiered.

[16] It didn't hurt that RKO owned the Hall.

at the famed Radio City Music Hall.[16] The movie opened to amazed audiences and rave reviews. The film would go on to become the second most watched film in theaters (behind *Gone with the Wind*) and on television (after *The Wizard of Oz*).

For my thirty-sixth birthday, my wife framed the *King Kong* print. Numerologically, thirty-six has almost no significance. That doesn't stop the poster from looking cool hanging in my living room.

Works Cited

Goldner, Orville and George E. Turner. *The Making of King Kong.* New York: Ballantine Books, 1975.

Hall, Mordaunt. "The Screen." *New York Times,* 30 Apr 1927.

One of the more opinionated people in an industry of opinionated people, RICK KLAW is perhaps best known for the popular column "Geeks With Books" in *SFSite. Geek Confidential: Echoes From the 21st Century*, a collection of his critical essays, reviews and other observations, was published in 2003 by MonkeyBrain, Inc.

His writings have appeared in *The Austin Chronicle, Weird Business, The Big Book of the Weird Wild West, Gangland, Michael Moorcock's Multiverse, Science Fiction Weekly, Nova Express, Electric Velocipede, KongisKing.net, Conversations With Texas Writers* and other venues.

Klaw lives in Austin, Texas, with his wife, a cat and an enormous collection of books. He is a frequent guest at conventions, where he can be seen nattering on about apes and pop culture.

King Kong and 1930s Science Fiction

James Gunn

THE 1930S WERE A PIVOTAL TIME for science fiction, setting a tone for the field, generating some of the most mythic and enduring stories—*King Kong* among them. Is it any wonder this genre became (arguably) the most brashly unbound and "American" literary and cinematic style of all?

I saw *King Kong* when I was ten. I remember that. I don't remember where I saw it. Probably at the Ritz Theater, a neighborhood movie house just a couple of blocks from where we lived in Kansas City. It may have been at the Benton, though. That was farther away and fancier—in the summer the Benton advertised that it was "cooled with ice." At the Ritz we simply endured the summer heat; nothing else was air-conditioned, including our house. There was no use complaining, even though 1933 was the beginning of the long drought, summer temperatures went up above 110 and we went to bed with wet wash clothes or dampened sheets. The theater was where magic happened.

King Kong was magical. Nobody had seen anything like it. *The Lost World* had dinosaurs and pteranodons, but that was released in 1925. It was a silent movie with subtitles and I didn't see it until much later. *King Kong* was sophisticated: it had actors who seemed to occupy their roles; it had Skull Island, it had the giant wall that kept out something huge and dangerous, it had stop-motion models of prehistoric creatures that looked almost real, and it had Fay Wray in the palm of a giant ape. The models didn't move quite right, but we believed in them and gasped when one of the dinosaurs picked a seaman out of a tree and when King Kong wrestled with a T. rex. We even sympathized with Kong in his chains. We didn't want him to kidnap Fay Wray's Ann Darrow again, but we secretly hoped he would escape his pursuers and get back to the island he had ruled for so long and from which he had been removed by science and treachery.

And we nodded in appreciation when Carl Denham added his epitaph to Kong's fall: "'Twas Beauty killed the Beast." You wouldn't find that kind of philosophical coda in *The Lost World* or in *The Invisible Man*, either (which annoyed us with its anti-science preachment: "There are things man was not meant to know").

As avant garde as *King Kong* seemed, and as thoroughly exciting and entertaining as we thought it, the movie did not happen in isolation. It was part of its times: the depths of the Depression during which one-quarter of the population was out of work, the drought that was laying the groundwork for the Dust Bowl, the collapse of the banking system, Prohibition and speakeasies, World War I veterans marching on Washington as part of the Bonus Expeditionary Force (evicted at gunpoint by Douglas MacArthur and Dwight Eisenhower), and a search for answers to an apparently insoluble problem: how the richest country on Earth could fall on such evil times. To all of this the movies provided some relief—two hours of fantasy adventure for a dime—and it was the background against which *King Kong* was created. It was very much a Depression movie, made for people hungry for entertainment as an escape from a world that was literally depressing, and in a context of economic struggle. In fact, Ann Darrow signed on to the project and Carl Denham signed her on only because of hard times: her failure to find work and his failure to draw an audience with less escapist fare.

Changes were occurring in science fiction as well. Between *The Lost World* and *King Kong* science fiction got a magazine and then two more, and a name. Hugo Gernsback, an immigrant entrepreneur from the Netherlands, added *Amazing Stories* to his technology magazines in 1926. At first he published only reprints, mostly from Edgar Allen Poe, Jules Verne and H. G. Wells, but within a couple of years he was publishing original fiction from authors such as Edward Elmer "Doc" Smith, Jack Williamson and Philip Nowlan. Then, in 1929, he lost his magazines to front men for Bernarr Macfadden and established new ones, including *Science Wonder Stories* and *Air Wonder Stories*, which he soon combined into *Wonder Stories*; he created the term "science fiction" in its first issue.

Meanwhile, editor Harry Bates suggested to the Clayton Publishing Company that they add science fiction to their thirteen other magazines. *Astounding Stories of Super Science* was born, and the magazine prospered from its offer of two cents a word on publication when the other two (*Amazing* and *Wonder*) were paying "a fraction of a cent a word and then only upon lawsuit," as Horace Gold described it. The scene was being set for the science fiction film.

It was not that the SF film was dependent upon printed science fiction, or drew from it (until much later), but that the SF film and printed science fiction emerged out of a similar hunger for what Sam Moskowitz later called "a sense of wonder." People needed to marvel and to dream. The world—roaring in the 1920s, grim in the 1930s—was pregnant with possibilities, particularly the United States with its eye to the future and its love of the new. But first it had to get through this inexplicable period of economic distress.

One way it got through it was with the pulp magazines. Frank Munsey invented the pulp magazine in 1896 when he turned *Golden Argosy,* his boy's magazine, into *Argosy* and then into an adventure magazine for adults that offered "192 pages of fiction for a dime." Other magazines emerged as competitors: *The Popular Magazine, The People's Magazine, Blue Book.* Then the pulp magazines began to specialize. First, Munsey produced *The Railroad Man's Magazine* and *The Ocean.* Finally, in 1915, Street & Smith published *Detective Story Monthly* and, in 1919, *Western Story Magazine* and *The Thrill Book* and, in 1921, *Love Stories.* In 1923, Jacob Clark Henneberger and J. M. Lassinger published *Weird Tales.*

Somehow adventure stories, even fantastic adventure stories, were not enough for the Depression years: heroes were needed. The first of the hero pulp magazines was *The Shadow*, an outgrowth of a radio show in which stories from *Detective Story Magazine* were read by a narrator known as The Shadow. *The Shadow* was followed by *Doc Savage, The Spider, Operator #5, G-8 and His Battle Aces* and others. My first experience with them occurred when my father brought home in the spring of 1933 a copy of the second issue of *Doc Savage,* followed by copies of the other hero pulp magazines. We all read them—my father, my brother and me, and maybe some of my uncles as well. In some ways they were better than the movies. Reading an issue took as long as a day, we could go back and read them again and they cost only as much as a single movie admission.

It must have been the following year, 1934, that I discovered science fiction magazines. I had come across a used-magazine store in downtown Kansas City. It was called "Andy's" and was presided over by an old man (by my youthful standards) in a green eyeshade who sat at the front of the store and grumbled that he couldn't make a living out of old paper. He wanted to sell his magazines for a nickel each; I didn't have a nickel, but I had lots of hero pulp magazines and I traded them, two for one, for copies of *Amazing Stories*, *Wonder Stories* and, best of all, *Astounding Stories*. In those magazines I discovered the same quality of adventure that I loved in the hero pulp magazines, but also something even more exciting: strange new ideas about creatures and people and the universe, and the wonderful things that might happen in the future. I fell in love with science fiction.

This also was the time of the futuristic hero comic strip: Buck Rogers, who began life in Philip Nowlan's two 1929 novelettes in *Amazing*, began appearing in the Sunday newspapers in 1930. *Flash Gordon* provided competition in 1934. Both became film serials, though *Flash Gordon* won the race to the theaters: it was released in 1936; *Buck Rogers,* not until 1939.

Science fiction was changing in other critical ways, as well. *Amazing Stories* bumbled along in the early '30s under the editorship of the ancient T. O'Conor Sloane, but published stories by Edmond Hamilton such as "The Universe Wreckers" (1930), and psychologist David H. Keller such as "The Cerebral Library" (1931). Sloane also published the superscience stories of John W. Campbell and the first stories of P. Schuyler Miller and Eando Binder, as well as a story by Howard Fast and one by John Beynon Harris (who would go on to fame as John Wyndham). The magazine's circulation fell; it went bi-monthly in 1935 and was eventually sold to the Ziff-Davis chain in 1938.

Wonder Stories also was being transformed. Under editor David Lasser, it published some remarkable stories by Laurence Manning, particularly "The Man Who Awoke" in 1933. Clark Ashton Smith published a series of stories, in his colorful prose, between 1930 and 1933, such as 1931's "The City of the Singing Flame." Edmond Hamilton published there as well, and Clifford Simak. John Taine (the mathematician Eric Temple Bell) began publishing there in 1931 with the three-part serial "The Time Stream."

Perhaps more important, editor David Lasser resigned in 1933 to devote all his time to the Socialist movement, and Gernsback, impressed by a new fanzine called *The Fantasy Fan*, hired its seventeen-year-old editor, Charles D. Hornig. Hornig set about reinvigorating the magazine and, in 1934, joined with Gernsback in creating the Science Fiction League, which organized SF fandom into local clubs, a move that encouraged the publication and distribution of fanzines and, eventually, local, regional and world conventions.

But the most important event of 1933 was the demise of the Clayton chain and the sale of *Astounding Stories* to Street & Smith. Although the price per word paid to authors was cut in half, the publisher was in good financial shape and the money was paid on acceptance. Moreover, F. Orlin Tremaine became editor, although Desmond Hall (who had been Harry Bates' assistant editor) did more of the actual decision-making, and introduced the "thought-variant" story with its emphasis on unusual new ideas. The first of these was Nat Schachner's "Ancestral Voices." The times they were a-changing.

Science fiction, like *King Kong*, had always attracted readers with colorful images, particularly its covers. Sometimes they featured futuristic marvels or other planets, but often they portrayed dinosaurs or bug-eyed monsters (later abbreviated, so frequent were their use, to BEMs) with scantily clad women in their grasp. The covers were false advertising: the stories inside almost never included BEMs or improbable couplings. Some squeamish young readers tore off the covers. But, like *King Kong*, those covers represented one aspect of science fiction: size, scope, imagination. The lesser magazines that were published during the 1930s and into the 1940s—at their peak, in 1939, there were eighteen of them—often resorted to such images, but *Astounding* preferred provocative ideas. Even *Astounding* played with size discrepancy, however: one memorable Kelly Freas cover (later adapted as a cover illustration for a Queen album) showed a giant robot holding a wounded (or dead) human in its palm.

What was most remarkable about the 1930s was what happened after *King Kong*. In 1934, *Astounding* serialized Doc Smith's "The Skylark of Valeron," the sequel to "The Skylark of Space." The same year it published "Colossus" by Donald Wandrei and "The Legion of Space" by Jack Williamson, "The Mightiest Machine" by John W. Campbell, "Sidewise in Time" by Murray Leinster, "Bright Illusion" by C. L. Moore and "Old Faithful" by Raymond Z. Gallun. Even more important, it published the first story that Campbell wrote under the pseudonym of Don A. Stuart, "Twilight."

Any one of these stories would have made 1934 a stellar year for science fiction, but together they represented an explosion of creativity such as science fiction would not see again until 1939. Only three of these were space epics—"Skylark," "Legion" and "The Mightiest Machine"—and they became classics of their kind. Mostly they were idea stories, startling in their innovation, and "Twilight," with its quiet, philosophic tone and literary style, pointed the way toward the Campbellian Golden Age.

Wonder Stories had a good 1934, too. Eando Binder published several stories, including two serials. Laurence Manning had five stories about the Stranger Club. Leslie F. Stone, Stanton Coblentz and Edmond Hamilton contributed stories. Donald Wollheim, who would go on to become a major editor and then a publisher of science fiction, published his first story. But the most significant event was Stanley G. Weinbaum's "A Martian Odyssey," which transformed the depiction of alien species and, in ways similar to "Twilight," the writing of SF itself. Science fiction was ready for a more literate, idea-centered, scientifically based literature, and John W. Campbell was preparing himself, although he didn't know it, to take over the direction in which SF would move.

In the world outside the magazines, Prohibition ended, the man accused of the Lindbergh baby kidnapping was brought to trial, Franklin D. Roosevelt succeeded Herbert Hoover, and the second Bonus Expeditionary Force was greeted by Eleanor Roosevelt instead of Douglas MacArthur. The Dust Bowl began in 1935 but Roosevelt's New Deal had begun to take hold as well, Social Security was enacted into law and acronyms began to litter the newspapers: NRA, WPA, PWA, TVA, NLRA....

Although events in Europe and the world were still distant from American experience, they cast their shadows on the coming decade. In 1933, Adolph Hitler was named chancellor of Germany and Stalin purged his Russian rivals. In 1934, Mao Tse-tung led his followers on the "Long March," and in 1935 Italy invaded Ethiopia and the League of Nations was helpless to intervene.

The state of the world was moving in two directions: in the U.S. the economy was beginning to recover; in Europe, even harder hit by the Depression and the aftermath of World War I, people were turning to more desperate measures, including political saviors. One could almost identify American confidence in science and in the ability of government to cope with economic problems with Carl Denham and the power of his gas bombs and chains to control primitive power, and the pent-up fury of the giant ape with Europeans breaking the bonds of civilization.

Sanity and science seemed to win in the American SF magazines. Campbell had been commissioned to write a series of articles for *Astounding* about the solar system, and eighteen of them were published after June 1936. In 1937, he was invited to become assistant editor and became editor the following May. He would recruit new writers—Isaac Asimov, Robert Heinlein, Theodore Sturgeon, A. E. van Vogt—and attract older ones, including Clifford Simak, Jack Williamson, Lester del Rey, L. Ron Hubbard, L. Sprague de Camp, Henry Kuttner and C. L. Moore, to his vision of a science-based fiction written in full consciousness of what was going on in the world of science, technology and politics. His dominance of the field for the next dozen years would later be called SF's "Golden Age."

Science fiction film, on the other hand, would enter a Dark Ages. *King Kong* had been preceded by *Just Imagine* (1930), *Frankenstein* (1931), *The Island of Lost Souls* (1932) and *Dr. Jekyll and Mr. Hyde* (1932). *Deluge* and *The Invisible Man* came out the same year as *King Kong*. All of these, including *King Kong*, had reflections of "the overreaching scientist destroyed by his own creation," as *The Encyclopedia of Science Fiction* put it. The "mad scientist" theme was a common element in SF films of the 1930s (and never completely absent in later years), and the great ape, stolen from his kingdom to be displayed as "The Eighth Wonder of the World," had elements of the mad scientist in its portrayal of Carl Denham's hubris. But it was the exception—it had this primeval force, this monster from the *id*, having climbed to the top of humanity's greatest erection, be finally destroyed by the forces of technology…unless, of course, as Denham said, his death was due to his doomed love for a human woman who fit into the palm of his hand.

The Bride of Frankenstein followed in 1935 and *Lost Horizon* in 1936, but then, except for the Buck Rogers and Flash Gordon serials, and another camp serial—Gene Autry in *The Phantom Empire*—the only significant event in SF film history of the 1930s was H. G. Wells' *Things to Come* in 1936. It was, of course, a major significant event, recognized by SF fans as the most sciencefictional of science fiction films. It held up a warning about the looming threat of war and its potential for destroying civilization, and it offered salvation from a group of scientist-aviators organized as "Wings Over the World." And it culminated in a technological future wonderland threatened once again (long before C. P. Snow and his "Two Cultures" lecture) by poetic rejection of progress. At the end, Oswald Cabal tells his friend Passworthy, after the Space Gun has shot Cabal's daughter and Passworthy's son into space, that humanity has a choice: to continue its pursuit of answers to the questions life poses or succumb to the eternal rest of death. And he concludes, "Which shall it be, Passworthy? Which shall it be?"

That was Campbell's message in "Twilight" and the philosophy behind the Golden Age, and SF fans recognized it as the true statement of SF's mission: to riddle the conundrums of the universe. It was the answer to the muscular passions and unbridled desires of the great ape: the victory, not of beauty over the beast, but of rationality over the forces of destruction.

Another significant SF film would not be released until 1950, when *Destination Moon* launched a new era of science-fiction filmmaking. *King Kong* had seemed like the centerpiece of a bright new period of fantastic films, but when the Army biplanes shot the great ape from the top of the Empire State Building, they shot down SF films as well.

Orson Welles terrified a nation in 1938 with his radio version of *The War of the Worlds*, and in 1939 New York opened its World's Fair, with a celebration of technology typified in Norman Bel Geddes' design for the American city of 1960, General Motors' "Futurama." Fairgoers who had visited it wore a button that read "I HAVE SEEN THE FUTURE."

But the Nazis invaded Poland in 1939 and the future was far darker than Bel Geddes could have imagined. It was like King Kong freed from his chains and, even though science finally won the war, the world would never be the same.

JAMES GUNN is an emeritus professor of English at the University of Kansas and director of its Center for the Study of Science Fiction. He is the author of a dozen novels, half a dozen collections of stories and a dozen books about science fiction, as well as the editor of nearly a dozen anthologies.

The Making of
King Kong

Bob Eggleton

O NE OF THE MOST REMARKABLE ASPECTS of
the 1933 film was its stunning visual experience. Its
visual effects were the most advanced of that time, dis-
playing a degree of realism that 1930s viewers had never
seen. And while we've advanced significantly since, the
film's atmosphere and scenic backdrops continue to inspire more awe than disdain. Bob Eggleton explains why
King Kong should be viewed as a work of art.

King Kong is simply one of the best fantasy films ever made. Now in its sev-
enth decade, it remains timeless despite brilliant advances in film technology, high-tech special effects and digital animation. One never gets tired of
watching it and even casual fans can discover new details in the film with
each viewing. And while younger audiences often disdain black-and-white
films, *King Kong* can't be viewed any other way. The flickering silver-screen
film stock itself is part of its mythos.

Willis O'Brien's name is integrally and appropriately intertwined with
this mythos. O'Brien was the special effects pioneer who used stop-motion animation to achieve a realistic feeling in not only the giant ape, but
in the various dinosaurs and creatures also seen in the film. Born in 1886,
O'Brien was involved in the making of early silent films such as *The Dinosaur and the Missing Link—A Prehistoric Tragedy* (1915) and *The Ghost of
Slumber Mountain* (1918), in which he began fine-tuning his stop-motion
animation technique.

Stop-motion animation is the process of creating articulated models which are then filmed one frame at a time. Parts of the model are moved carefully and minutely between filmed frames so as to create, in essence, a series of photographs. When shown continuously in sequence at film speed, these single shots give the illusion of a living, moving creature. A miniature landscape with multilayered glass paintings for the backdrop completes the very effective illusion. There were an astonishing 220 cuts of animation done for the original *King Kong*, though various censors and edits over time have caused this number to vary. Prior to *Kong*, audiences of the silent era had seen the fantastic sights of "living" dinosaurs, also thanks to Willis O'Brien, via the film *The Lost World* (1925). Though only made eight years prior to *Kong*, it seems far more primitive and less successful in terms of technique. *Kong*'s completely convincing world of visual effects, along with the advent of sound, left its 1933 audience forming lines around the block.

For *King Kong*, O'Brien had a staff of talented artists working with him. Illustrators Byron Crabbe, Mario Larrinaga and Duncan Gleason, as well as O'Brien himself, contributed stunning conceptual drawings of ideas and scenes based upon the initial script, in order to secure backing for producer/director Merian C. Cooper from RKO. At the height of the Great Depression, spending money on an outlandish film extravaganza, especially one in which the star was to be a giant gorilla on an exotic island, was not high on the list of priorities for the cash-strapped movie studios. Fortunately, the concept art helped sell the idea in many major ways. The drawings were also used as storyboards to design effects sequences and, in many cases, they stuck to them closely. O'Brien designed and then built the giant apelike creature and various prehistoric animals used in the film with armatures out of machine metal, including ball-and-socket joints, in order to duplicate real anatomical movement.

O'Brien hired Marcel Delgado to build the various detailed models over the metal armature using foam, latex and, in the case of Kong, a furry coat. To ensure realism, the foam was applied in a way that made its movements mimic the workings of muscles. Not only did Delgado create the titular Kong himself (several different models were created, which is why Kong appears subtly different in various scenes of the film[1]), but also a range of dinosaurs and prehistoric animals. These included a "carnivorous" Brontosaurus, a Tyrannosaurus rex, a Stegosaur, Pteranodons, an Elasmosaur, an unknown lizard with forearms but apparently no legs, several model humans Kong would either throw (or, in the case of Fay Wray, carry) and

---

[1] Though this was also due to the models having to be "stripped" and re-skinned nearly every evening, subtly changing the appearance of even the individual models from day to day.

most curiously, the fabled "giant spider" in the chasm that was unfortunately edited out of many prints of the film.

The technique was state-of–the-art at the time but is now simply explained and considered cumbersome and outdated. Miniature sets of lush forests, rock outcroppings and various buildings were constructed on tabletops to form most of the foreground of the shots. The middle ground was a flat tabletop where the model sat and was manipulated by hand as a different shot was taken of each action in a painstakingly long frame-by-frame process. The background consisted of multiple layers of painted glass which, when placed inches apart, gave the illusion of depth. If a live-action element was needed, it would be filmed and rear-projected onto the glass, thus giving the complete illusion of a person in the miniature scene. One improvement O'Brien was able to make over his previous work on *The Lost World* was the use of the traveling matte, which allowed for greater movement of elements in a scene and thus was more convincing.

What Cooper and co-director/producer Ernest P. Schoedsack wanted was an exotic island unlike anything anyone had seen so far, so they went for an over-the-top look with rich canopies of trees, including a sun-dappled, overgrown surface that is mysteriously foreboding yet begging for exploration. On this richly imagined island arrives the crew of a tramp freighter, the *Venture*, chartered by movie mogul Carl Denham looking to film his tale of "Beauty"—Ann Darrow—and the "Beast"—the legendary Kong.

A Brontosaur (or, more correctly, an Apatosaur) attacks the landing-party from the *Venture* as they cross a fog-enshrouded river. The creature is depicted not only aggressively destroying the raft and eating a few of the unlucky occupants, but also chasing a terrorized man up a tree and consuming him, as well. This is hardly the behavior of what we now understand from fossil evidence to be the strictly vegetarian Brontosaur. But this fact hardly ruins the action, mood or complete believability and scary thrill of the scene. With its glass-painted trees, fog and foreground vegetation, the scene positively drips with atmosphere as the Brontosaur chases the surviving crewmen onto the huge ancient log that bridges a mysterious chasm we soon discover is populated by an oversized, man-eating spider and several ferocious, two-legged lizards.

This scene (which was for many years doubted to exist, and can only be seen in the form of an old photograph that survived; the footage itself is suspected lost forever) was cut after a first viewing of the finished film. Cooper apparently felt it brought the pace of the scene to a screeching halt, though another story says studio heads wanted the film's number of reels to be shortened from fourteen to eleven, and still another version has a state film board demanding the horrifying scene trimmed out due to its excessively violent content. Unfortunately, we may never really know the truth.

Originally, Kong was to have a battle with several Triceratopses. A scene in which one of the crewmen is actually chased by one of the horned dinosaurs was partially filmed, but then dropped. Instead, Denham's men were to be chased onto the log-bridge by another prehistoric animal: a large two-horned mammal called an Arsinoitherium. However, Cooper suddenly decided he wanted a Styracosaur—another ceratopsian dinosaur—to do the chasing. In the end, due to running time and pacing, the whole scene was dropped and, through clever editing, the Brontosaur is what appears to chase the men onto the log.

Another dinosaur, this time a Stegosaur, appears from the far background as Carl Denham and the *Venture* crew go in search of Ann. As it charges, it attacks quite aggressively, creating a terrific scene in which the action unfolds in seconds. There is a visual glitch as the crew walks by the vanquished beast—it is obviously out of proportion to the humans in the scene—but the audience is so busy catching its collective breath that it hardly notices. The beast's spiked tail, thrashing reflexively as it dies, gives us one more good jump just as we thought things were quiet.

The Tyrannosaurus rex is perhaps the most iconic of Kong's opponents. It appears onscreen when the ape temporarily leaves his prize, Ann, in the crook of a tall dead tree in order to deal with the pursuers from the *Venture*. The dinosaur wanders quietly in from the lush background and leers hungrily at Ann until her screams alert Kong to the danger. As the two beasts attack each other, the Tyrannosaurus rex proves quite agile with its whipping tail and lizard-like movements. In truth, the tail would not have been that flexible, since it was, to the best of our knowledge, mostly used for pelvic stability and sometimes mating. While newly discovered paleontological information in recent years has made the dinosaurs in *King Kong* appear outdated from a scientific viewpoint, the creatures are depicted, romantically, as we think they *should* be. As Ray Harryhausen once commented, "Dinosaurs still looked better with their tails on the ground!"

The scene itself is absolutely terrific, featuring not only the live action of Fay Wray (as well as a miniature model of her), but mid-ground stop-motion action and a fantastic multilayered glass backdrop. Kong vanquishes the saurian beast by breaking its jaws and then, in a classic Willis O'Brien touch, pokes and plays with the flaccid jaw in an almost comedic way, just to make sure the creature is good and dead. Comically heightened by Max Steiner's music, the scene, and others like it, gives the ape character. It makes him more than a monster, and that endears him to us.

Finally, in what was perhaps the toughest and most breathtaking piece of animation in the film, Kong battles a Pteranodon attempting to make off with his fair lady. To create this scene, set atop Kong's lookout precipice, O'Brien had to suspend his winged beast from wires and create meticulous animation involving frame-by-frame camera shots while changing the positions of the Pteranodon and Kong models every other frame.

Following the success of *King Kong*, O'Brien went on to work on *The Son of Kong* (1933), for which Merian Cooper assembled essentially the same creative team for the somewhat smaller sequel to the original epic. O'Brien created not only the smaller and quite enchanting albino simian "son" (Denham only really assumes it is the son of Kong, as it is the second giant ape he has found on the island), but also a ravenous cave bear, a Styracosaur (held over from the first film) and a mythological four-legged sea monster.

81

Through the 1930s and 1940s, O'Brien continued to refine his animation skills, creating special effects for *The Last Days of Pompeii* (1935), and conceiving *The War Eagles* (a film about a lost race of Viking-like people who attack New York City atop giant eagles that was shelved due to difficulties with the project) and *Gwangi* (a story about a forgotten prehistoric cache of time in the Grand Canyon that also fell apart, though it eventually found some semblance of life almost three decades later, in 1969, in the film *The Valley of Gwangi*).

In 1949, Kong directors/producers Cooper and Schoedsack came to O'Brien with their next project, *Mighty Joe Young*, which was seen in some ways as a reworking of Kong without dinosaurs. In fact, Robert Armstrong returned to play basically the same kind of character. A young Ray Harryhausen, who had initially approached Willis O'Brien with a proposal to work for him, wound up doing a great deal of the actual animation on this film under O'Brien's supervision. Despite the film's comparatively lukewarm critical and box office reception, *Mighty Joe Young* was considered a vast advance in technique over *King Kong*.

Unfortunately, by the 1960s, movie studios considered stop-motion animation to be to too expensive to pursue. But *King Kong*—and the technicians and artists who worked on it, most prominently Willis O'Brien—had a giant influence on creative technicians and filmmakers through the following decades. It goes without saying what effect Ray Harryhausen's creations have had on the fantasy genre due to O'Brien's mentorship. In fact, Harryhausen said he learned the important secret of monster animation while working with O'Brien: even the most destructive monster must possess a little bit of pathos to allow it to connect with the audience.

The same is true for animators Jim Danforth, Phil Tippett and the late David Allen. Jim Danforth worked on various films in the 1960s and 1970s, including 1970's Hammer film *When Dinosaurs Ruled the Earth* when his friend and colleague Ray Harryhausen was unavailable. Phil Tippett took stop-motion animation one step further in the early 1980s while working at George Lucas' ILM special effects facility, calling it "Go-Motion" and adding a motion-control "blur" that gives traditional stop-motion more realism.

David Allen, in his animation work, even created a direct homage to Kong. He worked on the now-classic Volkswagen commercial in the 1970s that perfectly re-created Kong's epic battle on the Empire State Building. Instead of falling from it, however, the giant ape takes his girl and a captured plane, climbs back down, gets into his VW bug and drives away. In the early '90s, Allen also animated a segment of an IMAX film on special effects, re-creating Kong—this time in San Francisco—right down to the moving fur on his body. An inescapable side effect of stop-motion animation was that manipulating the models between shots left fingerprints on the fur. Fortunately, this side effect made the creature even more realistic, as the fur appeared to be moving on its own. Allen re-created the original Kong model, including the wavering fur, with eerie accuracy.

Even now, digital animation—which has largely replaced stop/go-motion work—still does not have the sense of "presence" that model work tends to create. Even the digital animators who made *Jurassic Park* and other films with dinosaurs candidly claim nothing quite gets the "personality" as much as model work. Ray Harryhausen, while a great admirer of digital animation, still rightly points out that "a model is something you can hold in your hands."

In 1996, New Zealand director Peter Jackson attempted to make a "new" version of the classic Kong story. While he did quite a bit of pre-production work and had a script, the film was shelved for one reason or another. In 2004, Jackson's stunning success with The Lord of the Rings trilogy and his Oscar win for Best Director proved that he, if anyone, could make the film happen, and *King Kong* was green-lighted for a Christmas 2005 release.

Thanks in part to the less-than-amazing Dino De Laurentiis *King Kong* remake of 1976, die-hard fans shudder at the idea of another potentially calamitous remake. However, Jackson has done much to calm the fears of Kong lovers by not only making his version a "period" 1930s film, but also using his Weta Workshop Ltd. and Weta Digital Ltd., whose excellent work was demonstrated in the Lord of the Rings trilogy, to re-create and build upon the classic look of *King Kong*. He has stated that Skull Island will be "over the top" and feature not the classic dinosaurs seen in the original film, but new variations on those species—a new kind of Ceratopsian as well as a Tyrannosaurus species called Vastatosaurus rex (Kong battles *three* of these in a stunning sequence!) Jackson has noted that evolution would have resulted in these changes had these creatures actually survived to the twentieth century in an isolated environment like Skull Island. It also appears that he plans to use a hand-tinted postcard look in places, to attain a more authentic period feel, while at the same time appealing to those who treasure the very depth and richness of the black-and-white original. The look of Jackson's Kong appears to be vastly different but no less inspiring than 1933's. This new Kong is a "gentle giant" with the fierce stance of a silverback gorilla and eyes that emote, speaking in ways verbalization cannot, and a scarred, broken face showing he's truly living in a brutal land. Kong himself will be portrayed by actor Andy Serkis, filmed in a motion-capture suit similar to the one he wore as Gollum in the Lord of the Rings trilogy. This gives Jackson the ability to actually "direct Kong" as he would an actor. The suit has points which register with a computer, recording the wearer's movements and giving effects artists a template to work with. Serkis' black-suited body is then replaced by a completely digitally animated Kong, complete with Serkis' movements, thus attaining a sense of a living creature.

Both the 2005 and the 1933 *King Kong* utilize their own era's state-of-the-art animation techniques. The new *King Kong* will not only be a cornerstone in special effects like its 1933 predecessor, but also act as a testament to the longevity of a legacy. As Ray Harryhausen himself so eloquently stated regarding not only the careers, but the "muses" of creative artists, sculptors and filmmakers: "Where would we be if not for *King Kong*?"

BOB EGGLETON is a successful science fiction, fantasy and landscape artist. In his twenty years of putting brush to canvas or board, he has won nine Hugo Awards and twelve Chesley Awards, as well as various magazine awards, and his art can be seen on the covers of magazines, books, posters and prints, and of late, stationery, drink coasters, journals and jigsaw puzzles. He has also worked as a conceptual illustrator for movies and thrill rides (including the Academy Award–nominated animated film *Jimmy Neutron: Boy Genius*) and illustrated two books of experimental artwork about dragons, *Dragonhenge* and *The Stardragons*. *Primal Darkness: The Gothic and Horror Artwork of Bob Eggleton* is currently available from Cartouche Press, and work has already begun on Bob's next collection of recent art works, *Dragon Cosmica*.

Improbable Antics
Notes from a Gorilla Guru

Dario Maestripieri

YOU'D THINK ONE APE was as good as another. You'd be wrong. And a man in an ape suit? Doesn't even compare.

Long before the Walt Disney Company's animated production *Beauty and the Beast*, there was *King Kong*. In both stories, the ferocious beast is an angry and loveless prince (or king) who spends his life terrorizing his countrymen until he falls in love with a charming beauty that brings out his tenderness and need for love. At the end of the Walt Disney film, the hideous beast becomes strikingly handsome, marries the beauty, and they live happily ever after, whereas at the end of *King Kong*, the beast still looks ugly and gets shot at the top of the Empire State Building. The explanation for these disparate endings is that in the Walt Disney movie, the beast is a human who is temporarily transformed into a repulsive monster by a spell cast by a wicked witch. Breaking the spell and returning him to humanity is simply a matter of a few words of heartfelt devotion from his True Love. In the other movie, the beast is an ape, and although evolution by natural selection broke the spell and turned apes into humans, that process took a few million years to occur—definitely longer than the attention span of the average moviegoer. Thus, in the movies as in the real world, the ape ends up getting shot despite the fact he has a romantic heart and is vulnerable to developing crushes on hot, young chicks just like the rest of us.

Whether, in the end, Kong is monster or victim is difficult to say. But whether or not he is depicted as retaining characteristics faithful to the world of primates is clear from a primatologist's point of view. Although

85

successful in some regards—and a darn good story—both movie versions of *King Kong* generally fail in portraying a gorilla worthy of scientific review: in 1933 because of the lack of extensive available knowledge and in 1976 because of the relative disinterest in it.

Given that a variety of different animals, including spiders, snakes, sharks, birds and even domestic cats and dogs, have figured prominently in horror movies, it is no surprise that a movie was created in which the scary monster was an ape. But why a gorilla? There are four extant species of great apes: gorillas, chimpanzees, bonobos and orangutans. Given what we now know about the behavior of these apes, chimpanzees would seem to be the ape of choice for a horror movie depicting graphic animal violence. Adult male chimpanzees are aggressive and carnivorous primates that hunt and prey upon monkeys and murder and cannibalize other chimpanzees, including young and helpless infants. When given the chance, they have also been known to savagely attack humans and devour their body parts.

For an X-rated movie with graphic sex scenes, bonobos or orangutans would be the ape of choice. Bonobos are well known for their intense sexuality and tendency to engage in copulatory activities in any possible position and with individuals of any sex or age. The specialty of male orangutans is to sexually coerce female orangutans as well as, according to some unverified reports, the females of our own species. Gorillas, on the other hand, are peaceful, slow-moving, leaf-eating apes that make ideal subjects for nature documentaries but do not have anything in their behavioral repertoire that would land them a leading role in any film sporting more than a PG-13 rating. Gorillas are often given the "most boring primates to watch at the zoo" award by students. At the zoo, they are also known for their habit of eating their own feces or regurgitated food—not the kind of behavior anyone would want to see on the big screen. But what we know now about the behavior of great apes, and especially gorillas, we did not know in the 1930s when the first *King Kong* movie was made. At that time, we barely knew that gorillas existed.

There are two basic kinds of gorillas: lowland and mountain gorillas. Lowland gorillas were officially discovered in 1846 by two missionaries, Thomas Savage and Leighton Wilson, who collected gorilla skulls and sent them to anatomists Richard Owen in England and Jeffries Wyman in Boston to be analyzed (Schaller 1964; Willoughby). Savage and Wilson also had a few encounters with gorillas, and described them as "exceedingly ferocious and always offensive in their habits" (Schaller 1964, 4). The reputation of the gorilla only worsened after American explorer Paul du Chaillu arrived in Africa in 1856 and began shooting them. Du Chaillu gave gorillas a heaping dose of bad publicity. When narrating his adventures in Africa, he described the gorilla as "a hellish dream creature...half-man and half-beast, which we find pictured by old artists in some representations of the infernal regions" (Schaller 1964, 5).

At the turn of the century, after numerous explorers had discovered and shot many lowland gorillas, the focus of attention shifted to Central and Eastern Africa where rumors had emerged that another species of gorillas existed. The first mountain gorilla was found and immediately shot in 1902 by a German officer named Oscar von Beringe. (The mountain gorilla's scientific name is *Gorilla gorilla beringei*, in his "honor.") Between 1902 and 1925, fifty-four more mountain gorillas were killed in the Ugandan region of the Virunga Volcanoes alone (Schaller 1964). In many cases gorillas were killed during scientific expeditions; in those days, studying animals in their natural environment involved shooting them first.

One of the first attempts to study wild gorillas with modern observational methods was made by a zoologist named Robert L. Garner in the 1880s. Intimidated by du Chaillu's descriptions of the gorillas and expecting to be attacked by these fierce creatures, Garner built a large cage for his own protection and spent hours "in captivity" on the floor of an African tropical forest (Schaller 1964; Bourne). Needless to say, the only animals that attacked Garner were mosquitoes, against which the cage offered little protection. He saw few or no gorillas, but his presence in the forest probably provided great entertainment to many species of monkeys and other animals, which lingered in front of his cage, observing this strange creature and his bizarre behavior (probably one of the first monkey studies of human behavior in the wild).

It wasn't until 1959, long after the making of the original *King Kong*, that anyone succeeded in getting close enough to mountain gorillas to observe their leaf-eating habits and generally peaceful lifestyle. This somebody was George Schaller, one of the greatest field biologists of the twentieth century (Schaller 1963). Schaller's study was successful in part because it was built upon the foundation that, as Schaller himself wrote, "The serious researcher must discard most published information about the behavior of free-living gorillas. Much of it is sensational, irresponsible and exaggerated prevarications, with little concern for the truth" (Schaller 1964, 2). In most documented encounters between humans and gorillas prior to Schaller's study, people only saw a moving shadow or heard the sound of a crashing branch as the animals fled. In only a few cases did people actually see a silverback male beat his chest, roar and display a bluff charge against intruders, the behavior that gave rise to the myth of the ferocious gorilla (Schaller 1964). The rest is *King Kong* history.

The idea for the first *King Kong* movie allegedly originated when co-director/co-producer Merian Cooper had a dream about a giant gorilla attacking New York City. In the movie, the fifty-foot-tall gorilla was represented by miniature models that were only eighteen inches high and the film was shot using stop-motion photography.

Despite the now-archaic effects used to simulate the giant ape, there were many aspects of this Kong's behavior that were true to life. The miniature is anatomically appropriate for an ape (i.e., the length of his arms relative to the body is that of an ape and not a human) and, on several occasions, King Kong walks on his knuckles the way a real gorilla would. After beating his chest during his first onscreen appearance, he creates similar displays in appropriate contexts: e.g., before and after his fights with the dinosaurs, and more generally when he is angry at the world. Real gorillas beat their chests to scare intruders or male rivals, and these displays may be accompanied by threats or actual fighting.

Unfortunately, the fighting scenes, which are frequent in the 1933 movie, are where the similarities with real gorilla behavior end. Most egregiously, while fighting with a Pterodactyl and a Tyrannosaurus rex, King Kong exhibits the moves and punches of a professional wrestler performing on *WWF Saturday Night Nitro*. It turns out that the animator himself, Willis O'Brien, had been a boxer, and choreographed the fight between King Kong and the Tyrannosaurus rex.

In the 1976 Dino De Laurentiis/John Guillermin remake, King Kong was instead played by an actor wearing an ape suit. Although the movements of the 1976 King Kong are much less forced than those of his stop-motion predecessor, they are also more human. The movie literally makes fun of itself for it: In one scene, King Kong takes Dwan away from the sacrificial altar and back to his nest, destroying a few trees in the process. Jeff Bridges' character points to the path taken by the ape and asks another fellow, "Who the hell do you think went through there? Some guy in an ape suit?" Exactly. The guy's name was Rick Baker.

We do not see much naturalistic gorilla behavior in the 1976 version. King Kong beats his chest once, upon his arrival at the sacrificial altar with Dwan, and that's all. For the rest of the movie, the giant ape holds a perfect upright posture, walks bipedally and swings his arms and fists like a man. When he is on top of a building with Dwan, he throws objects at the soldiers as if he is playing bocce.

The rubber face mask worn by Rick Baker gives King Kong a respectable gorilla appearance and, more importantly, allows for the expression of emotions. Since King Kong does not talk, he only communicates with the other characters and with the audience through his facial expressions. Thus, to express love and tenderness when giving Dwan a shower under the waterfalls, he smiles and purses his lips like a big baby. When he becomes jealous of Dwan and her lover Jack, he shoots them a bad look.

When his plans for ecstasy and bliss with Dwan take a wrong turn, he is overcome with anger and resentment. And how does the enormous gorilla show his anger? He rolls his eyes, throws his head back, opens his mouth and screams—in a very un-apelike fashion. In the 1933 film, King Kong's roar was created by combining a lion and a tiger's roar and playing it in reverse. In the 1976 remake, the origin of the roar is unclear, but King Kong roars with exaggerated frequency throughout the film, including when his mouth is closed and sometimes even when he is off camera.

Sexuality is another area in which the portrayal of King Kong, particularly in the original version, falls far short of realistic. During the sequence in which King Kong peels off Ann Darrow's clothes (a scene initially censored but later restored), King Kong has an intrigued look on his face as he takes off her shirt, pokes and tickles her with his index finger and then sniffs it. I doubt that these scenes were inspired by observations of gorilla behavior made by missionaries in the nineteenth century. Until Schaller's study in the late 1950s, however, gorillas and other apes had a reputation not only for being violent, but also for having voracious sexual appetites, representing "man in the most debased condition, a slave to vice and his own unrestrained inclinations" (Maple 31). Critiques of the 1933 movie noted its rich sexual symbolism: the skyscraper is an obvious phallic symbol, and it is no coincidence that King Kong climbs to the top of the tallest skyscraper on the planet to make himself known to the world (Morris and Morris).

It is ironic, however, that a gorilla like King Kong was used as a champion of male sexuality, because male gorillas are known to have a short penis and small testis size relative to their body size when compared to the other apes. When biologists in the 1970s took the time to study the genitalia of various primate species, they discovered that for species in which both sexes are promiscuous and males compete with one another to inseminate and fertilize females, testicles are large, whereas in monogamous species in which females typically mate with only one or few males, testicles are small. Large testes produce more sperm, and the more sperm the higher the chance of successful insemination during competition with other males and their sperm. Among the great apes, chimpanzees and bonobos have a very promiscuous mating system and therefore males have large testes relative to their body size. Gorillas, however, live in small harem groups, in which mating is monopolized by the silverback male. Because

---

[1] Incidentally, human males have a large penis but small testicles relative to their body size and in comparisons with other primates, thus suggesting that sperm competition has not been a prominent feature of human evolution despite claims to the contrary.

sperm competition is not intense for gorillas, their testis size is relatively small (Baker).[1]

The person who first discovered that gorillas had small testes was probably the American explorer Paul du Chaillu but, according to some, he removed the genitals from the dead apes he brought back from Africa to make his stories of gorilla aggressiveness and sexuality more convincing (Morris and Morris).

With all the nature documentaries on gorilla behavior that have been filmed since the 1976 *King Kong* movie (many of which are titled "Gentle Giants"), it is likely that the behavior of the new King Kong will be more naturalistic and apelike than his predecessors. With the availability of digital technology, he will probably look more realistic as well. Other Hollywood productions featuring great apes that were filmed in the pre-digital era typically used the approach employed in the 1976 version. The chimpanzees, gorillas and other apes featured in the various *Planet of the Apes* and *Tarzan* movies, for example, were usually actors wearing ape suits. In some *Tarzan* movies (e.g., *Greystoke: The Legend of Tarzan, Lord of the Apes*) however, there are scenes in which the adult chimpanzees played by actors are mixed with live young chimpanzees to make everything more realistic.

Incidentally, any real chimpanzees that appear in Hollywood movies are adolescents; adult chimpanzees are simply too dangerous and uncontrollable to be used on any movie set. Similarly, the chimpanzees performing in circus acts are typically youngsters as well. Because young chimpanzees are docile and playful animals that can be easily trained to wear human clothing and make funny faces, chimpanzees have traditionally had a reputation for being friendly animals. When relatively recent studies of wild chimpanzees in Africa reported the occurrence of hunting, murder, infanticide and cannibalism, our view of these apes changed dramatically. The violent nature of adult male chimpanzees in particular has been captured on film and been the subject of books with apt titles such as *Demonic Males* (Wrangham and Peterson). Our views of chimpanzees and gorillas, therefore, have changed inversely as we have learned more about both.

Although the environment and the behavior of gorillas and other apes in recent movies look increasingly realistic, inaccuracies still abound, such as showing African apes living side by side with capuchin monkeys, which are found only in South America (e.g., *Congo* or *Outbreak*). Some of these inaccuracies are probably inevitable, and part of what makes these movies entertaining. Indeed, the first King Kong lived on the wrong continent, fought with dinosaurs and fell in love with a female of the wrong species— a clear misfit in every way. As Peter Jackson re-creates the giant ape, with thirty extra years of research and modern-day CGI miracles at his disposal, we can only hope that what he makes up for in accuracy, he will not lose in appeal.

Works Cited

Baker, Robin. *Sperm Wars*. New York: Basic Books, 1996.

Bourne, Geoffrey H. *Primate Odyssey*. New York: GP Putnam's Sons, 1974.

Maple, Terry L. "Primate Psychology in Historical Perspective." *Captivity and Behavior: Primates in Breeding Colonies, Laboratories and Zoos*. Eds. J. Erwin, Terry Maple and G. Mitchell. New York: Van Nostrand Reinhold, 1979. 29–58.

Morris, Ramona and Desmond Morris. *Men and Apes*. New York: McGraw-Hill, 1966.

Schaller, George B. *The Mountain Gorilla: Ecology and Behavior*. Chicago: University of Chicago Press, 1963.

———*The Year of the Gorilla*. Chicago: University of Chicago Press, 1964.

Willoughby, David P. *All About Gorillas*. Cranbury, NJ: AS Barnes and Co, Inc., 1978.

Wrangham, Richard and Dale Peterson. *Demonic Males*. Boston: Houghton Mifflin, 1996.

DARIO MAESTRIPIERI earned his Ph.D. in psychobiology from the University of Rome, Italy, in 1992. He is currently an associate professor of comparative human development and evolutionary biology at the University of Chicago. His research interests focus on the biology of behavior, and in particular on physiological, ecological and evolutionary aspects of primate social behavior. Dr. Maestripieri has published over 100 scientific articles and book chapters and recently edited the book *Primate Psychology* (2003, Harvard University Press). He was awarded the 2000 Distinguished Scientific Award for Early Career Contribution to Psychology from the American Psychological Association and is the current recipient of a Career Development Award from the National Institute of Mental Health.

Darwin, Freud and King Kong

Joseph D. Miller, Ph.D.

TAKE A MAP OF SKULL ISLAND. It's actually a map of your *brain*. Don't get it? Grab a compass and some tracing paper. A pith helmet and machete. Read on, and explore.

King Kong was the first and probably greatest of the "Big Ape" movies and, over the years, its story has inspired analysis in terms of race, culture, feminist theory and nearly every other lens through which a text can be studied. It is entertaining and perhaps instructive to examine Kong through the "looking glasses" of Freudian psychology, neuroscience and evolutionary biology as well. Here, we will take a look at all three, then extend our analysis to the second of the "Big Ape" movies, *Mighty Joe Young*, and to the prime example of the "Big Lizard," Godzilla.

The key construct of Freudian theory is that a *superego* (read: civilized behavior) dominates an *ego*, which behaves according to perceived pleasure and pain. In turn, these conscious processes usually dominate an unconscious *id*, which is synonymous with our most base and ancient impulses. Freudian theory is, according to Karl Pribram, the first neuroscience theory, although clearly a theory largely created in the absence of empirical data about the brain. Still, there is an amazing analogy between the simple constructs of Freud and the widely accepted neuroanatomical model, Paul MacLean's triune brain.

MacLean's model is basically a neuroanatomical three-scoop ice cream cone. The first scoop is what he called the R-complex, or reptilian brain— essentially, the brain stem. Here MacLean placed the simplest drive states,

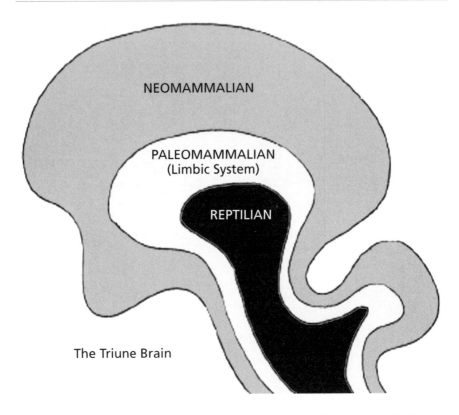

NEOMAMMALIAN

PALEOMAMMALIAN
(Limbic System)

REPTILIAN

The Triune Brain

in strong analogy to Freud's *id*. The next scoop in the cone is the limbic system, the great mammalian invention, all the forebrain structures responsible for the generation of emotional behavior. This, once again, is very analogous to Freud's *ego*. Finally, the topmost scoop is the cerebral cortex, the latest evolutionary development—characteristically very large in primates, particularly in humans. The cortex is the locus of thinking and reasoning, essentially the neurological substrate of the various strictures society places on human behavior, and an excellent instantiation of Freud's *superego*.

How can these simple concepts enliven our understanding of *Kong*?[1] There is reason to believe that psychoanalytic theory is not a terrible approximation of human behavior, or at least neurotic behavior. But the patient needs to be ignorant of Freud's theory, else he begins to act according to Freudian precepts due to the power of suggestion (the psychoanalytic

---

[1] Karl Jung points to the deep connections between psychoanalytic theory and the archetypes of myth. And Claude Levi-Strauss would study not "how men think in myths, but how myths operate in men's minds without their being aware of it."

term is *iatrogenesis*), suggesting that using this theory to analyze a film whose makers were cognizant of Freud's teachings (as almost everyone is today) would be fruitless. The '30s, however, were a simpler time, with the large majority of people—script writers and directors included—largely unaware of Freud and certainly unaware of the neuroanatomy which seems to correspond to much of Freudian theory. So it is a legitimate undertaking to analyze an iconic movie like *King Kong* for signs of such universal psychological constructs and their anatomical substrates.

Early in the movie we learn of Skull Island, the remote home of the god Kong. The island is divided into roughly three parts: First, a sandy beach area where the native humans (read: cerebral cortex, or *superego*) reside, separated from the domain of Kong by a massive gate, perhaps created by the Egyptians, the denizens of Angkor Wat or some mysterious "lost race" (a common trope in the adventure fiction of the '30s). Beyond these "doors of perception" lies the second part, Skull Mountain, the domain of Kong (read: limbic system, or *ego*). Kong's domain in turn overlooks the third part, the jungle realm of the dinosaurs (literally the reptilian brain and once again synonymous with the *id*). So what we see is that the very geography of Skull Island closely corresponds to the constructs of Freudian theory and their neurological correlates.

The relationships between the denizens of these three domains reflect the workings of Freud's *superego*, *ego* and *id* as well. The native population controls (though "barters with" may be a more accurate term) Kong, who in turn reigns over the island's dinosaurs. On Skull Island, *superego* talks to *ego* and *ego* talks to *id*, all in a kind of linear progression, which actually captures much of the hierarchical structure of the nervous system—in which projections from cortex to subcortical limbic structures are denser than those to the brain stem and projections from limbic system to brain stem (and from brain stem to limbic system) are as comparably dense as those from cortex to limbic structures. The *id* (saurian R-complex) never directly invades the domain of the cortical *superego*; such intrusion is mediated by Kong, the limbic *ego*.

We see a similar kind of cortical-subcortical mediation between the natives and Kong. The natives ceremonially sacrifice[2] a woman every year to Kong, which seems to placate him—to "keep him in his place." A psycho-

[2] It is never precisely clear what Kong does with these sacrifices. But in psychoanalysis there is a deep connection between death and sex. To a lesser degree many psychologists posit the overconsumption of food as a compensatory response to sexual deprivation. Since both drives, sex and hunger, when satisfied, ultimately stimulate the "pleasure center" (or more properly the dopamine projection to limbic regions), a deep connection between the two makes sense. Thus, Kong's sexual urges may in part be satisfied by human sacrifice. We never see a "Lady Kong," although the subsequent movie, *The Son of Kong*, suggests that Kong may have at some point found another outlet for his sexual urges as well.

analyst would say it is the social rules of civilization which control the self-centered desires of the *ego*, which in turn reflect the primal urges of the *id*. Here, Kong's "marriages" sate his sexual desires (reflective of the mating urge)—the regular sacrifice of brides keeps Kong from breaking down the wall in search of other ways to satisfy his needs.

This social contract is strictly upheld until Ann Darrow's appearance on the scene.[3] Ann appears to be a new concept for Kong. He does not eat her, but he does diddle her in a famous and subsequently censored scene: the white woman subjugating the savage beast through her sexuality rather than her "good taste." Kong becomes her protector from the other beasts of Skull Island, and in so doing his subordination to the dictates of the *superego*, in this case romantic love, is assured. But even this rather one-sided contract is broken when Jack Driscoll rescues Ann from Kong's lair. Subsequently Kong bursts through the giant gate into the native domain, the *ego* wresting control from the *superego*. But Kong fails to secure the love object, in Freudian terms, and is forced to submit again to the *superego*: this time the white adventurers with their gas bombs, representing a restraining cortical influence superior to the native society's, a kind of super-*superego* reminiscent of Kipling's "white man's burden." White society will civilize Kong even if native society fails.

In New York Kong continues in subjugation to the *superego*, the civilization which places him in chains. But eventually his emotional reaction to the photographers' flashbulbs and his jealousy of Jack Driscoll, his competition for Ann's affections, allows him to burst the strictures of the *superego* and, temporarily, escape. But even having broken the chains that hold him, he is still a slave to that greatest construct of the *superego*—idealized romantic love. He regains Ann and carries her to the top of the Empire State Building, once again bringing to mind the triple ice cream cone of MacLean's triune brain, with the Empire State Building, the largest instantiation of the phallus in that era, standing in for the *id*, Kong personifying the *ego*, and the machine-gun armed biplanes that rise above him representative of the ultimately triumphant *superego*, our social cortex. But of course it is not the airplanes that truly bring Kong to his knees, but his prior surrender to the charms of romantic love, perhaps the most powerful of our social inventions. It wasn't Beauty killed the Beast, as Denham indicates; it was Love.

Compare the uneasy neuropsychological relationships in *Kong* to those in its theatrical descendant, *Mighty Joe Young* (a ten-foot-tall midget com-

---

[3] We learn from the native chief that the going rate for Ann is six native girls, indicating the racist values of the era. The underlying assumption seems to be that a native girl is more primeval or limbic than a white woman and hence less effective in mastering Kong; that is, the *ego*.

pared with Kong's fifty feet). By the film's 1949 release, movie censorship was in full flower; nevertheless, the subtext is that Mighty Joe Young is the emasculated pawn of the crypto-dominatrix Jill Young. Joe has grown up with Jill, the older sister to his younger "brother," who subjugates his desires entirely by simply singing "Beautiful Dreamer." (Music soothes the savage limbic system!) Such a mechanism is necessary to suppress even the faintest hint of incest, a much greater Freudian concern than the mere miscegenation threatened in *Kong*. Here the dominance of the *superego/cortex* over the *ego*/limbic system is nearly total in comparison to the Ann Darrow/Kong relationship. In perhaps the most famous scene, Jill Young plays the song on a platform which gradually rises to reveal Joe, in Atlas mode, supporting it—a graphic depiction of the first two scoops of MacLean's triune ice cream cone. The only time Joe escapes this repression is under the influence of that well-known cortical suppressant, alcohol. But the *ego*'s moment is brief and Joe is quickly bundled back to Africa to continue a life of cheerful sexual suppression, where of course the primacy of the always white *superego* (i.e., Jill) is constantly acknowledged.

Darwinian evolutionary theory may be simply expressed in one sentence: individuals who exhibit reproductive fitness are selected for over time. From a Darwinian perspective both *Mighty Joe Young* and *King Kong* depict impossible biology. Kong would have phenomenal problems simply walking on two legs and maintaining appropriate metabolism, body temperature, etc. Giantism is sometimes seen in geographically restricted island populations, but a fifty-foot-tall ape is well beyond the possible biomechanics of anything except a Brontosaur! And Kong seems to have sprung *de novo*; there is no breeding population of giant apes on Skull Island—although a later movie, *The Son of Kong*, implies this cannot be the case.

In evolutionary terms it is a waste of energy for sexual relations to occur between different species since, by definition, fertile offspring cannot result. So at first glance Kong's infatuation with Ann Darrow makes little sense. And of course size does make a difference.[4] Nevertheless, Kong becomes enamored of Ann and protects her from various prehistoric beasts. Does this make any evolutionary sense? Actually, Ann may be a supernormal stimulus for Kong—a stimulus that represents a magnified version of the same attractors Kong would look for in a suitable mate, creating in Kong a hypersexual response. Such supernormal stimuli have been shown to be effective in many mammalian species, including our own: it is possible that our glorification of supermodels and Playmates (in which, for

---

[4] Editor's note: See Adam-Troy Castro's essay in this volume.

instance, the swollen breasts that indicate fertility have been taken to extremes) may tap into similar neurowiring.

But this begs the question: Why should supernormal stimuli occur at all? The best answer at present is that such stimuli are fortuitous combinations of characteristics which, on their own, have much lower sexual appeal but are relatively common in the population and have accumulated considerable fitness over evolutionary time. Thus it is a matter of probabilities that such characteristics will sometimes combine to produce a more powerful gestalt. A supernormal stimulus which facilitates reproduction will be selected for: a combination of wide hips (an indicator of relatively easy birth) and large breasts (a possible sign of effective milk production and ease of suckling) in the women of Raphael's time would presumably have had a particularly high degree of fitness because of the primitive nature of obstetric and pediatric nutritional care during that period. Ann was more endowed in this sense than most primates, although the argument is weakened by the fact that we know nothing of the secondary sexual characteristics of female Kongs!

In the case of Mighty Joe Young, Joe is effectively neutered by music, as well as his near-sibling relationship with Jill Young. Effectively, the issue of sexuality never comes up, even though adult apes are highly sexual creatures in the "real world." Apes raised in captivity may express considerable sexual interest in humans, perhaps because of confusion in species identity. But the climate of censorship at the time would have precluded any consideration of this issue. Furthermore, it is possible that interspecies sexual attraction would have been perceived, hard as it is to understand such a mindset today, as condoning interracial relations. Far better to keep the African pacified with song!

Even more interesting in terms of science and its intersection with the film is the battle between Kong and the Tyrannosaurus rex. Actually, this should have been a "no contest" since Tyrannosaurus rex only got to be about twenty feet tall; a fight between them would have been akin to a wrestling match between Shaquille O'Neal and a munchkin from the *Wizard of Oz*! Nevertheless, we now know that mammals as large as dogs (such as *Repenomamus giganticus*) actually preyed on small dinosaurs some sixty-five million years ago—during the same era in which the first primates appeared. It is possible that some primates may have likewise preyed on small dinosaurs. But more importantly, the contest was a brilliant reification of the interaction between the *ego* and the *id*, and may indicate a possible historical underpinning for the *ego*'s dominance over the *id*: early primates would have been largely lacking in differentiated neocortex—read *superego*—but probably had a well-functioning limbic system—read *ego*. In fact, the theme of Kong triumphing over the dinosaur was present in the earliest conception of what the film would be. Director Merian C. Cooper originally wanted to use an ape miniature struggling with a Komodo dragon as the basis of the film.[5]

Perhaps the iconic clash between *ego* and *id*—i.e., monkey and lizard—is *King Kong vs. Godzilla*. Here, Godzilla, fifty meters tall and a much better match for a now forty-five-meter-tall Kong than T. rex, battles Kong to the "death." In the end both creatures are submerged beneath the waves, but in the final frame we hear Kong's battle cry...and nothing from Godzilla.[6]

While it seems fine for apes to beat the stuffing out of lizards, humans (like the majority of the hapless crew who rallied to go after Ann) do not seem to do so well. If this century's dinosaur films (the various Jurassic Park films and even *The Lost World*) have taught us anything, it is that all human protagonists can manage is a kind of draw with the big lizards. Perhaps (unlike *Homo flores*) we require a proxy in order to defeat the truly primeval, a notion which gains some support from psychoanalysis, neuroanatomy, evolutionary history and the cinema!

Throughout human history, war has depended on two things: dehu-

---

[5] Ironically, recent research has indicated that our immediate hominid ancestor, the Indonesian three-foot-tall "hobbits" of Flores (*Homo flores*) actually subsisted on a diet that included Komodo dragons. Thus, art imitates (nearly) life! (Editor's note: See Robert A. Metzger's essay in this volume for a lengthier discussion of *Homo flores* and its implications for Kong.)

[6] Actually, in the Japanese version, Godzilla's cry is also heard! Both monsters presumably live to fight another day.

manization of the enemy (identification with the sub-human, as in reptilian?) and an energizing hatred of that dehumanized enemy. This is a sociological analog of the triune brain, the emotional *ego* mediating the cortical plan to subjugate the externalized *id*. But it is also clear that on the battlefield soldiers often find that the "enemy" is not so different, not so inhuman, and therefore becomes difficult if not impossible to kill. In anthropological terms the Other becomes us.[7] The cortical plan is subverted by the "upfront" experience of the *ego*/limbic system. Kong cannot bring himself to kill Ann; instead, he protects her. And in *Homo sapiens* the *ego* is not an always reliable mediator of the cortical design, perhaps to the credit of our species. When we circumvent the immediacy of mediation by the *ego* (e.g., long-distance bombing of villages in Viet Nam, which required no face-to-face contact between pilot and villager), we retain the cortical plan, but we lose the possibility of that unrestrained "quality of mercy" of which the Bard speaks.

And so King Kong, for all the destruction he represents, serves a purpose—as *ego*, he mediates between the *superego* of the cerebral cortex and the *id* of the R-complex. And in that, he is not irredeemable. As a creature of emotion, he is capable of ignoring both *superego* and *id*. The *ego* can defy the dictates of the *superego*, as Kong does when he attacks the natives of Skull Island, and it can override the drives of the *id*, as Kong does when he chooses to protect Ann rather than kill or eat her. In the *ego*'s ability to identify with others emotionally there lies an immediacy, and an integrity, that neither *id* nor *superego* can boast—one that can elevate an ape above his baser instincts, and make him more noble than his captors. It is after all the airplane, that remote control of our social *superego*, that is proximally and literally Kong's downfall. But when King Kong falls, the "up close and personal" bystanders show a final empathy for an Other not so different in the end from our limbic-driven selves. For it was ultimately Love, not Beauty or *superego*, that killed the Beast.

---

[7] Most cultures are xenophobic "in clubs." In fact, most cultures have an exclusive name for themselves which may be translated as the People, suggesting that all Others are not really human. But the camaraderie of personal battle dissolves the distinction, which can be seen in the Western tradition at least as far back as Homer's *Iliad*.

Works Cited

Freud, Sigmund. *The Ego and the Id.* New York: Norton, 1990.

Levi-Strauss, Claude. *The Raw and the Cooked.* New York: Harper and Row, 1969.

MacLean, P. *The Triune Brain in Evolution.* New York: Plenum Press, 1990.

Pribram, K. H. and M. M. Gill. "Freud's 'Project' Reassessed." *Contemporary Cognitive Theory and Neuropsychology.* New York: Basic Books, 1976.

JOSEPH D. MILLER, PH.D., is an associate professor in the Department of Cell and Neurobiology at the Keck School of Medicine at USC, as well as the director of pharmacology for the medical school. He is a neuropharmacologist with research primarily in the fields of circadian neurobiology, sleep and stem cell research. In addition, he is a science fiction critic of long standing and has been a fan of science fiction in literature and in cinema for over forty years.

Dragon's Teeth
and Hobbits

Robert A. Metzger

FORGOTTEN ISLANDS, impossibly oversized apes, *living* dinosaurs...*King Kong* is a fantasy of the first order. Isn't it? Robert A. Metzger has some awfully compelling evidence to the contrary.

King Kong is fictional.

Oh, that is what *they* would like you to believe.

You see, King Kong is actually real.

Now I'm not talking about the *King Kong* brought to the big screen in 1933, telling the tale of the poor mutant ape kidnapped to New York City for his big debut, who storms offstage, girlfriend in hand, and then makes his fateful climb to the top of the Empire State Building, only to be riddled with bullets and eventually splat on the cruel streets of Broadway like so many other hopeful young actors. That was the Kong brought to New York by Carl Denham, the moviemaker/explorer *character* in the *King Kong* movie. This was as close to the actual tale as Merian C. Cooper, the real life moviemaker/explorer, creator of Kong and inspiration for the fictional Carl Denham, dared to bring to the American public of 1933. What I'm talking about is the *real* King Kong, a creature who lived on an island in what is now part of Indonesia. But I'm getting ahead of myself.

First consider the historical context of the theatrical *King Kong*.

Only a scant eight years before the release of *King Kong,* the United States of America was divided by the Scopes Monkey Trial, in which the theory of evolution (or the Bible, depending on your perspective) was put on trial. If America could not handle the concept of modern man evolving from a more primitive form of man, Cooper knew that America could never accept the true story of Kong. So as a compromise, with a kind of shot fired across the bow to waken America's imagination, he teased the movie-watching public, suggesting that in distant and exotic lands, there still lurked things *unknown*.

America was not ready for the truth, a truth that the explorer Merian Cooper had pieced together from the mysterious East through legends, eyewitnesses and archeological evidence. Never during his life did he suggest that King Kong was real, but from our twenty-first-century perspective, it is quite easy to put the puzzle together, and show that something amazing did exist in the unexplored islands of Indonesia and that, if one carefully examines the clues left by Cooper, the truth may be revealed.

CLUES

If one realizes that Merian Cooper was very careful in the creation of *King Kong* and its dialogue (mostly written by Ruth Rose, the wife of his partner in film and adventures, Ernest B. Schoedsack), then a whole new level of interpretation of the film is possible, leading to critical insights into the nature and origin of the *real* King Kong.

The first question to ask is as to the location of King Kong's home—Skull Island. Although never explicitly detailed, the movie offers a major clue, giving the ship's location when Denham reveals his map of Skull Island to the captain and first mate Driscoll—they are at a latitude of two degrees south and a longitude of ninety degrees east, which we are correctly told puts them west of Java (the large, northernmost island of present-day Indonesia).

Furthermore, Denham then tells them that Skull Island is located southwest of Java, and the captain, surprised to hear this, replies that there is nothing in that direction for thousands of miles. Again this is correct. Taking a direction due southwest from the west coast of Java would carry their ship across better than a thousand miles of the Indian Ocean, finding no islands, until they eventually hit Western Australia.

However, if the ship were to travel just a bit more west than south, it would clip the southern islands that make up the eastern chain of Indonesia—in particular, the Lesser Sunda Islands. Merian Cooper was quite familiar with these islands, and they would have been critical in his piecing together of the Kong legend.

Cooper had *King Kong* (or *The 8th Wonder of the World*, as he originally envisioned the title) on the drawing board for many years before RKO Stu-

dios gave him the go-ahead to start production. Long before he had decided to use stop-motion animation to create Kong and the other inhabitants of Skull Island, it had been his plan to go to Africa, capture the largest gorilla he could find and then transport that gorilla to the only location on Earth that still had dinosaurs.

Yes, dinosaurs.

In the 1920s, the closest thing that anyone could find to dinosaurs (long before archeologists and paleontologists started to believe that the surviving dinosaurs evolved into birds), was to be found on the Sunda Islands of the Malay Archipelago (of present-day Indonesia)—in particular, Sumba, Flores and Komodo Islands. In fact, this region, called the East Nusa Tenggara (NTT) province, consists of 566 islands, many of which to this very day are uninhabited and unexplored. It was Cooper's original plan to bring his gorilla to these islands and have it battle a real Komodo dragon, or whatever other fierce dinosaur-like creatures he could find. With that footage in hand he then planned to return to Hollywood to complete filming and then splice everything together.

The explorer Cooper knew the Sunda Islands quite well; he was knowledgeable about the fantastic creatures that lived there, as well as legends of creatures that science had not yet discovered.

But the rapid development of stop-motion animation in the '20s and early '30s made the expensive expedition unnecessary; Kong and the other creatures could now be created on the soundstage. Cooper never brought his gorilla to the East Nusa Tenggara province. But he did bring back the legends and myths of that part of the world in the creation of his fictional Kong.

LEGENDS

Anything can be had in the Chinese apothecaries found throughout Asia—including those in the East Nusa Tenggara province. One of the most remarkable medicinals ever used by Chinese pharmacists is derived from the teeth of dragons. By the beginning of the twentieth century it had been recognized that one of the best places to dig for fossils in all of Asia was not some forbidding location in Outer Mongolia, or the headwaters of the Yangtze, but the back rooms of Chinese apothecaries—the practitioners of ancient Chinese medicine having been collecting fossils for thousands of years. Dragon's teeth were a rare but known commodity to these shops. In 1935, just two years after the release of *King Kong*, the anthropologist G. H. R. Von Koenigswald obtained one of these dragon's teeth. Upon investigation, he discovered it did not belong to any dinosaur, lizard or even mythical dragon species, but to a primate—it was a huge tooth from an unknown hominid. Since that initial identification made by Westerners (Asians having been aware of these so-called dragon's teeth for millennia), jawbones and thousands of teeth of this extinct primate have been discovered throughout Asia. Based on teeth and jaw measurements, this primate was huge, possibly over ten feet tall, and has been named *Gigantopithecus blacki*. While most anthropologists believe climate change and the encroachment of modern man resulted in the extinction of this creature tens of thousands of years ago, there are others who are not so sure, believing that this creature survives into modern times, and is the basis for the legend of the Yeti of the Himalayas and the Sasquatch of the Pacific Northwest.

An explorer such as Cooper would have been well aware of these teeth, and would have possibly even examined them himself. To anyone with a critical eye, it would be obvious that these were not teeth from a dragon, but from something human-like, and something extremely large. This is the first legend to consider.

But this is not the only legend of strange primates lurking in the hidden places of Asia. We can move right to the East Nusa Tenggara province for another legend—tales of a primate quite different from that of *Gigan-*

topithecus blacki. The locals of Flores Island (one of the few remaining island homes to the Komodo dragon) tell a legend of the *ebu gogo*, believing that this creature exists deep in their jungles and in the caves that riddle the sides of local volcanoes. The name *ebu gogo* means "the grandmother who eats everything." Described as furry little people, only three feet tall, with overly long arms, these creatures were not considered to be otherworldly demons or evil spirits, but quite dangerous pests. They not only carried off crops and animals but, on occasion, even babies. The legend of these creatures has existed for centuries—the very first Dutch explorers of the region, from 300 years ago, returned to the West with tales of these creatures.

Only a legend?

Most thought so until just a few years ago, in 2001, when what is now being called the greatest archeological discovery of the last fifty years took place. In a cave on Flores Island, archeologists discovered the remains of small humanoid creatures. These creatures are now being called *H. floresiensis*, but most of the on-site archeologists have named them *hobbits*. They had brains the size of chimpanzees', stone tools and fire, and when hunting in packs were able to take down not only the small elephants that once inhabited Flores (Pygmy Stegadons), but also the local Komodo dragons, beasts that outweighed each hobbit by a factor of ten. Bones of these creatures only 13,000 years old have been discovered, indicating that these creatures were occupying Flores at the same time as modern man.

Imagine the explorer Merian Cooper, his imagination fired by legends of mighty ape creatures and miniature people and all those unexplored islands of the Indonesian peninsula. It was not by accident that Cooper sailed his fictional explorers in the direction of the East Nusa Tenggara province.

COOPER'S BREADCRUMBS

Let's examine *King Kong* a bit more carefully.

Carl Denham tells Captain Englehorn the story of how he obtained the map of Skull Island, getting it from a Norwegian freighter captain who made it after coming across a canoe with a group of six natives whose lone, dying survivor told him about the island from which they'd escaped—Skull Island. This island had a huge wall built across a sandy peninsula, constructed by a civilization long vanished, and behind this wall lay mysteries the modern world has never seen.

Denham suspects the mighty Kong lurks behind that wall.

So off they go, heading southwest from the western coast of Java, traveling through fog, amazingly able to navigate exactly to the location of this island based on the tale of a dying native as told to a Norwegian captain.

A bit too good to be true. How handy that all actual witnesses from Skull Island are dead. How handy that the Norwegian captain is able to understand the language of a dying native from an unknown island. Even more amazing is that the native either knew the exact longitude and latitude of Skull Island, or else his description of the ocean journey was so detailed that the Captain was able to determine its longitude and latitude from the tale alone.

Highly suspect.

Why would the otherwise meticulous Cooper, who gave the exact latitude and longitude of the ship's position when Denham first shows the map, make up an unbelievable story of natives, a Norwegian captain and a ship that, sailing off in a general southwest direction into a bank of fog, is able to hit so close to Skull Island that its crew can hear the natives of the island chanting before they actually spy the land?

Such a plot hole can only be deliberate.

Cooper must have known exactly where the mythical Skull Island was located and which of the 566 islands of the East Nusa Tenggara province was the homeland of primates both large and small. He obviously chose not to tell, to keep both the secret and the creatures of Skull Island safe from the outside world.

And what of these creatures?

The film gives more clues.

Carl Denham, his crew and the blonde wannabe starlet Ann Darrow all arrive at Skull Island, come ashore and sneak up on the locals who are doing a dance around a terrified native girl—their song unintelligible except for the word *Kong* which is repeated over and over again.

Certainly remarkable, but insignificant compared to what rises up behind the natives—the legendary wall of Skull Island. Not only is the wall exactly as shown by their map, but there is a massive door sunk into the center of it. One look at the locals and their dance, and the explorers conclude that these people could not possibly be the folks who built the wall—a much more advanced civilization had to be responsible for its construction.

The captain suggests the wall may have been built by Egyptians—an obvious ruse to confuse the viewing public. However, there is some truth in the deception. What the captain is alluding to is the sheer size, scope and great age of the wall—something that can only be comparable to one of the other wonders of the world, the Great Pyramid. So while the pyramids may have been built by millions of Egyptian slaves, just who—or *what*—could have built the wall?

THE BIGGEST CLUE OF ALL

Is there something about that mighty wall dividing Skull Island that doesn't seem quite right? It's a subtle thing, a design quirk that might not even catch your eye, a *wrongness* that you can't quite put your finger on.

Think doors.

The doors in your house are about a foot taller than the average person—and this is because they are designed for people to walk through. Think about the door in that massive wall on Skull Island. If that wall was built to keep King Kong inside, then why would someone build a door that is just the right size for him to walk through?

If people built that wall, wouldn't it make sense for there to be a people-sized door? My goodness—it takes several people to just draw back the locking bolt on the doors, and most of the tribe to push the thing open. Doesn't make much sense, especially when you consider that even if the door is opened, there is no real need for Kong to use it.

Cooper goes to great trouble to show us just how ineffective such a wall would be in containing King Kong. By the end of the movie the audience has seen King Kong scale the Empire State Building one-handed, while being subjected to the skull-cracking scream of Fay Wray's Ann Darrow.

The Big Ape could practically jump over the wall, and would have no difficulty at all in climbing over it. It is obvious that the wall was never intended to keep King Kong *inside*. There is no denying the logic of it. Now all we have to do is take the next step. So just what was the real purpose of the wall?

The purpose of a wall is to keep something away from the wall's builder. But this is obviously not Kong—think about something smaller, a pest that would destroy crops, steal harvested food and generally make a nuisance of itself. Think about something to which the wall would represent a real barrier.

Well?

Yep—*H. floresiensis*, the all-devouring runt of the hominid family tree.

That wall was designed to keep hobbits behind it.

So just who built the wall to keep the hobbits trapped inside?

Again, look at the wall. Who would build a wall with such a doorway? There is no way that any standard human, standing 5-6 feet tall, would waste the time with such a massive door. There is only one logical candidate available—Kong.

I'm not suggesting that King Kong built the wall—he doesn't have the brainpower for such an effort. But as our explorers point out, this wall was built by some long-vanished ancient civilization.

How about *Gigantopithecus blacki*?

All the pieces fit. Imagine sometime before the dawn of recorded history, 10,000 to 20,000 years ago, on one of the 566 islands of the East Nusa Tenggara, where there lives a gentle race of *Gigantopithecus blacki*—farmers, plant eaters, trapped on Skull Island and safely isolated from the marauding *Homo sapiens* that are covering the planet. But all is not well on Skull Island—not only do Gigantopithecus have all these meat-hungry dinosaurs to contend with (as we see in *King Kong*, even the dinosaurs that should be herbivores, such as Stegosaurus and Brontosaurus, are some strange meat-eating variant) but hordes of these evil little hobbits.

What to do?

Build a really big wall. And on those rare occasions when you need to go inside, make sure that you have a Gigantopithecus-sized door. Makes sense. And what happened to this tribe of Gigantopithecus? Well, I would suggest that the wall was both their salvation and demise. Again, we need to consider the many clues that Cooper gives us. Remember that when he shows us the map of Skull Island, the region of the island outside the wall is little more than a *sandy* peninsula.

Obviously the Gigantopithecus did not have enough land to support a diverse and stable population. Trees were probably cut for firewood, and to clear land for the growth of crops. But after generations of tilling the same soil, the land would have eventually become exhausted, less and less food would have been able to grow and the population would have imploded through a combination of starvation and warfare over dwindling resources. We have ample evidence of such population implosions on island ecologies throughout the world: Easter Island, for example, once had abundant enough resources and a large enough population to support the building of thousands of statues. But the destruction of forests and intrinsically poor soils on tropical islands resulted in a population crash; in this case, not a single person had survived on Easter Island by the time Westerners discovered it.

And this is most likely what happened to the Gigantopithecus of Skull Island. As the food supplies dwindled, each generation would have become more and more nutritionally deprived, resulting in severe malnutrition and eventually leading to brain damage in Gigantopithecus embryos. As a result, each subsequent generation would slide further and further back the evolutionary ladder, until what had once been a proud race of *Gigantopithecus blacki*, a people who had been able to build a magnificent wall, would have become little more than a handful of gorilla-like creatures, what I would call *Gigantopithecus kong.*

And when there was nothing left to eat on their side of the island, they would have been forced over the wall, to fend the best they could in those savage lands, regressing even further back into barbarism—becoming meat eaters themselves. And of course we know what the most plentiful source of meat must have been—hobbits.

But how long could an annoying race of little hobbits have lasted against the now meat-hungry race of *Gigantopithecus kong*? A few generations at best, and then the hobbits would have been gone (anthropologists estimate this occurred about 10,000 years ago on the East Nusa Tenggara island of Flores), and *Gigantopithecus kong* would have had nothing to eat at that point except dinosaurs. Evolution was still in play, favoring the biggest, toughest *Gigantopithecus kong*, those that stood the best chance of taking down a big meat-eating dinosaur. After several thousand years, what you have left is a creature twice the size of the gentle *Gigantopithecus blacki*—an inbred, mentally decayed animal operating under the misguided impression that if it could only mate with a human (preferably a blonde), then its race could be renewed. By the time Western explorers arrived only a single member of that species was left—King Kong.

This is undoubtedly how Cooper pieced together the story, from legends that local islanders told, from mysterious items found in Chinese apothecaries, from walls that could have only been built by huge creatures and from sightings of the few pitiful hobbits to have survived into modern times.

This is a prehistory never suspected—one that runs totally counter to the creation story of the Bible. This is undoubtedly the tale that Cooper would have wanted to tell, but an America not ready for the truth, coupled with a studio on the brink of bankruptcy, unable to take the risk of generating a controversy with Bible fundamentalists, forced Cooper into producing the politically correct monster movie that we have today.

But you now know the truth.

The King Kong created in 1933 is fictional.

But *Gigantopithecus kong* may still survive on some unnamed island in the East Nusa Tenggara, dreaming of days long past when his relatives built mighty walls, hobbits trembled at their passing, and Skull Island was a true Garden of Eden.

ROBERT A. METZGER is a research scientist and a science fiction and science writer. His research focuses on the technique of Molecular Beam Epitaxy, used to grow epitaxial films for high-speed electronics applications. His short fiction has appeared in most major SF magazines, including *Asimov's*, *Fantasy & Science Fiction* and *SF Age*, while his 2002 novel *Picoverse* was a Nebula finalist, and his most recent novel *CUSP* was released by Ace in 2005. His science writing has appeared in *Wired* and *Analog*, and he is a contributing editor to the *Science Fiction Writers of America Bulletin*.

King Kong
Behind the Scenes

David Gerrold

DAVID GERROLD TAKES US behind the scenes of the original film, introducing us to the *real* Kong...and Ann, the bold, young co-star he loved....

The soundtrack begins with a scratchy buzz, then we see a badly framed industry leader counting down to:

Black and white, flickering, grainy, scratched, a terrible old print of one of the most exciting sequences in the original 1933 classic, *King Kong*. This is a full shot of the great gate of the natives—Kong is slowly pushing it open as the natives run screaming in terror.

As the great ape comes stamping through, suddenly the music becomes a full stereophonic orchestra, color floods the image, the screen swells to a full 70mm—and Kong, the most magnificent ape of all, comes charging, roaring, bellowing into the native village to wreak havoc upon their homes. The sequence runs through its most exciting shots, and then, as it peaks, we hear a voice say, "Cut, cut, cut!"

The camera pulls back and we are looking at a back-lot set. Extras, dressed as natives, mill around with bored expressions while the director, Ernest B. Schoedsack, calls Kong aside for a conference. We see the two of them discussing something in the script; Schoedsack is speaking in low tones, Kong is replying in deep, guttural grunts. Kong nods his head knowingly, Schoedsack pats the ape's arm reassuringly and the huge twenty-foot ape shambles back onto the set and back into position, while an assistant director hollers, "All right, places, everybody."

Schoedsack calls, "Let's try another take. Lights, please. Camera. Action!"

And the filming continues, with Kong smashing his way through the rest of the native village. We climax with Kong picking up one of the natives, popping him into his mouth and biting his head off. (This is one of the famous "missing scenes"—eventually rediscovered and restored.)

"Cut. Print. That's a take," Schoedsack calls. "Next set-up, please."

We go to a wider angle on the set. We see Kong retiring to a large chair with his name on the back. He starts paging through a copy of *Variety*, circa 1931. An assistant director confers with Schoedsack in low tones, "We gotta do something about all the extras he's eating. Central Casting is getting suspicious."

And we go to titles:

KING KONG: BEHIND THE SCENES

Open on Fay Wray, an elegant older woman, being interviewed by an off-screen reporter.

She is reminiscing about the first day she reported to work for Merian C. Cooper and Ernest B. Schoedsack.

At that time, they had just begun working on a new picture that all of Hollywood was buzzing about....

Dissolve to 1931. A young Fay Wray (dark-haired) coming onto the soundstage for the first time and being introduced to her co-star, young Kong—a hulking twenty-foot ape.

"I remember Kong as being very good-natured, very eager to please, but very, very naive about life in the big city. He let people take advantage of him something awful. Even though he'd been in Hollywood for two years before being discovered by Mr. Schoedsack—Mr. Schoedsack had seen him in Schwabs eating a four-foot banana split—Kong never became hard or cynical like so many other young actors whose careers were faltering, because he never lost his optimism, so he never fell for the whole 'Hollywood' thing. Even afterward, the fame never went to his head. He was always his own quiet self—I think that's what I liked about him the most."

We see Fay Wray shaking hands with Kong, who is carrying a script under one arm. "I'm looking forward to working with you, Mr. Kong."

Kong gives one of his familiar guttural grunts in reply.

She twinkles, "And you can call me Fay—"

And we see the first beginnings of the love affair between Kong and Fay, right here in their first meeting—she can't take her eyes off him, and he is equally entranced by her. Voiceover narration continues, "If only I had known what lay in store for both of us...."

We see the dailies:

The shot is Kong battering at the gates of the wall—this is the view from his side, before he has managed to push the great doors open. The dailies are in black and white, of course, and there is the usual run of outtakes.

We see Kong leaning patiently on the door while a slate pops into foreground. Offscreen voice calls, "Action," and he turns and knocks politely.

We hear producer and director comments over all this. "Well, you can't fault his manners."

Slate and second take. Kong knocks a little harder, but still not in character. (The audience knows what the shot should look like—they're feeling what the director is feeling now.)

Producer: "I don't think he understands the scene...."

Slate and third take. Kong finally begins to knock properly. An extra falls off the top of the wall.

Producer: "Oh, shit—"

Director grunts.

Producer: "He's awfully hard on the extras, isn't he? How many does that make?"

"Six. I think."

Slate and fourth take. We see Kong getting a little more fidgety in the background between takes.

"Action!"—and he begins banging on the wall again. This looks like a good take, until part of the wall—the wrong part—collapses, revealing stagehands and lights behind it.

Director: "That's when we broke for lunch."

Slate and fifth take. We see director and Kong conferring softly, director acting out the motion, Kong nodding. Re-slate. Kong begins again.

"I don't know. He just doesn't seem to have the feel for it."

"He's young—give him a chance."

"What about that little Italian kid—Dino whatshisname? The one with the rubber suit?"

"No, no, I think this will work out better in the long run. Give Kong a chance."

Slate, and next take. Kong falls on his ass.

"He was getting tired there, but I think we can cut away, then cut back and use the stuff from the other side of the wall."

End of take, setting up for next one, camera still rolling—

"Hmm, I must have forgotten to call a cut."

We hear the extras jeering Kong, calling him a "big monkey." We see Kong finally getting honestly angry—and he bashes down the wall exactly as we remember him doing it from the classic film.

"Hey—!"

Fay Wray narrating again:

"That was Kong's screen test. He wasn't a very good actor at first, it was all very new and strange to him to be in the movies, and he had a lot to learn—but Mr. Schoedsack was very patient and kind, and Kong was a fast learner. There was something about him, a raw power that couldn't be denied. I had to dye my hair blonde for the first day of shooting, and ..."

We see Kong's famous entrance scene re-created for the watching cameras—the first time the theater audience sees him as he comes crashing through the forest, parting trees, and as he catches his first glimpse of Fay Wray....

Fay: "There were fourteen takes—"

We see a montage of Kong reactions—excited, stunned, happy and so on.

"He was very pleased when he saw me as a blonde; he thought it did wonders to bring out the color in my cheeks."

We see Kong and Fay Wray talking softly between takes, she holding a Coke in one hand, he holding a barrel.

"Kong was just a big, overgrown kid—the theater audience didn't realize it at the time, but he hadn't even reached his full growth. In fact, he grew another four feet while the picture was in production, which explains why he looked taller in the New York scenes.

"We were in production for two years. But at the beginning, he was very shy and needed a lot of coaching. He had a tendency to overact on some of the subtle scenes, and not be big enough on the more dramatic shots."

We see Fay and Kong sharing a quiet moment together.

"Kong also had a terrific sense of humor...."

We see Fay re-creating the famous scene with Robert Armstrong, where he is making the first screen tests of her aboard the ship. She is wearing a long, white dress, and Armstrong is exhorting her to, "Look up, up, now you see it, it's huge, it's horrifying—"

We cut to a wider angle and we see Kong standing off to one side, watching the take—and making grotesque faces at Fay.

"He used to try to make me break up during shots."

In the shot, Fay starts giggling, and Kong delightedly slaps his thighs.

"He thought that was great fun. Mr. Schoedsack didn't dare bawl him out for it in front of everybody, but you could tell he was annoyed. I think Kong must have been very lonely at that time. He was always on the set—even on days when he wasn't needed, he was always there. I think he just didn't have any other place to go. And he felt at home on the soundstage. As if we were his only family. I guess I felt sorry for him, at first."

Fay finishes the take and rejoins Kong.

"Later on, I grew to see the nobler qualities of this very misunderstood actor—"

Fay narrates her first meetings with Bruce Cabot, and we see an innocent and charming boy-girl relationship developing between them; it is not serious, but the moment between them is one of those moments so easily misinterpreted.

We see Kong entering the soundstage at an inopportune time, and abruptly seeing his co-star spooning with her "other leading man."

Kong's face darkens and he sulks off the set....

In the next take, we see Kong losing his temper and punching down a scaffolding with some natives on it—another one of the famous missing scenes—but now we know why Kong was so mad.

Narration: "We had some trouble in planning the ending of the picture. For one thing, we weren't sure where to stage it...."

We see shots of Kong holding Fay Wray atop a variety of 1933 landmarks: Radio City Music Hall...Grand Central Station...the Chrysler Building...the Statue of Liberty...

"...but none of them seemed to feel right. Finally, someone remembered that the Empire State Building was due to be finished soon, and it was going to be the tallest building in the world. Out of desperation, because we couldn't think of anyplace else, we decided to stage the ending of the picture there. It seemed like a good idea at the time."

We see the Empire State Building, still uncompleted, Kong climbing it slowly—

Fay Wray narrating: "One of the best-kept secrets was that Kong was very much afraid of heights—but there was no other way to shoot some of the scenes for the ending, except to go to the newly completed Empire State Building and actually shoot them there."

We see Kong and Fay Wray on top of the Empire State Building, makeup men working on both of them, then hurriedly leaving the scene. We see a camera plane circling nearby. An assistant director with a radio set signals them for action, and we see a take of the "original" ending of the movie.

"Ann Darrow is on the roof of the Empire State Building, threatening to jump. Kong comes up to the top in an attempt to save her, thus proving he is not a monster at all, but really a very good guy at heart. The closing shot is the two of them watching a tranquil sunrise over 1933 New York, fadeout."

The first take isn't good, however, and while we reset for another take from the camera plane or perhaps a camera dirigible, Kong and Fay Wray talk over their difficulties.

Grunt, grunt.

"Kong, don't you see—we can't go on meeting like this."

Despondent grunt.

"All this sneaking around, hiding from other people—"

Very despondent grunt.

"Your family doesn't like me at all. And there's the religious differences. How would we raise the children? And all the social pressures. And there's another thing—"

Grunt. Grunt. I don't want to hear it.

"It would mean the end of your career. You know how prejudiced people can be. I don't mind giving up my career, but I can't let you deprive the world of a great talent—"

Kong is very upset. Grunt, grunt, grunt, grunt. He turns away from her.

"Oh, please—don't talk like that. You know you don't mean it."

Grunt. Grunt. I do too.

"Kong, don't you see—it's over. It's bigger than both of—well, it's too big, anyway—"

Kong rages—

In the camera plane, we see the director and cameraman. Cameraman says he's ready, the director says, "Roll 'em."

Back on the tower, Kong is still raging angrily at Fay Wray.

The assistant director calls, "Action," but Kong ignores him. Ditto Fay. "Kong," she says, "I know it's hard, but it has to be this way."

Grunt. Grunt. I can't live without you. And he turns to jump—

"No, don't—"

He turns back to her, reaching, imploring—

She reaches for him—

And he loses his balance—

And falls—exactly as we remember him falling in the 1933 original.

Fay screams, horrified. The makeup men and assistant director have to hold her back to keep her from throwing herself off after him. "Oh, God, no—"

Down on the street, we see Robert Armstrong push his way through the crowd, and someone behind him says, "He fell—"

And Armstrong says, "Oh, no. 'Twas Beauty killed the Beast."

Next to him, an assistant director notes, "Hey, that's a good line."

Fay Wray's voiceover narration continues: "Of course, we had to change the ending of the original picture. Kong was supposed to rescue me; now he dies in the attempt. Mr. Schoedsack used the film they had already exposed, and the wonderful Mr. O'Brien superimposed in all these biplanes, so his experiments with stop-motion animation paid off after all.

"Of course, there were all those terrible rumors that circulated for years afterward that Kong hadn't really died, that his death had been faked, and that he'd been living in secret up in Benedict Canyon for all this time—the fact that no one was allowed near his body and that the funeral was very private seemed to prove those claims—but I was there, I loved Kong more than all the millions of his movie fans, I loved him more than anyone, and if he were still alive, I would certainly know it." She is very, very wistful. "Even today, so many years later, I still put a wreath on his grave every year."

The angle widens and we see Fay Wray looking small and sad and obviously in a great deal of pain. "I guess Robert Armstrong was right...I guess beauty did kill the beast."

As the interview concludes, we hear a car pull up, and a door slam off screen. Fay says, "Oh, that's my son coming home now."

We hear a familiar heavy footfall, followed by a very familiar grunt. All off screen.

Fay says, "He's just like his father."

And we fade out.

DAVID GERROLD is the author of numerous television episodes, including the legendary "Trouble With Tribbles" episode of *Star Trek*. He has also written for *Land of the Lost*, *Babylon 5*, *Twilight Zone*, *Sliders* and other series. He has published forty-five books, including two on television production. He taught screenwriting at Pepperdine University for two decades. He has won the Hugo, Nebula and Locus Awards. A movie based on his autobiographical novel, *The Martian Child*, is now in production.

III

The Philosophy of King Kong: Thinking about the Great Ape

Of Gorillas and Gods
The Kong-flict of Nineteenth-Century Thought and Twentieth-Century Man

Charlie W. Starr

*K*ING KONG IS OFTEN SEEN as a conflict between the primitive, as represented by Kong, and the civilized world. But in Charlie W. Starr's view, this is all wrong. Far from an icon of the *primitive*, Kong symbolizes the unbounded ambition of Modern Man....

"And the Prophet said, 'And lo, the beast looked upon the face of beauty. And it stayed its hand from killing. And from that day, it was as one dead."
　　　—OLD ARABIAN PROVERB, quoted at the beginning of *King Kong*

"It was a woman in the flower of her age; she was so tall that she seemed to him a Titaness, a sun-bright virgin clad in complete steel, with a sword naked in her hand. The giant bent forward in his chair and looked at her.

'Who are you?' he said.

'My name is Reason,' said the virgin.

'Try now to answer my...riddle. By what rule do you tell a copy from an original?'

The giant muttered and mumbled and could not answer, and Reason set spurs in her stallion and it leaped up on to the giant's mossy knees and galloped up his foreleg, till she plunged her sword into his

heart. Then there was a noise and a crumbling like a landslide and the huge carcass settled down; and the Spirit of the Age became what he had seemed to be at first, a sprawling hummock of rock."
—C.S. LEWIS, *The Pilgrim's Regress*

I'm sure many of us were surprised by Peter Jackson's choice to move from the stately world of Middle Earth to the savage jungles of Skull Island. Rather than taking up *The Hobbit* (the prequel to his monumental Lord of the Rings films), as many had hoped, he opted for a remake of *King Kong*. Perhaps, having worked with hobbit-sized people for six years, his penchant for actors of varying size moved him to want to direct a larger star (trolls, I suppose, just weren't big enough). That he said no to *The Hobbit* didn't surprise me—even I might have been sick of Middle Earth after six years and three films. But why *King Kong*? What fascination is there to be found in an *Übergorilla*, for Jackson or for his audiences? The greater surprise for me came when I began researching Kong's history. I knew of the original 1933 classic and its 1976 remake, of *The Son of Kong* and *Mighty Joe Young* (and its more recent redux). But I was surprised to find, or had nearly forgotten, the dozen or so additional spin-offs in film and television, everything from Japanese monster movie shtick (how could I forget *Godzilla vs. King Kong*?) to pornographic camp, to a children's cartoon series. That's when it hit me. Nothing keeps its pop-culture staying power, especially not for seventy years, but that it somehow resonates with the masses, connecting with a large group of people in a way that defies analysis (even when it was first released, the original film had an impact, breaking all box office records of its day). This *Kong* thing had to mean something.

Karl Jung gave us the concept of inborn, archetypal (or foundational) images, part of a universal human unconscious that wells up into our conscious understanding through art, literature and myth. And in these images is incarnated a primal understanding of hidden patterns in Being itself. To first view an archetypal image—a serpent, a paradisal garden, a hellish underworld—is to experience something absolutely familiar to us in a picture or story we've never before seen. In *King Kong* we're presented an archetype as old as Enkidu and the Sumerian harlot in the *Epic of Gilgamesh*: the Beauty and the Beast myth. But neither Jung nor the great myth gurus Frazier or Campbell ever discovered an archetypal story featuring a giant gorilla.

The image of a mighty ape resonates like an ancient archetype in the mind of modern culture, as if we've invented a new element among those rock-bottom atoms that form the chemistry of all human experience. Dragons and giant serpents have long roamed our imaginative past, but in 1933 a new image emerged, brought to life in one of the first mythic films in history. In Kong we have a new Beast for Beauty to subdue. He entered our cultural consciousness in the '30s, but his origins hearken back to the previous century. And though his image may float in semiconscious recesses of the imagination, he is born of scientific rationalism, conscious deliberation and cold philosophical abstraction.

King Kong is indeed a mythic story. It is a parable of Modernity, a vision of twentieth-century humanity bequeathed to us by nineteenth-century thought. In short, *King Kong* is a parable of nineteenth-century thinking's legacy to twentieth-century culture, what we call *Modernity*: a vision of man which elevates us to godhood while turning us into animals, which raises the human spirit to the heights of Divinity, but only by denying the existence of Humanness and Spirit. It builds a tower to heaven, our own Empire State Babel, but forever denies the Beast the heavenly bliss of marriage to the Beauty. *King Kong* is the story of Modernist man's vision of what humankind is: a mighty god who turns out to be an oversexed gorilla.

TRANSCENDENCE OR ASCENDANCE

The difference between Pre-Modern and Modern thinking has been described in terms of dichotomies: faith vs. skepticism, superstition vs. rationality, religion vs. science. All wrong—examples of what Owen Barfield called the modern predilection to "chronological snobbery." The real difference has been a top-down vs. bottom-up approach to pursuing knowledge.

Pre-Modern thinking was dominated by a belief in Transcendence. This isn't merely a belief in God and religious faith: Plato's philosophy, foundational to Western thinking, argued that everything from abstract ideas (like Reason, Truth, Justice and Goodness) to physical objects themselves was rooted in a higher, Transcendent reality. Knowledge, in their paradigm—their complete system of thought—was a thing to be discovered, not determined. The shift away from Transcendence began with René Descartes (1596–1650). Again, the change did not come because of science or skepticism, but because of the Cartesian approach to knowing. Descartes shifted the seat of knowledge to the individual human mind. He did not, himself, reject Transcendence; he initiated a methodology of thinking that would lead others to do so. The resulting paradigm, born of the Enlightenment, was Modernism—and with it came the bloodiest century in human history.

King Kong is a parable of that paradigm.

DARWIN AND THE APE

Carl Denham, maker of adventure documentaries, takes an expedition by ship to the South Pacific. His goal: to make "the greatest picture in the world, something that nobody's ever seen or heard of." How like Darwin who, a century before, documented creatures unseen in his South Pacific sea voyage to the Galapagos Islands. What he returned with was indeed something no one had ever heard of.

We cannot underestimate the impact of Darwin's *The Origin of Species* on Western thought. Though alternatives to Divine Creation had previously been entertained in the history of philosophy and the shorter history of science, none of them were taken seriously. Certain questions are foundational, among them the question of Existence. Till Darwin, the most widely received answer was a top-down answer: the *Immanent* (or immediately visible) universe was rooted in a *Transcendent* source (primarily thought of as a Creator God). But Darwin proposed an intellectual framework for biological processes which eliminated the necessity for a Divine/Transcendent/Non-Materialistic origin to the universe. He suggested a bottom-up explanation for existence, an idea no one had ever before "seen or heard of." Like the New York marquee's description of Kong, Darwin's theory was a veritable "Eighth Wonder of the World."

The Darwinian element of the parable continues in the description of the island. It is, first of all, a place known by its most prominent feature: a mountain shaped like a skull. Certainly among the chief images that shape evolutionary vision are skulls, those of the so-called human-ape hybrids dug up by heroic Leakeys in Africa (where Denham made most of his movies) and argued to be links in a chain of natural history. Furthermore, this island contains a wall built by a forgotten civilization from the ancient past but kept in repair by superstitious natives who fear what's on the other side: a Darwinian past—a primordial jungle of dinosaurs and death. The wall stands as the metaphor of superstition and rejection, of a Gothic civilization intent on hiding itself from Darwin's evolutionary cosmos (and Freud's animalistic *id*, as we'll see).

The ship's captain and first mate ask Denham what it is the natives fear behind the wall. Denham replies that it is something "neither beast nor man." That's what Darwin gives us: humanity no longer born of a Divine spark in a paradisal garden, but by survival of the fittest in the jungle slaughterhouse of natural selection. The ship's crew experience this world firsthand: more than a dozen deaths are dealt out among people and beast alike. (It's a wonder enough dinos survive on the island to propagate with Kong on his constant killing rampage.) All but two of the crew prove unable to survive, apparently having lost too much of their animal nature. Most important, though, is Kong, "neither beast nor man," symbol of the Darwinian definition of the human race as handed to the twentieth century. In it, humanity descends from its special place in God's creation but rises from the slime to stand on its own two feet (*Homo erectus* indeed), a king of the natural world like Kong, the anthropomorphic ape (he smiles, grasps his throat, and rubs his eyes like a human), who loves the beautiful woman. Darwin's gift to Modern Man's self-myth was a vision of man as neither man-the-Divine-creation nor merely an insignificant beast.

NIETZSCHE AND THE GIANT

Nietzsche's contribution to the *Kong* parable was the death of God (which doubtless came as a surprise to the Almighty). Nietzsche saw, in Darwin, the foundation for the destruction of top-down morality. In a biological explanation for existence, a whole new ethical system was required. With God no longer necessary to explain the universe, not only should the moral foundation of culture shift, but morals themselves. Every Transcendent thing—God, Ideals, Morality—was human invention. Reality was survival of the fittest, and the new morality had to be born of this reality. The will to power was Nietzsche's new ethic. He claimed that Christianity had given rise to the good of the masses: values like meekness, patient suffering and forgiveness, in which only the unprivileged, the disenfranchised, could find solace. The new Darwinian world proved that power, aggression and ascension—the values of the privileged, aristocratic few—were true to human history.

But of course such ethics are only for the elite. Selection of the fittest means that some must rise above the masses. In fact, the goal of humanity ought to be the purposeful continuance of its evolution: the production of the *Superman*. This is not the elevation of all men to greatness; aggression and ascension mean the few will rise above the masses, will step on common men to do so (as Kong literally does). God is greatness, conflict, war and the sacrifice of the many to the will of the one. This *Superman*, this giant among men, is Nietzsche's final ethic. Freedom and democracy are its great enemies, and in hindsight we know that he laid the philosophical foundations of Fascism.

The parable of *Kong*, then, is a parable of a giant, kicked up from the average by Darwinian processes to become a giant among men, a god. Says Denham, "Did you ever hear of Kong?" to which Captain Englehorn replies, "Why, yes. Some native superstition, isn't it? A god or a spirit or something?" Denham calls Kong "[a]ll powerful, still living...holding that island in a grip of deadly fear." In Kong, the human spirit is elevated to godhood, but since Darwin has eliminated the divine spark in humanity and Nietzsche the existence of Divinity altogether, the giant is an anthropomorphic ape, a *Homo gigantus*, whose only Transcendence is extreme savagery and strength. In true Nietzschean fashion, however, modern man conquers this god. Seeing the strength in Kong, Englehorn says, "No chains will ever hold that." But Denham replies, "We'll give him more than chains. He's always been king of his world. But we'll teach him fear." Kong's captors drag him to a new jungle, one of steel and concrete, where, true to prediction, he cannot be held. *Superman*, the great Darwinian Beast, breaks his chains to wreak havoc on the lesser creatures of his new realm and climb the jungle heights of Manhattan. Using Darwinian nature, Nietzsche gave Modern Man a vision of himself as capable of replacing God. But once God is dead and Transcendence along with Him, Man's ascent slams into the ceiling of his material, his natural self. And as big as that self may be, it is, in the end, still only an animal.

FREUD AND THE RAPE

According to Sigmund Freud, that animal is a horny one. If, through Modernist thinking, Darwin killed creation and Nietzsche God, Freud killed the existence of a human soul. As Darwin believed that humanity ascended out of creatures less complex, so Freud believed that human personality ascended from unconscious regions of the mind (or we might more accurately say *brain* since a completely materialistic view of the cosmos must deny the existence of a mind). At the base of human personality was a subconscious *id* which, like its animal predecessors, was chiefly concerned with survival and procreation. All human behavior, in Freud's thinking, could be reduced to aggression and sex: dominate your environment and continue your species—survival of the fittest. Morality and civilization, then, were mere products of a more evolved *superego* which struggled to keep the *id* in check.

Freud's vision of the human animal is a perfect example of Modernity's rejection of Transcendent vision in favor of a bottom-up approach. At the beginning of this essay, I quoted from C. S. Lewis' philosophical allegory *The Pilgrim's Regress*. In the story, the giant "Spirit of the Age" is challenged by the beautiful woman "Reason" to solve a riddle: "By what rule do you tell a copy from an original?" The giant cannot answer and is slain. Lewis said every age had a blindness, a preconceived way of looking at reality, of which the people of that age were completely unaware. Among others, the great blindness of the twentieth-century West has been a failure to know the source of human ideals and experiences.

Where, for example, does love come from? Do human beings love because love is an evolutionary inflation of the instinct for sex, or do they love because Love is a quality of Spirit that permeates the universe from the heights of heaven (or, if you prefer, from a higher Transcendent Reality) down to the very act of biological procreation? Is morality the product of a herd instinct—an attempt by the mass of human animals to control the alpha males—or is Goodness an absolute, a Transcendent Concrete as real and necessary for governing the human condition as are the laws of physics? And what about our longing for an afterlife: is it simply the survival instinct gone steroidal in an over-developed cerebrum, or, is it that, just as hunger proves the existence (if not the immediate presence) of food, so our hunger for Transcendent Life proves its existence and attainability? Whence the copy, and whence the original?

If we look at reality from the top down, with Plato and Christ and the long-standing vision of Pre-modern thinking, then Beauty, Goodness and Love are Transcendent Realities, more real than atoms, more dense than a collapsed star. But if we look at reality from the bottom up with Darwin and Freud, beauty and love are illusions of an over-evolved sex drive, and morality and spirit are illusions of an over-developed survival instinct—they are all mere wish-fulfillment. So which is the copy, and which is the original?

Kong is a creature built from the bottom up at the art-deco height of the Modernist vision, when Nietzsche's own hideous creation, Adolf Hitler, had only begun his rise to smash the utopian longings of the age. Kong is the beast of the *id*, whose longing for the beautiful woman is mere lust. She exists in the story to satisfy voyeuristic desire; without her, there can't even be a movie. As Denham says: "All right. The public wants a girl, and this time, I'm gonna give 'em what they want." And though Denham swears to Ann that he has only honorable intentions, Driscoll, the ship's first mate, understands the disturbing power of her sexual presence onboard an all-male sailing ship. She is a "nuisance" and the ship is "no place for a girl." Women, he claims, "just can't help being a bother. Made that way, I guess."

Yes, made (through natural selection for the sake of survival of the species) to raise male sexual desire and its accompanying aggression by their mere appearance. The crew gawk at her from every available perch. Denham notes that once even the toughest man "gets a look at a pretty face," he inevitably "cracks up and goes sappy." Voyeurism, and the woman reduced to image, to property, become dominant themes in the film. Denham himself is on a lifelong quest to capture images. He admires Ann's choice of the "Beauty and the Beast costume" which she chose because it was the "prettiest" and will create the image of her he wants for his film.

When the crew arrives on the island, the "white men" (and woman) of the West are witness to a marriage ceremony. "Holy mackerel, what a show!" exclaims Denham as he tries to capture the images on film. But the bride is more property than person, a half-naked sacrificial offering to the desires of the island's hairy king. When the tribal chief sees Ann, he offers six of his own women in trade, and when he is refused, he exercises his role as alpha male and takes her against her will. In a ceremony that looks as much like an orgy as a sacrificial ritual, the natives offer Ann as a bride to Kong.

Kong's anthropomorphic expressions—wide eyes and wide tooth-filled smile—indicate that he is as attracted to Ann as any man. He protects her with furious vengeance and, upon reaching his mountaintop cave, strokes her body with a clumsy finger, tearing off pieces of her clothing (the sexual imagery is even more obvious in the 1976 *Kong* remake, where the heroine ends up topless and Denham's counterpart, Wilson, flat out says that Kong "raped" her). Thus, the "Beauty" in this Beauty and the Beast story is an object of lust, obtained by violence, and possessed for the purpose of rape.

The theme of satisfying voyeuristic lust does not end in the movie with the rescue of Ann. In a role reversal, Kong becomes the object to possess, an "eighth wonder of the world" held in chains to be ogled by Western audiences. Denham steps out onstage in a Broadway theater and says to the audience, "I'm going to show you the greatest thing your eyes have ever beheld. He was a king and a god in the world he knew, but now he comes to civilization, merely a captive, on show to gratify your curiosity." The power of the *id* is subjugated by the civilizing *superego* for the sake of gratifying lust in a civilized veneer, the "lust of the eye." Neither man nor beast, Superman that is only an animal, creature of the *id* whose only desires are sex and aggression—Kong is the image twentieth-century Man had of himself, received from his nineteenth-century fathers. Those in the audience are, in fact, looking at themselves.

BEAUTY AND THE TRANSCENDENT

Is a vision of Transcendence merely wish-fulfillment? Our longing for greatness may be born of subconscious aggression, but perhaps its source is a Divine spark in a truly existing central soul. And Love may be born of the sex drive, but perhaps its roots are eternal. If there is a single best argument for the existence of Transcendent Power governing human being, it is another human longing: the desire for Beauty, a hunger which a bottom-up approach *can* explain but not in so compelling a way as to satisfy our experience of it.

King Kong is not merely the story of a beast. There is a beauty in the equation, and the film itself belies its Modernist vision. Neither Kong nor Driscoll, nor perhaps even Darwin, Nietzsche or Freud, can long stand against the Beauty that is Ann. You see, "the public, bless 'em, must have a pretty face to look at," and there isn't "any romance or adventure in the world without having a flapper in it" (says Denham). But what do romance and adventure have to do with Darwinian biology or Freudian psychology? Sex and aggression, I suppose. Over-evolved desires turned into wish-fulfillment. Except that those desires cannot explain actions that go against the instincts for survival. As the proverb at the film's beginning suggests, Beauty can kill the Beast.

The controlling theme of *King Kong* is spoken by Denham in reference to his own movie: "It's the idea of my picture. The Beast was a tough guy too. He forgot his wisdom and the little fellas licked him." The "little fellas" are Nietzsche's mass/majority, who try to contain the *Superman*. The "wisdom" is the philosophy of man handed to Modernity by Darwin, Nietzsche and Freud. And the Beauty is that longing for Transcendence that defies the wisdom of Materialist Man. Most especially, this longing defies Man's sense of self-preservation. Backstage before the New York show Denham tells reporters, "Kong could've stayed safe where he was, but he couldn't stay away from Beauty." Modern Man rejects Transcendence and then risks destruction in his quest to have it back.

Ann is the "golden woman" to the island natives, more valuable than six *normal* women (racial interpretations aside). She is the figure of Divine Presence at her marriage to Kong: in one moment, as we look back through the doors at the altar to which Ann is tied—this just before the doors are shut—her outstretched arms and S-bent form mimic the figure of Christ in traditional crucifixion images. More than the object of lust, Ann is the object of longing; she is heaven come to an earth which has written heaven from its rational belief. Consider her power even on our popular culture: few people remember the names Robert Armstrong (who played Denham) or Bruce Cabot (Driscoll). Conversely, the character name Ann Darrow is all but lost, while the actress Fay Wray endures in our cultural memory as the Beauty who tamed Kong.

HEAR THEN THE PARABLE...

King Kong is a parable of Modernism, specifically of the definition of humanity handed to the Modern world by its nineteenth-century intellectual forefathers. Kong is Modernist Man, rejecting Transcendence and God and thereby elevating himself to the place of godhood (of power) by reducing himself to the place of an animal. Simultaneously he destroys those Transcendent concepts—Beauty, Divinity, Goodness, Love—which gave his life meaning, while longing to have them back.

The parable culminates atop the Empire State Building, the Babel-like tower built by Modern Man to his own godhood. There Kong climbs to the edge of heaven, that high throne like his island mountain, only to find that heaven is gone, replaced by a naked sky populated no more by winged angels, nor even living Pterodactyls (creatures from which he could easily save his Beauty). Instead demonic biplanes, lifeless machines, now inhabit his cosmos; he cannot defeat the Materialist world he has created, where all life is but machine and thus the strongest machines shall claim godhood over him. Having rejected Transcendence, he can neither keep his throne of Divinity nor join in marriage to his Beauty. He cannot save her, and so he leaves her atop the unconquerable tower, lost forever to his evolutionary jungle. Like Lucifer, he falls to a hell of his own making (but that was only a fable, wasn't it?—and this only a movie), there to die and become meat for the survival of the fittest worms.

Modern Man began to die in the sixties, though a few intellectual vestiges yet remain. But if we do not learn the lesson of the *Kong* parable, it will not be the Modernist nightmare—nuclear holocaust—that kills us, nor machines that fly. Nor will it be religious fanaticism as many in a post-9/11 world fear may be the case. Religious fanaticism gives us the paradoxical horror of holy war, but Secular/Materialist fanaticism gave us Hitler, Stalin, the Khmer Rouge and forty million dead. This is the lesson of the *Kong* parable: the real danger is a return to philosophical systems that reject Transcendence for Materialist/Evolutionary visions of humanity and morality. To reject Beauty is what will kill us. Such is Denham's profoundly sappy conclusion: "Oh no; it wasn't the airplanes. 'Twas Beauty killed the Beast."

CHARLIE W. STARR teaches English, humanities and film at Kentucky Christian University in Eastern Kentucky, where he also coaches soccer and makes movies with his students and family. He writes articles, teaches Sunday school and has published two books, one on Paul's letter to the Romans, the other a science fiction novel entitled *The Heart of Light*. His third book

Honest to God is due out from Navpress in the summer of 2005. He enjoys writing, reading classic literature and watching bad television and movies of every kind. Charlie describes his wife Becky as "a full of life, full-blooded Cajun, who can cook like one, too." They have two children: Bryan, who wants to be the next Steven Spielberg, and Alli, who wants to be the next Jacques Cousteau.

Why Does My Daughter Love King Kong So Much?

Adam Roberts

O NE OF THE MOST DISTINCTIVE THINGS about Kong is his size. With diminutive blondes clasped in meaty paws, the sheer difference in scale is both terrifying and somehow compelling. To be in the grasp of such an all-powerful, incomprehensible creature, completely at its mercy, is just so...well, just imagine how your children feel!

The first thing I did, when I was approached to write an essay for this collection, was to buy the DVD of the 1933 *King Kong* to refresh my memory of what the film was about. Watching it through a couple of times I discovered something interesting, or interesting to me, at any rate. My three-year-old daughter—whose favorite films to date had been *Finding Nemo*, *Shrek* and the live-action *Peter Pan*, and whose cinematic taste I therefore felt I had pegged as being determined by bright colors, fast inventive storylines and a child-based emphasis—absolutely loves *King Kong*. She was wholly absorbed in it when we watched it together. When it was finished she wanted immediately to watch it again. She has now watched it dozens of times. The fact that it's an old film, and monochrome, and lacks most of the elements conventionally thought of as kid-friendly, does not bother her. When we watch the *Wizard of Oz* together she insists we scene-flip through the black-

and-white section to get to the first brightly colored appearance of Munchkin Land. But with *Kong* she sits wide-eyed the whole way through.

It occurs to me that this is a film that speaks eloquently to her on a deep level; and this in turn makes me think again about my own critical understanding of the text. I have always, without thinking very deeply about it, gone along with the critical consensus that this film is actually about race and imperialism rather than a stroppy simian mashing up Manhattan, which is how most ordinary people take it. But thinking about it in the face of my daughter's passion I have to wonder the extent to which those topics (fascinating and important though they are) are likely to grab her attention.

So why does she love it? There is, I think, a short answer and a long answer. The short answer is five words long and begins the next paragraph. The longer answer takes up most of the rest of this essay.

King Kong is a fairy tale. I don't mean this in the loose sense that it is a fantastic and entertaining story of the sort that beguiles the attention of children (although saying that describes the film very well); I mean it in a strict sense. This movie is a combination of two core fairy tales, "Beauty and the Beast" and "Bluebeard." But this is not anything new; earlier critics, and even characters in the film itself, make this point—at the end of the film Carl Denham insists, with plangent and deliberate melodrama, that it wasn't the planes that destroyed Kong, "'Twas Beauty killed the Beast."

In "Beauty and the Beast," the beautiful heroine is held captive by a beast but learns that he is actually a handsome prince under a bestial spell. In "Bluebeard," the beautiful heroine marries a hairy husband only to discover that he has previously murdered and perhaps devoured his seven (or, in some versions, many more) brides—just as, in *King Kong*, the first sight we see on Skull Island is of the natives preparing yet another trembling "bride of Kong." Bluebeard is destroyed: in Perrault's version of the myth, the heroine calls out from the highest tower of her husband's castle, at which point her brothers hear her and ride in to rescue her, killing Bluebeard in the process. In *King Kong*, of course, it is Jack Driscoll, Ann Darrow's true love, who clambers up the highest pinnacle of Kong's natural stronghold, and Kong is incapacitated rather than being killed immediately; but the film leaves us in no doubt of Kong's murderous and indeed human-devouring capacities.

Critics have long debated the resonance of this fairy-tale underpinning, but it would clearly be too simplistic to see Kong merely as a type of "ogre," a monster to be battled with, over whose defeat we can triumph. In the words of John Brosnan and Peter Nicholls:

The classic status of *King Kong*, which has become one of the great mythopoeic works of the twentieth century, has probably much to do with the ambiguous feelings—much as with its fairy-tale model, "Beauty and the Beast"—created by the film toward Kong himself: terror at his savagery; admiration for his strength, naturalness and effortless regality in his primeval surroundings; and pity for his squalid end—the most memorable of all cinematic images of Nature destroyed by the City.[1]

This ambiguity is one of the reasons that the movie leaves us, as viewers, with the sense that it is actually about more than its surface storyline. The narrative, though gripping and pace-y, is rather puerile. Indeed, by way of dignifying their passion for the movie, critics have argued almost without exception that this story is only the pulp-adventure form taken by a more interesting and buried true meaning: that whilst the film appears on the surface to be about a giant ape fighting a bunch of dinosaurs and then wrecking New York, in fact it is about "sex," "race" or "a self-reflexive mediation upon the burgeoning cinematic art of the spectacular." We may choose to agree or disagree about these readings, but they are not necessarily wholly incompatible.

Perhaps this film *is* about sex but, if so, it is only because "Bluebeard" and "Beauty and the Beast" are also, in a sense, about sex. As a "bride of Kong," Darrow has good reason to scream when her bestial Bluebeard-like husband snatches her in his great hairy hand. Perhaps the beast will eat her up, as he is shown eating several other characters in the film. But what, generally speaking, is the real significance of the ogre's appetite for eating people? Marina Warner's excellent analysis of fairy tales, *From the Beast to the Blonde* (1994), spells out the subtext:

> In myth and fairy tale the metaphor of devouring often stands in for sex: ogres like Bluebeard eat their wives, we are told, even though the story itself reveals their bodies hanging whole in the secret chamber, apparently uneaten; Beauty ... is terrified that the Beast will eat her, as he eats other creatures.[2]

King Kong is certainly a film with a palpable erotic charge: something emblematized by the flimsy and indeed practically transparent dress that Fay Wray wears in this pre–Hays Code film, a dress which is later ripped

---

[1] John Brosnan and Peter Nicholls, "King Kong," in John Clute and Peter Nicholls (eds), *Encyclopedia of Science Fiction* (2nd ed., London: Orbit 1993), 668.

[2] Marina Warner, *From the Beast to the Blonde: on Fairy Tales and their Tellers* (London: Chatto 1994), 259.

to even flimsier shreds by a visibly excited Kong. As the only woman in the party, Wray becomes the focus for erotic fascination by the crew, as well as by the natives of the island and Kong himself. Critics have often argued that the threat represented by Kong, the literal consumption of Ann, is symbolically that of Ann being raped. The notion that Kong constitutes a symbolic type of racist caricature, hyberbolically huge, violent and necessarily sexualized, results in the most common critical interpretation of the film: that it is actually about the racial anxiety of white America of the 1930s, the fear of sexual miscegenation.

I have problems with this reading; however plausible it is for the context of segregated America of the 1930s, it has much less purchase today—indeed, if it holds true then it tends to paint the film in a deplorable and frankly repellent light. The thought of black men and white women having sex no longer horrifies us (especially since "us" today includes men and women of multiple races and ethnicities). To describe black manhood in terms of a bestial, hyperbolic simian-ness is an offensive and unpleasant libel, and only the most moronic racists would actually insist upon the identification of "black man" and "ape." I want the film to be more than a racist libel, and I believe that it is.

Let me be more specific: it is only possible to read the film through the lens of race if you, as a viewer, bring to the film a series of (nowadays thankfully exploded) racial stereotypes and assumptions. But to read the film as being about *scale*, as about the relationship between the small and very big, the viewer need only have the experience of what it is to be a very small person in a world in which everything is threatening and huge—and everybody has that experience, for that is the experience of being a child nipping through the jungle of early life with its bellowing, stamping, towering monsters called "adults." One thing of which little children are acutely aware is that, whilst some of the time these "adults" are absorbed in their own mysterious concerns, there are times—both thrilling and scary—when "adults" will notice the child, fasten their gaze upon her, perhaps chase after the child (who runs away squealing with mingled delight and fear), perhaps pick her up and carry her away, maybe threaten to eat her up, even pretending to sink their fangs into her neck or tummy. The threat is always averted, though it is frequently renewed. But the crucial thing is this: from the child's point of view this acting has nothing to do with "race," a concept baffling to young children, just as it has nothing to do with sex (prepubescent as they are, sex is a blank in the mental life of the very young). It has to do with primal apprehensions of the world.

So it is in this sense that we should call *King Kong* a fairy tale. It is a film *about the perspective of childhood*. Many fairy tales do carry an erotic charge, of course, but it is an inchoate one, an apprehension of sexuality that relates less to the actual experience of sex and more to the nebulous sense of sensual connection and pleasure. For children the key locus of sensual pleasure is not sex but rather food. Children are deeply interested in food, especially in the more sensually pleasurable foods, the sweet and the succulent. They understand appetite in its intensity and its profound satisfactions principally through the trope of eating. From their point of view *of course* Kong stuffs people in his enormous mouth and munches them: what else would he do with them? Of course he gets excited doing this; who wouldn't?

Little children also understand intense and overwhelming emotions, particularly rage (as anybody who has tried to weather the totalizing tantrum of a two-year-old can attest), and love. That these are the poles of Kong's own emotional world is no coincidence. To quote Marina Warner again:

> This cannibal motif conveys a threefold incorporation: sexual union, by which a form of reciprocal devouring takes place; pregnancy, by which the womb encloses the growing child; and paternity, which takes over the infant after birth in one way or another. Fairy tale princesses enclosed in towers are themselves metonymically swallowed up. One of Marie-Jeanne L'Héritier's tales, *La Princesse Olymphe, ou l'Ariane de Hollande*, describes how Olymphe is abandoned on an island where a monster roams who devours young women.[3]

Sound familiar?

So: I want to suggest that this film is primarily about this disjunction between big and little, something that resonates with all of us at a deep level because of our experience of precisely that circumstance.

This is the reason why fairy tales in particular, and children's literature as a whole, are so full of disjunctions of size—why children love hearing about encounters with giants (like Jack and his Beanstalk, or that other Jack who earned the name Giant-Killer), as well as with tiny little people (Thumbelina, Tinkerbell and other fairies and borrowers). It is for this reason, too, that *King Kong* appeals to my three-year-old daughter.

It is for this reason too, that the literary and cultural tradition of the little-big is so extensive. Perhaps the most famous example of what I'm talking about here is Jonathan Swift's *Gulliver's Travels* (1726), in which Gulliver gets to see things from Kong's perspective in the land of the Lilliputians and from the perspective of Ann Darrow in the land of the Brob-

---

[3] Warner, 260.

dingnagians. It's lucky for him that these two peoples are the respective sizes they are; the Lilliputians are quarrelsome and warlike, quick to anger, and Gulliver is rather protected by his relative enormity. The Brobdingnagians, on the other hand, are calm, civilized and by and large kindly, taking pains not to squash him. When we are with Gulliver in Lilliput we become empathetically huge with him, which means we look down with condescension upon the petty bickerings and runnings-around of the rest of puny humanity. This is the perspective of the comic satirist, able to make a series of witty points about the triviality of political society. But when we are among the Brobdingnagians we become empathetically tiny with Gulliver, and we suffer with him his continual fears that (encountering a gigantic harvestman), "with the next step I should be squashed to death under his foot, or cut in two with his reaping hook." Accordingly the satire of the Brobdingnagian section is darker, more penetrating and less lighthearted or witty. In Lilliput we are amused at the folly of international politics, where two nations could go to war over something as negligible as from which end of a boiled egg the meat should be eaten. In Brobdingnag, despite the fact that the Brobdingnagian court is far more sane and rational than the Lilliputian one, Gulliver's response is far more visceral. His disgust of the human body is vividly rendered; for instance, there was "a woman with a cancer in her breast, swelled to a monstrous size, full of holes, in two or three of which I could easily have crept and covered my whole body," or, in a more famous example, as he observes the beautiful Maids of Honour naked:

> They would strip themselves to the skin and put on their smocks in my presence...which, I am very sure, to me was very far from being a tempting sight, or from giving me any other emotions other than terror and disgust. Their skins appeared so coarse and uneven, so variously coloured, when I saw them near, with a mole here and there as broad as a trencher, and hairs hanging thicker than pack-threads.[4]

This is the crucial point about *King Kong*: it is the question of whether we see the events of the film from the point of view of the miniature humans, or of the giant ape himself. From the latter perspective, New York becomes something like a marvelous playground in which we can act out our repressed anger—smash up trains like toys, grab whom we choose and mount the Empire State Building like a climbing frame. From the former,

---

[4] Jonathan Swift, *Gulliver's Travels* (1726; ed Peter Dixon and John Chalker; Harmondsworth: Penguin 1967), 151, 158.

however, it is the hideous intimacy of Kong's face leering down upon us as he bears his enormous fangs; it is the fearful, exciting presence of the towering adult, impinging on the jewel-bright, tiny world of childhood. I don't think it has ever yet been noted that the core premise of *King Kong* is already contained within *Gulliver's Travels*: a giant ape seizes a fearful human, takes a strange fancy to his captive and carries him or her to the top of a tall building, from which the human is eventually rescued. As Gulliver relates:

> The greatest danger I ever underwent in that kingdom was from a monkey... [who came] peeping in at the door and every window. I retreated into the farther corner of my room, or box, but the monkey, looking in at every side, put me into such a fright.... After some time spent in peeping, grinning and chattering, he at last espied me, and reaching one of his paws in at the door... dragged me out. He took me up in his right forefoot, and held me... and when I offered to struggle, he squeezed me so hard, that I thought it more prudent to submit... he suddenly leaped up to the window... walking upon three legs, and holding me in the fourth, till he clambered up to a roof that was next to ours... the monkey was seen by hundreds in the Court, sitting upon the ridge of a building....[5]

In France, Voltaire, clearly impressed by the imaginative possibilities of Swift's story, wrote his own version: *Micromégas* ("Littlebig," written 1730, published 1750) in which two gigantic space aliens—one of them five kilometers tall—visit the Earth and converse with what are to them microscopic natives. But despite its serious and creditable message, that the enormity of the cosmos dwarfs humanity, Voltaire's work is barely read today. Swift's novel, on the other hand, became one of the most popular in the literary canon—particularly, by the nineteenth century, as a book given to children, although in a tastefully expurgated version. And there is justice in that, for the brilliantly realized alterations in size and scale speak most strongly to children, who have direct experience of what it is to change size rapidly and to move amongst giants. Swift's greatest successor wrote directly for children: Lewis Carroll penned *Alice's Adventures in Wonderland* (1865), a book which folds Gulliver, the Lilliputians and the Brobdingnagians into one person, Alice herself, whose charming reasonableness in the face of her bizarre lurches from miniature to gigantic helps her through a landscape of miniature doors too small to step through and pools of tears large enough in which to swim.

---

[5] Swift, *Gulliver's Travels*, 161-2.

There is an explicitly identified *dream*-logic to Alice's little-big alterations, and it is one of the strengths of *King Kong* that it too never entirely
abandons dream-logic. Any appearance of rational coherence to the plot
disintegrates before five minutes of contemplation. As fans have observed
from the first release of the film, it seems counterintuitive that the inhabitants of Skull Island should build a wall to keep Kong out and then fit a
door in the middle of it large enough for Kong to step through. And the
wall itself—large though it is—would surely have presented little obstacle
to a creature capable of shinning up the enormously taller Empire State
Building, a feat he manages without even using both hands. Nor is it apparent how Kong is transported back to New York; the expedition, after
all, did not come prepared to encounter a gigantic ape. If he were stowed in
the hold, what would stop him from smashing free? Anchor chains would
be much less secure than the steel bands which he snaps off onstage in
New York; the gas bombs that incapacitated him on the island could presumably not be detonated at sea without damaging the ship. Besides, the
voyage to the island took six weeks; if Kong was kept unconscious for so
long a time he would surely have starved. But in another sense, to dwell
on the movie's inconsistencies is to miss the film's point. The landscape
and transitions of the film have a dream-like *rightness* to them; they make
sense to our subconscious, and so ninety-nine out of a hundred viewers
do not question them.

Another brilliant child-centered fantasy dream world is that of *Little
Nemo in Slumberland*, American graphic artist Winsor McCay's comic strip
from the early decades of the twentieth century. Nemo is a little boy who
dreams bizarre and wondrous things, always waking in the last panel of
the strip. Very often in this marvelous text Nemo imaginatively enters into
both the fear of the very little before the very big and the liberation of ex-
periencing the world as a giant experiences it; all the ponderous props of
adulthood are reduced to toys.[6]

"Flip Makes Trouble in a Little Place" (1912) sets the amoral Flip loose
in Midget City:

Like Kong in New York, he is looking for a princess; and like Kong, he
ends up wrecking the dollhouse-like buildings, even ripping them up and
hurling them at Doctor Pill, who is trying to stop him. Flip is in effect anticipating Kong's riotous rampage through New York City; he is acting out
the sort of joyously unfettered tantrum for which every child's subconscious yearns. When Doctor Pill smacks him for straying into Midget City,

---

[6] Winsor McCay, *The Complete Little Nemo in Slumberland: Vol 5, In the Land of Wonderful Dreams* (ed. Richard
Marschall, Mark Johnson, Cole Johnson; Seattle WA: Fantagraphic Books 1991), 45, 61.

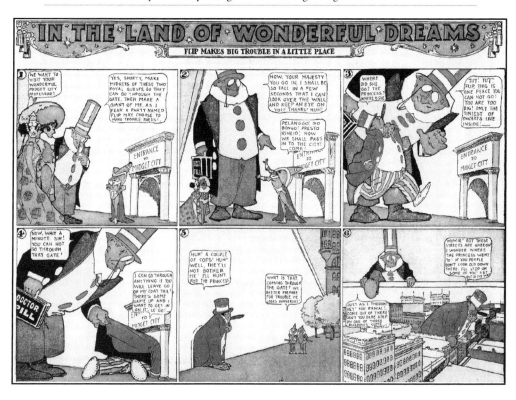

Flip responds by hurling the building at the grownup ("You know what I'm going to do? I'm going to soak you with this skyscraper!").

Winsor McCay understood the psychic underpinnings of a child's fascination with scale. In a different strip, "A Ride on the Wonderful Cow That Jumped Over the Moon," the point of view is not Kong's (as it were) but Ann Darrow's. Nemo and four of his companions are captured by a giant clown, who leers down at them. "Oh! Look what a face!" cries Flip, before he is devoured:

What is especially interesting in this penultimate panel (the ultimate panel, as always, has Nemo waking to a scolding from his mother: "Quit yelling in there and go to sleep!") is the mixture of horror and delight amongst the potential victims of this ogre: dream-Nemo begs, "Don't eat him up!" whilst the Imp looks on delightedly, "Whee ha ha!"

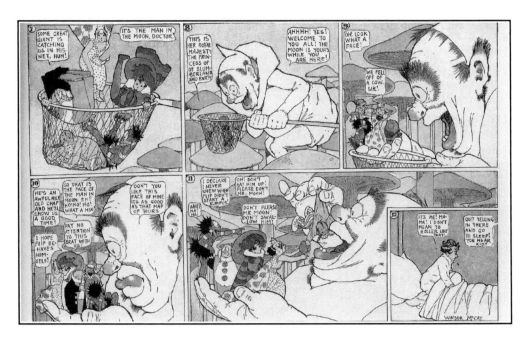

Children understand the pleasure that eating things entails; they are fond of sticking anything of an appropriate size in their mouths. As any parent will attest, little children are Kong at the dinner table just as they are Kong amongst their toys. At the same time they are Denham, Driscoll and Darrow amongst the world of towering grownups. It is this fluid sense of the scale of existence, and children's delight at any text that dramatizes the juxtaposition of the big and the little, that explains why so many children love dinosaurs. A film like *Jurassic Park* orients our perception around the child's as the stomping adult-monsters roar and roam, but the child with his or her toy dinosaur becomes the monster himself—larger than even a T. rex, roaring and marching through the other toys.

I'm arguing, in other words, that *King Kong* deserves to be regarded as a classic of children's literature. More than that, however, the film's ongoing appeal to generations of adults is a direct result of their ability to empathize with the dynamics of size they experienced as children. The film's simple but eloquent articulation of the terrors and the exhilarations of *size*, its core understanding of the significance of scale, has rarely been bettered.

ADAM ROBERTS was born in 1965. He has a day job, as professor of nineteenth-century literature at the University of London, and has published a variety of academic criticism; he also writes science fiction novels and parodies. He is married with a young daughter and lives just west of London, UK. Sometimes he beats his chest and runs roaring around the sitting room chasing his daughter in the manner of King Kong. She runs away screaming, but actually she's enjoying herself. She hasn't summoned the machine-gunning airplanes yet, at any rate.

'Twas Stupidity Killed the Beast

Keith R. A. DeCandido

KEITH R. A. DeCANDIDO has heard the "Beauty killed the Beast" theory; he just doesn't believe it. If we'd just look at things logically, he says, the real culprit becomes obvious.

> "'Twas Beauty killed the Beast."
> —THE FINAL LINE OF *King Kong*

What a load of hooey!

The final line of *King Kong* is often cited as a powerful moment, the coda to the tale that has gone before. A riff on the name of the fairy tale—recorded in the eighteenth century by both Gabrielle de Villeneuve and Jeanne-Marie Le Prince de Beaumont, and made famous to modern audiences by Jean Cocteau, Ron Koslow and the Walt Disney Company onscreen—the line draws on a powerful archetype, that of true love transcending the physical, and the monster taken in by beauty. The theme can be found in classic literature from Mary Shelley's *Frankenstein*, where the monster is fascinated by the beauty of the world, of life, of literature, only to find that it's forever denied him due to his ugliness, to the Greek myth of Cupid and Psyche, with its theme of a love that can never be. It's a powerful metaphor, one that bespeaks tragedy and pathos.

And it's still a load of hooey.

It wasn't beauty that killed the beast, it was all those planes flying around the Empire State Building that killed the beast, and they did a right good job of it, too.

While the most remembered thing from the 1933 film is probably the visual of the giant ape atop the Empire State Building, the second most remembered is probably that last line, spoken by Carl Denham, the filmmaker whose actions are the catalyst for the plot. The very first comment on *King Kong* on the Internet Movie Database (as of this writing) is "Who among us can forget the classic ending line ''Twas Beauty killed the Beast.'?" The line is cited as the theme of the movie. The poor, deluded monster—much like Shelley's creature or the monster from the Cocteau film—is unable to attain the true love that he has found and, as has been the fate of those whose love cannot be consummated throughout storytelling history, dies for his troubles.

It is not surprising that so many have been taken in by this interpretation. Tragic love stories are the stuff of Hollywood legend, though American movies tend more toward a happy ending—the conclusion of Disney's 1991 *Beauty and the Beast*, for example, where the beast is changed into an attractive young man and gets to live happily ever after with Belle, just as the beast does in the original fairy tale. But love stories have always been ones that capture the popular imaginations, whether we're talking tales told around the campfire, the plays in Shakespeare's time, or the movies and TV shows of the twenty-first century.

Denham himself is aware of that power. When he meets with Driscoll and his crew at the outset of the film, before they hare off to Skull Island, Denham talks about how he's received pressure from critics and viewers to "sex up" his films. Prior to this, none of his films, which have become increasingly less popular (though some of that may be attributable to the Depression), have had a female presence.

In fact, Denham literally brings Ann Darrow in off the street in order to achieve this goal. His entire motive for even having her along is to provide a sexy story, one that will make his film more marketable. He isn't interested in having her act, or even in her playing much of a role beyond being a pretty face, which is why he grabs the first pretty woman he finds. He doesn't want somebody who might actually think for herself; she's just a means to an end.

The opening of the movie shows Denham's motivations straight off. He only wants Darrow there as a distraction, really—or, more accurately, a hook. Her pretty face will bring people in so he can make the film he wants to make, which is about the eighth wonder of the world, found by the heroic Carl Denham on the mysterious Skull Island.

Faced with his star attraction lying dead in a heap at the base of the Empire State Building, after causing considerable panic and disarray, one cannot blame Denham for trying to cast an inevitable air to the sad end of the monster, done in by unrequited love for the lovely Darrow.

There is, however, absolutely no reason to believe a word he says. He's trying to cover his own ass. Think about what he's facing in terms of charges—reckless endangerment at the very least. And he'll probably be responsible for whatever property damage Kong inflicted on the city of New York. So he's got every reason to spin this his way.

Meanwhile, let's look at what actually happened, through a proper anthropological lens rather than through the filter of what makes a good moving picture.

The tribe on Skull Island had a very ritualized culture. The sacrifice of a young woman to Kong was obviously a practice that was deeply ingrained in their society, one that had long been accepted among them. When the boat first arrives on the island, the tribe is in the midst of just that ritual, and its usual outcome is clear: the sacrifice goes through the massive doors to her fate, and Kong continues to leave the people alone.

In 1998, a movie called *Phoenix* was released. It starred (among others) Ray Liotta and Jeremy Piven as police detectives in the titular city, and at one point they're discussing *King Kong*, which is Piven's favorite movie. Liotta points out the ridiculousness of the fact that the giant double doors somehow keep Kong away from the tribe, yet later in the movie Kong is scaling tall buildings in New York City. So how, exactly, were those big doors—which weren't much taller than Kong himself—supposed to keep him in check on Skull Island?

It's a hilarious scene, especially thanks to the crestfallen look on Piven's face as Liotta deconstructs his favorite movie, but there's an easy answer to the question: The doors weren't there to keep Kong out.

Sure, Kong *could* have scaled the big doors. But why would he want to? His life was orderly and constructed and pretty well set. He gamboled about on the island with his fellow monsters, no doubt had all the bananas he could eat, and every once in a while the little humans sent him a plaything. All fine and dandy—until Denham showed up.

Actually, things were still fine at first—this time the sacrifice was a little paler than the usual, and dressed differently, but what the hey. The routine was essentially undisturbed.

What changed things was when Jack Driscoll and the rest of the crew rescued Darrow from Kong's clutches.

Up until then, the sacrifice came through the doors and never came back. The wall wasn't a prison or a barrier, but simply a boundary between where the humans lived and where the big monsters lived. The only time that boundary was crossed was when the sacrifice went through the door.

Now some pale-skinned strangers had come to mess that up. They stepped through the door and violated the proper order of things. Naturally, Kong took poorly to it.

That was what set in motion the chain of events that led to Kong's fatal plunge. Kong was violently removed from his natural habitat, first metaphorically when Darrow messed with the program, then literally when he was absconded with and taken to New York. Likely neither Denham nor the ship's crew realized exactly what they were doing, or if they did, they didn't care—and it's hard to say what's worse, ignorance or malice. The result, however, is the same.

One might then question: If Kong didn't have warm, squishy feelings for Darrow, if he didn't have unrequited love in his heart, why did he go after her when he got loose on the streets? But his behavior is much more satisfactorily explained by his going for what was familiar in a sea of unfamiliarity than by desire for a pale woman a tenth his size.

Everything Kong knew was gone. His pastoral jungle had been replaced with a concrete one. The sights, sounds and smells were all completely different than what he'd known all his simian life. The people and creatures he cohabitated with on Skull Island were nowhere to be found. Worse, he was treated, not with respect or with reverence, but with fear and loathing. With all that, there was only one familiar item: his most recent sacrifice.

In the face of all this, can anyone blame the poor beleaguered ape for making a beeline for the one thing he can still make sense of?

And, in the absence of a tall tree to climb, he instead climbs the tallest building, where he is treated with more fear and loathing in the form of airplanes that bring him down.

Denham's reasons for having Darrow present are misdirection, truly. He wants to fool people into thinking he has a love story. At first, it's to get people to see his picture. At the end, it's to lend an air of tragedy to the disaster that his picture has become—to prevent the exposure of his own stupidity in going in and removing Kong from Skull Island in the first place.

And it worked. H. L. Mencken's words come to mind: "No one in this world, so far as I know...has ever lost money by underestimating the intelligence of the great masses of the plain people." Denham sold his audience a love story because any other explanation for the ape's rampage and death would have cast the blame on him. Denham's own ignorance caused the problem, and he preyed on the ignorance of the general populace to cover it up.

Similarly, people bought the film by Merian C. Cooper and Ernest B.

Schoedsack as a love story rather than a film about a monster. And, just like with Shelley's *Frankenstein*, in the end, the monster isn't the outsized, ugly creature—the humans who doomed it are.

KEITH R. A. DeCANDIDO is the author of dozens of novels, novelizations, short stories, comic books, eBooks and nonfiction in the universes of *Star Trek* (in all its incarnations, plus some new ones), *Serenity*, Marvel Comics, *Farscape*, *Warcraft*, *Xena*, *Buffy the Vampire Slayer*, *Andromeda* and many more. Find out insufficient information about him at his Web site at DeCandido.net.

Ann, Abandoned

Adam-Troy Castro

A NN'S BEEN KIDNAPPED in the middle of the night as a sacrifice to dreaded Kong. Rather than going after her, Denham and Driscoll decide that discretion is the better part of valor...and pack up to go home to find a new blonde! There's no rescue party coming; Ann is on her own. What happens next? This won't be pretty.

Author's Introductory Note: Gross inconsistencies of scale in King Kong's many film appearances—which provide him with heights ranging from as little as fifteen feet in scattered shots of the original film to several hundred in some of his Japanese work—force me to establish official measurements before I can proceed. The following speculations assume for the sake of argument that Kong is exactly fifty feet tall. Fanatics nursing their own preferences can fiddle with elements of this thesis to accommodate both smaller and larger figures. —A-TC

If all good stories come down to the choices made by their characters, the movie *King Kong* comes down to the decision to rescue Ann Darrow from the giant ape. Everything else hinges on that choice: from the pursuit through the jungle, to the capture of Kong, to the final rampage in Manhattan, to the battle with the biplanes. Had Carl Denham and Jack Driscoll decided to cut their losses, on the practical if less than heroic grounds that an island with one giant monster might well have others and that a rescue mission was likely to cost many more lives than the one at risk (as it in fact did), then their participation in Ann Darrow's story would have ended, and any story following the rest of their lives would have been a bleak study in guilt, recriminations and posttraumatic stress disorder. But what about Ann? Had she remained in Kong's custody, what would have happened to her? The most likely possibility is, of course, an early death.

After all, the natives of Skull Island have been through this kind of thing enough times for the dispensing of virgins to evolve into a well-established, and highly elaborate, societal ritual, and for Kong himself to learn what their drums and chants mean. They've probably handed the great gorilla any number of unwilling young ladies over the years, with a frequency that does not say a hell of a lot for the general life expectancy of Kong's women.

To be sure, not all the danger comes from Kong himself. As you recall, he has to do battle with several monsters just bringing Ann back to his crib. He fights so many battles on her behalf during the course of this one day that it's hard not to imagine how frequently he'd start home with some screaming young lady only to have her plucked from his paws by some giant snake or Pterodactyl. One can even imagine circumstances in which the ladies failed to prize his services as protector and ran away from him into the gaping mouth of something more interested in lunch than amour. Given the difficulties involved, maybe Kong never quite managed to keep a bride out of harm's way long enough to tramp all the way home and store her away someplace where she wouldn't be hurt. Maybe his entire love life up until now had been a long series of such cruel bereavements, leaving him so cranky and frustrated that the hair-trigger temperament he displays throughout the film suddenly makes a whole lot more sense.

But then, Kong himself is just as dangerous as his environment. Real gorillas are by and large gentle beasts, but they have the emotional stability of four-year-old children, and they throw tantrums that amount to going after one another with deadly force. Who's to say Kong wouldn't get irritated at Ann's incessant screaming and throw her across the jungle in a fit of pique? He might feel bad about it later, but that would be little consolation to Ann. Or worse, given the simian attention span, who's to say he wouldn't leave her in a high branch somewhere, get distracted by something shiny and completely forget about her until long after she'd perished from fever or hunger or thirst?

Maybe the phenomenon that eventually doomed all of Kong's previous brides was not his lust, or his malice, but his boredom: his inability, common among many human males as well, to maintain interest in the well-being of his mates once they were living on his side of the threshold.

In any of these circumstances, Ann's fate worse than death is likely to be a short one. Kong will continue to be the single loneliest ape on the planet, and the tribe down below will continue to serve as his dating service.

But what if she lives?

We have to be careful with our assumptions here. Kong is not a gorilla. He looks like a gorilla and he behaves a little bit like a gorilla, but we know he's not a gorilla: he lives far away from any known gorilla habitat, and his size (and, in some of his appearances, upright posture[1]) are both alien to the species. When we call him a gorilla, and treat him like a gorilla, as we will from this point on, we do so out of convenience and lack of any other more appropriate term.

But we can draw some parallels.

One of the most famous gorillas known to science is the talkative Koko, who was trained to communicate in American Sign Language. A few years ago Koko asked for a pet and was rewarded with a kitten she dubbed All-Ball. The cat was frightened of Koko of first, but the pair eventually bonded, playing and sleeping together in a perfect owner-pet relationship. When All-Ball died for reasons that were not Koko's fault, the great ape went into mourning and remained inconsolable until another kitten was provided.

Koko proved perfectly capable of modulating her great strength to accommodate All-Ball's relative fragility. This is, of course, a necessary skill for any species that cares for its own young. You can't take care of a baby or child without acute knowledge of its extreme vulnerability at your hands. To be sure, this all-important sensitivity remains subject to variables like the competence, temperament, commitment and emotional health of the parents. In the singular case of human beings, our emergency rooms, family courts and morgues all provide ample proof that we're far from infallible at putting that necessary level of sensitivity into practical effect. Still, it is that potential which allows any parenting species to survive past a single generation. And our ability to raise small pets, as surrogate young, depends entirely on that potential...even if, like hamsters squirming to escape the hands of their owners, the pets in question have little interest in reciprocating our affections and devoutly wish to be elsewhere.

We already know that Kong is dedicated to protecting Ann from predators. Maybe he'd be just as conscientious when it comes to feeding and sheltering her. Maybe, given the opportunity, he'd get her someplace nice and protected, with enough sun to keep her warm and enough water for her to drink and enough soft grass to keep her comfortable. Maybe he'd lock her up for her own good and let her out only when he was ready to play with her and keep her area clean so it didn't smell up the place too badly. Maybe he'd

---

[1] Further speculations in this essay will assume those appearances (where he was performed by human beings in gorilla suits) in error. Our Kong moves like a gorilla of natural dimensions, which is to say rarely upright, for the most part using the knuckles of his hands for support. Although the Bronx Zoo does have one gorilla capable of walking significant distances with a human being's posture—or at least had, the last time I was there—that one seems to be a one-of-a-kind oddity and can be discounted.

provide enough kind, loving attention to keep her alive and healthy, if not happy, for something approaching the rest of her natural lifespan.

Admittedly, with no company other than an insanely possessive fifty-foot gorilla, but still.

She might even come to like it.

This is not as much of a stretch as you might think.

There's a well-known phenomenon called Stockholm Syndrome, named after a real-life case in which bank employees were held hostage by brutal criminals for several days. The thugs had guns and threatened to use them, but whenever they were not actually threatening physical harm, they also engaged in small talk, rewarded cooperation with freedom from abuse, doled out small comforts and provided food and water. The hostages, cut off from any societal context, soon came to identify with, and feel deep affection for, their captors.

Stockholm Syndrome becomes more and more likely in isolation. Prisoners permitted the opportunity to commiserate with other people are able to make use of that reality check and thus more easily retain the awareness that they're being mistreated. By contrast, some battered wives, locked away in their homes for years without ever being allowed contact with friends or family or anybody but the brutes who slap them around, become pathetically grateful for every moment of relative kindness. They come to treasure every fleeting second of peace as de facto evidence of love.

Imagine how much more isolated Ann would be.

Imagine living in a sustained state of terror with nobody but the big guy for company.

Imagine needing to cooperate with him to avoid his rages, receiving kindness from him only when she obeyed.

Imagine needing to stay close to him in a nightmarish jungle where he presented the only oasis of relative safety, feeling relief in tight situations whenever he showed up to whip the ass of an intruding giant snake.

Further, imagine never, ever again encountering another human being capable of looking at her funny whenever she made passing comment about the big lug's better qualities.

It might take weeks or it might take months or it might take years. Conversely, it might only take days. (That's how long it took the Stockholm hostages.) But sooner or later, Ann would come to depend on Kong, submerging any trace of human independence out of the deep awareness that she was only safe when he was around.

And eventually, she'd imprint on him out of sheer self-preservation.

Inevitably, she'd come to love him.

Yeah, I know. This is getting to be a bit distasteful.

Can't be helped. It's inherent in the situation.

Follow the thread to the only place it goes, and it gets worse.

I can only promise that at the end it gets a little bit better.

Let's talk for a bit about what living on Kong's terms would do to her.

First, she'd have to read him. She'd observe the various nuances of his body language and simian facial expressions, and from this discern how to avoid the terrifying consequences of rage or abandonment.

She'd classify his bad moods according to symptom and severity and figure out when it would be useful to try to cheer him up and when it would be better just to keep her head down and try to go unnoticed.

She'd recognize his good moods the same way, and reserve all non-urgent business for those times when he was likely to be receptive.

And she'd have to learn how to make her own needs known. There would be any number of times when she'd need to let him know she was hungry, or thirsty, or cold, or sick, or in need of protection, or, for that matter, lonely.

How would she do this?

Not in writing. Duh.

And likely not in human speech. Given enough time, Ann might be able to provide Kong with a comprehension vocabulary of a few words, but she needs to be understood by him much more than he needs to be understood by her. After all, the second she disappears down some big snake's gullet, he just sighs and treks down the hill for another native girl.

So it's highly likely that she'll pick up gorilla communication.

She'll learn that direct eye contact is taken as a challenge and is a very bad idea. She'll likely learn the same thing about the human smile: a friendly expression to us, but a hostile baring of teeth to many apes.

She'll learn the squeal of protest and the chatter of happy excitement.

She'll come to suppress her human gestures, expressions and movements in favor of their gorilla equivalents, which are more likely to be understood and less likely to be dangerously misinterpreted.

Necessity will require her to do this more every day.

The more she adapts to this kind of behavior, the more she will be rewarded with security, food and Kong's version of affection. The more she resists and tries to preserve her human ways, the more she will be punished by the whims of an ape who can't understand why she continues to resist.

Years without regular encounters with other human beings to keep interpersonal skills in practice will likely cause her human language skills to atrophy. One thing we've learned from hermits is that those who don't forget how to speak entirely grow awfully rusty at conversation. The words feel alien to their tongues. One can imagine Ann, discovered decades later by a subsequent visitor to Skull Island, communicating in half-formed sentence fragments as she strains to explain what has happened to her. Given enough time, trauma and imprinting, she might even lose her language skills entirely.

And that's not all she'll forget.

Living in Kong's household, according to Kong's standards, communicating with him using his sounds and gestures, being rewarded and/or punished according to his preferences, surviving only because of his good-will and looking up to him (literally) as the source of all things that make survival possible, she will also grow accustomed to gorilla sanitary standards and gorilla modes of behavior.

Here's a snapshot of Ann and Kong, as they might look ten years after Denham abandons the woman to the giant gorilla's mercies.

Kong is doing what most alpha male gorillas do, all day long. He's sitting on his rump in the center of a clearing, sometimes scratching himself, sometimes yawning, sometimes shifting positions to catch the sun or a patch of shade. He looks like he's just vegetating, but in reality he's performing a function vital to his family. He's serving as the symbol of strength and protection, providing leadership by his very presence, as he keeps constant track of all the sounds and smells that might warn of an unwanted intrusion by predators.

Ann squats a short distance away, yawning. She's not the girl we remember. Her clothes, tattered within the first day of her captivity, are gone completely. Her hair is straggly, unkempt and well down her back. As she munches on a fruit, we see that she's lost teeth. After a moment, feeling restless and out of sorts, she whimpers, rolls on her back, scratches her belly and, knuckle-walking, because she rarely stands upright anymore, ambles over to Kong, taking care to lower her eyes so he knows that this approach is not a challenge. She hesitates until a grunt from him provides her with permission to proceed. Squatting at his side, she commences grooming him. Given Kong's immense size, this is a job likely to take many, many days: it's like window-cleaning on a skyscraper, in that the only reward of finishing the top floor is to start at the bottom again. That's all right. It's pleasurable for him, and she feels more secure when he's happy. It's not like she has anything better to do. After a few seconds she finds a tick. She removes it, sniffs it and eats it. Then she continues, emitting the occasional coo of interest.

She is, in short, a gorilla.

She likely remembers being human.

But one hopes not.

One can only pray she thinks she's happy.

Some readers are saying, "Ewww."

Sorry.

I can only assure you we haven't reached rock bottom yet.

Not even with this next bit, which is itself pretty icky.

I can only promise that it gets better by the end.

It's time to talk about interspecies sex.

Mass stampede for the exits.

Sorry.

Kong's interest in Ann Darrow, and in all the brides provided by the natives of Skull Island, has always been explicitly about sexual longing. He can't have a female of his own species, so he sublimates.

Question: Can he do anything but look?

The most tempting assumption is that his parts, and hers, are incompatibly sized, so incompatible that she's not in any danger of suffering serious or fatal injury from a failed attempt to fit Peg A into Hole B. The scale is so off that there's not even any point in trying. In such a case, she's actually fortunate he's ten times her size, and not, let's say, twice, as a sufficiently frustrated ten-foot gorilla might actually go for it and do her some serious damage.

If we're right about this, then Kong is the gorilla equivalent of a frustrated guy with no prospects other than pleasuring himself and needs Ann present only to serve the same function as, let's say, a *Playboy* centerfold. Something to look at, and think about, while he takes care of the job—excuse me—at hand.

(This may not be entirely true. After all, assuming as we have that Ann actually gets into her new life as Kong's bride, we don't need that much sicker an imagination to picture the kind of intimate services a horny ape can demand of a mate one-tenth his own size. But these are not rewarding details on which to dwell. We can leave them to the fevered contemplations of those predisposed to travel down that road. You sick bastards, you.)

Anyway: the greatest likelihood, by far, is that Kong's passion for Ann will never be fully consummated. She will be spared *that* fate worse than death, at least.

And if you buy that, you can stop here and move on to the final section.

But there remain more fanciful possibilities.

Including, among them, the distant but very real possibility that Kong's parts, and Ann's, are compatible after all.

159

Kong's plumbing is not visible at any point in any of his film appearances. This is primarily because of the reasonable assumption that nobody in the audience really wants to see it. (Except you. Yes, you. There. We know who you are.) But it's also rendered invisible, by his thick coat of fur...a phenomenon that would argue that it's fairly small.

Perhaps even disproportionately small.

Perhaps even... *pathetically* disproportionately small.

Fairy tales are filled with stories of giants living on top of beanstalks, or towering ogres living inside of caves, with understanding wives of merely human dimensions.

Kong might belong to the same tradition.

He might be built like a human. Or at least enough like one to place co-itus within the realm of physical possibility.

Again, one sincerely hopes not, for Ann's sake.

Seriously: Ewww.

But even though this journey has taken us through increasingly extreme levels of unlikelihood (from the chances of Denham and Driscoll abandoning her, to the chances of her surviving more than a couple of days, to the chances of her adapting to life with Kong and now to the chances of them being able to mate), the unquantified nature of the variables involved[2] still leaves the prospect of regular relations between the two at least theoretically within the realm of possibility.

We need to acknowledge it.

It's our own fault, just for starting down this road.

Which brings us to our penultimate speculation. I promise you, this is as far as we descend before we emerge into an area of relative light. Forgive us for being thorough, and feel free to skip ahead to brighter possibilities.

Assuming that Kong can mate with Ann in more than name...

...can they reproduce?

Ewww! This guy's sick!

No, he's not. Just thorough.

And while we might not want to think about it, impregnation is not totally outside the realm of possibility.

In nature, it's very possible for animals of separate but closely related species to produce offspring. Sometimes it requires enthusiastic animal

---

[2] Heck, on the basis of the first film, we can't even confirm Kong's malehood at all. We just assume it because of the regal title and surly attitude. A later sequel, *King Kong Lives*, provided an obviously female member of the species with great big prominent breasts, but even that establishes nothing, as the Kong we know might just be flat-chested.

husbandry on the part of human caretakers, but it can happen. Lions can breed with tigers, horses with donkeys and zebras, and dogs with wolves. In a few cases, as with the crossbreeding of some of the big cats, the off-spring are just barely viable and doomed, if they live at all, to endure a life-time of poor health. Other times, as with mules, they're strong but sterile.

Human beings, who are genetically much more closely related to the chimpanzee than horses are related to donkeys, do have the potential to contribute to such a hybrid.

As of this writing, nobody, as far as we know, has ever attempted the ex-periment.[3]

A successful human/gorilla hybrid is far less likely, but that's where we come up against Kong's many unknown variables. After all, as previously established, he's probably not actually a gorilla, just something very much like a gorilla which human observers find convenient to call a gorilla. We don't know what he actually is, where he stands on the evolutionary scale or just how closely he's related to *Homo sapiens*.

Again, the overwhelming odds hold actual impregnation impossible or at the very least extremely difficult.

But the odds don't completely exclude the possibility.

Kong is after all a hypothetical creature, with a hypothetical genetic structure, not established for certain in any of the films made about him.

Kong and Ann might be genetically compatible.

And if we assume, as we have, that she survives long enough for it to happen, and that they're physically compatible enough to permit insemi-nation if not actual penetration, and that the offspring is at least potential-ly capable of life, and that Ann is capable of carrying the fetus long enough for it to survive outside her body,[4] then the mountains of Skull Island might well see a new generation of the Kong family.

Ann might very well live out her days functioning as brood mother for little Kongs.

And one can imagine the aghast reactions of Carl Denham and Jack Driscoll, living in comfortable if troubled retirement many decades later, when a subsequent expedition to Skull Island returns with evidence of flat-faced, semi-sentient giant apes, distinguished by their unusually shrill screams and luxurious blonde hair. One imagines them sitting side by side in some old-age home somewhere, catching the news on television and

---

[3] Who would admit it?

[4] One can only hope, for Ann's sake, that its fetal development conforms to the limitations of her own human anatomy as opposed to a giant gorilla's or some genetic compromise of a size, and further that its growth to Kongian dimensions occurs at some point following infancy. Preferably after weaning, or else Ann will have a hard time of it.

slowly turning toward each other with matching looks of dawning unhappy realization. "Oh, no," Denham gasps. "You don't think—"

I've now taken you past abandonment, past imprisonment, past severe psychological trauma, past sexual servitude and past the spawning of monstrous hybrids. The road has been a dark one indeed, up until now, but we needed to take the journey through these shadows in order to examine the final question, which provides us some point of relative light.

To wit:

What if all of the above proceeds from the most pernicious of false assumptions?

What if Ann Darrow is actually stronger than we think?

What if she's stronger than Kong?

Of the many traits that permit one will to dominate another, only some are based on physical superiority.

In his dealings with the lower animals, mankind has always traded on intelligence.

Think of the creatures we routinely command, who could easily prevail over us in any contest of sheer strength.

Horses, for one. Allowed sufficient provocation, any horse can kill its rider. By and large, they don't.

Oxen, for another. They're powerful beasts. We make them pull plows.

I once stood beside an eight-hundred-pound tiger, with no bars between us, and laid my hand on its back, feeling the coarse texture of its fur while its keeper kept it silent with nothing but the threat of her own disapproval.

I know of a man who cares for a Florida panther, who sits beside it, feeding it by hand, while it purrs from the attention.

I've seen other men and women command bears. I've stood meters away from a woman who barely topped five feet as she directed an immense elephant capable of reducing her to a mash to stand on its hind legs before her, patiently awaiting her permission to sit.

This is not a specialized skill. Indeed, it's fairly common. Think of domestic dogs. Think of how many of them are big enough to do us serious damage when they want to. Think about how few of them do. Think about how many human beings happily share their homes with huge, fanged predators, and who willingly trust those predators with small children. Think about the confidence we must hold in our own capacity to control such creatures, to not only endure their presence but also to treasure them as members of our own families.

There are difficulties. Just ask Siegfried and Roy.[5]

But key among human attributes is our ability to manipulate.

Kong clearly has the upper hand in the early stages of the relationship. At that point, Ann seems no more than a screaming ninny, and frankly, it's hard to blame her. She reacts exactly as most of us would. But it's hard to maintain total irrational terror, even in the face of a totally nightmarish situation. Sooner or later the terror winds down and we find ourselves forced to take stock.

Ann would start using her brain.

And that would mean exerting all the influence at her disposal to establish a will of her own, in Kong's eyes, rewriting the rules bit by bit until he started taking his cues from her.

His ability to mash her flat with a shrug wouldn't matter nearly as much as her refusal to take his crap.

It's not as unlikely as it sounds. We all know small dogs that boss around big dogs. Petite little women who call the shots over hulking men. Diminutive wise guys who control big dummies. It's called Authority: it has little to do with actual power, and it's what enables people in jodhpurs to command creatures three times their body weight with claws and fangs.

It's the same phenomenon that allowed a jungle girl posited in another movie to order about another big gorilla named Mighty Joe Young.

It doesn't even require physical punishment. All Ann has to do, to condition Kong, is shower him with affection when he pleases her, and withhold it when he doesn't. She can't allow him to set the rules, however easy that may seem in the short term. That way makes him Lord and Master and reduces her, eventually, to the shuffling ape-pet we've already examined. She has to set the criteria herself and stick by them, making him conform to her standards instead of the other way around.

She might not realize it in time. That's what makes her situation so dicey, especially since Kong has a pretty formidable will of his own.

But with the proper application of human intelligence, it's very possi-

---

[5] On the other hand, an animal trainer I met recently, who claimed to have been among the experts brought in to investigate Roy Horn's "mauling," adamantly insisted that the incident was not a mauling at all. He pointed out that the tiger in question had four-inch-long fangs and that the bite marks on Roy's neck were less than a quarter-inch deep. Had the cat wanted to, he said, it could have closed its jaw all the way and bitten Roy's head off. All by itself, the shallow nature of Roy's wounds argues for another explanation. And indeed, upon examining a video of the incident, he observed that the tiger grabbed Roy's wrist three times, trying to pull him offstage, before Roy slumped and the cat took him by the neck instead. Once offstage, the cat immediately released Roy and withdrew without argument while backstage personnel rushed to help its now immobile master. The explanation offered by my acquaintance the animal trainer? Roy had a stroke onstage. Far from attacking him, the big cat sensed it coming and tried to help, carrying him off in the same way it would carry off an injured cub. Which is relevant here only because it illustrates the degree of influence a human being can have over an animal capable of reducing him to his component parts. What prevents Ann from exerting the same kind of influence over Kong?

ble that by the time a few months have passed, Ann will be ordering him around, instead of vice versa.

And that opens up even more interesting possibilities.

Imagine that a year has passed since Kong and Ann disappeared into the jungle. The scouts of the native village, who keep a sharp eye on the horizon, report signs of the great ape's return. The elders sigh. It has been so long that they had dared to imagine themselves free of the terror forever. But now it's time to select another virgin for the wedding ceremony.

They pick a girl. They light the torches. They pound the drums.

Kong appears at the village gate.

But this time there's a blonde woman sitting cross-legged on top of his head, clutching tufts of his hair to hold herself steady as he makes his way past the trees. The clothing she wore the previous year is tattered and frayed, but still recognizable. Not diminished at all, but somehow more than she was, Ann looks healthy and confident and regal, uncommonly pleased with herself as she murmurs something to Kong.

Kong grunts and halts in mid-step.

The jungle drums stop. The village elders stare.

Ann waits until all the din has subsided, looks them over, spots this year's squirming sacrificial bride and barks: "Untie that girl!"

Sooner or later, Ann would make it back to civilization. I'm sure of it.

Sooner or later, she'd confront Denham and Driscoll. I'm sure of that, too.

It doesn't take much imagination to figure out just what she'd have to say to them.

Or just how inadequate their excuses would sound to her…and to her new friend.

ADAM-TROY CASTRO'S short fiction has been nominated once for the Stoker Award, twice for the Hugo and five times for the Nebula. The author of four *Spider-Man* novels and several books of short stories, he advises readers to check out his upcoming paperback, *Vossoff and Nimmitz: Just a Couple of Idiots Reupholstering Space and Time.* Adam lives in Miami with his long-suffering wife, Judi, and a rotating collection of cats that now includes Maggie the Cat, Uma Furman and Meow Farrow.

Scream for Your Life

James Lowder

*K*ING *KONG* DEFIES THE NORMAL CONVEN-
TIONS of the horror film. Horror, after all, has a
specific formula. The world is disrupted by the appearance of a monster. Terror ensues. The monster is vanquished and the social order is restored, at least until
next time. In *King Kong*, however, there is as much horror in the everyday streets of New York as there is in the
jungles of Skull Island...and nobody wins....

Moviegoers who paid fifteen cents to see *King Kong* when it hit theaters in
March 1933 probably expected a film firmly rooted in the exotic adventure
tradition, exemplified by such recent hits as *Trader Horn* (1931) and *Tarzan, the Ape Man* (1932), or even the 1931 gorilla-grabs-the-girl flick *In-
gagi*, with elements from the successful silent adaptation of Arthur Conan
Doyle's *The Lost World* (1925) thrown in for good measure. Producer-di-
rectors Merian C. Cooper and Ernest B. Schoedsack had established their
reputations with the expeditionary documentaries *Grass: A Drama of the
Wilderness* (1925) and *Chang: A Nation's Battle for Life* (1927), and early
ballyhoo surrounding *King Kong* gave audiences every reason to believe
their latest project was similar in its spirit of exotic adventure, if more fanciful in its dramatic content. For the movie's Los Angeles premiere, at Sid
Grauman's famous Chinese Theatre, an elaborate stage show preceded the
movie. This prologue was titled "A Scene in the Jungle" and included such
set pieces as the "Eccentric Dance of the Zulus" and the "Gathering of the
Tribes," with musical support provided by a "Chorus of Dusky Maidens
and African Choral Ensembles."

The film that followed Grauman's elaborate and predictable jungle-themed prologue was something unsettlingly different. To be sure, showman Carl Denham's quest to uncover the mystery of Skull Island and his encounter with the natives residing in that strange and isolated place were, on the surface, familiar story elements to fans of jungle pictures, or Cooper and Schoedsack's own expeditionary documentaries. The encounter with the charging Stegosaurus resembled many a scene in popular safari films, with the doomed saurian in place of a lion or rhino. Kong's capture and rampage through New York surely inspired a feeling of *déjà vu* in those who'd seen the stop-motion Brontosaurus' building-rumbling jaunt through London in *The Lost World*.

Unlike all those earlier pictures, though, *King Kong* was suffused with an almost overwhelming sense of unease, a genuine spirit of terror that characterized the film as a horror movie, no matter how RKO or theater owners tried to sell it to the public.

Horror had done big business in the years leading up to *Kong*'s release, especially Universal's twin 1931 smashes, *Dracula*, directed by Tod Browning, and *Frankenstein*, directed by James Whale. *Kong*'s initial screenwriter, Edgar Wallace, studied those films, along with several other successful horror pictures, as part of his preparation for the assignment. But the elements of disquiet in *King Kong* are more pervasive than those found in the Universal classics. In those movies, the unnatural typically intrudes upon the natural world embodied as a monster or madman intent on destroying the carefully constructed social order. In the end, defenders of this endangered idyllic world of daylight and reason defeat the darkness. Van Helsing and his codified rules for combating the undead spell the end for Dracula, and the united nobles, burghers and peasants corner and destroy Frankenstein's Monster—at least until demand for sequels prompt their timely resurrections. Terror's defeat ushers the romantic leads into a future of marital bliss and economic security, in a bright and hopeful world where order reigns triumphant.

In Merian Cooper's earliest notes to RKO studio executive David O. Selznick, the monstrous title character had been dubbed the "Giant Terror Gorilla." Like Dracula and Frankenstein's Monster, Kong is a successful figure of menace. If not exactly unnatural, he and the other gigantic creatures that tromp through the film are hyper-natural threats—embodiments of Nature in long-forgotten, primal forms. As threats, they're made all the more eerie and unsettling by their sometimes lifelike, sometimes jerky and mechanical movements on the screen. Even the plot woven around the Giant Terror Gorilla appears to follow the successful but well-worn pattern employed by other horror films of the day. Kong threatens to wreak havoc

on the civilized world, even while foiling the course of true love. Eventually the beast is brought low by a combination of superior weaponry and clever, if reactionary, thinking, and his death finally allows the unification of the romantic leads. Yet none of the story elements or thematic juxtapositions, or even the Giant Terror Gorilla himself, function in *King Kong* quite as expected, and the film's pervasively gloomy, even fatalistic, tone sets it apart from contemporary horror fare.

From the opening scene, showman Carl Denham is revealed as reckless and seemingly unconcerned with human life. He's packed the *Venture* with enough ammunition to blow up New York harbor, without bothering with the proper permits. When Weston, the theatrical agent, can't provide him with a girl for his latest project, he charges off into the night to find one. His search takes him from the waterfront to a crowded soup line at a rescue mission. He had already described the women he finds there to first mate Jack Driscoll before leaving on his quest for a would-be starlet. "Listen," Denham drawls, "there are dozens of girls in this town tonight that are in more danger than they'll ever see with me."

Driscoll correctly notes that the dangers of Depression-era New York are ones the women understand, as opposed to the exotic perils to which Denham might subject them, but they are dangers just the same. The soup line women are sad, shuffling things, worn down by their strife, either too old or too coarse for Denham's plans. When the showman sweeps Ann Darrow into his arms, after self-interest drives him to rescue her from a fruit vendor's accusations of theft, she can't resist because she's so weak from hunger. Ann remains wary of the showman's offer of work and adventure; she's seen other predators eager to exploit pretty girls fallen on hard times. And while Denham's offer is "strictly business," it's just as exploitive, just as dependant upon Ann's desperation, as the more lurid propositions to which she alludes during the diner scene.

Like Ann, Depression-era audiences would have suspected Denham's offer of instant show business fame, recognizing that the world of poverty was not the only one promising peril. By 1932, films like George Cukor's *What Price Hollywood?*, which examined the seedier side of show business and the potentially high cost of stardom, had begun to crop up among the wide-eyed cinematic fairy tales about movie producers discovering fresh-faced stars at the corner drugstore. But those same audiences would also recognize Ann had little choice but to accept the offer, not if she wanted to save herself from sliding into indigence.

Thus the "civilized" world of *Kong* is established as a quite different place from the neat little drawing rooms and baronial estates of *Dracula* and *Frankenstein*, the sheltered bastions of privilege the heroes must defend from the creatures of the night. In *Kong*, the dichotomy between order and chaos is not so neat. Danger lurks everywhere, and the façade of civilization has worn so thin the darkness has already begun to creep in, well before our first glimpse of the monster.

To an audience entering the dark of the movie theater seeking escape from the harsh realities of the Depression, this New York sequence was cold comfort indeed. During the same month as *Kong*'s premiere, newly elected president Franklin D. Roosevelt delivered his now-famous First Inaugural Address, warning the country that the only thing they had to fear was fear itself. And fear was rampant. The previous year had seen the Depression at its worst, with unemployment at a staggering twenty-five percent and the stock market down eighty percent from where it had been just four years earlier. The soup line Denham scans for likely stars was a familiar sight to *Kong*'s earliest audiences—the specter of destitution threatening Ann—one with which they trafficked daily.

The audiences could only hope that the destination to which Ann escapes, the exotic locale to which Denham promises to whisk her, would be surprising, yet ultimately rewarding. Instead, Ann's flight from the grim mundane world of the Depression leads her, and the audience, to a nightmare landscape comprised of one startlingly gruesome scene after another.

The dinosaur sequences in *King Kong* are consistently cruel and bloody. When Denham and the crew defeat the charging Stegosaurus, they shoot it several times, including a final close-up blast that causes the then-helpless monster to writhe in pain. The brilliantly choreographed battle between Kong and the Tyrannosaurus rex ends with the giant ape rending the dinosaur's jaw, the monsters' roars supplanted on the soundtrack by the prolonged crunch of the fatal attack. When Driscoll, in pursuit of Ann and her captor, stumbles across the dead T. rex, he finds a gigantic vulture perched atop the corpse, picking at its still-oozing wounds.

In the village on Skull Island and the streets of New York, Kong's rampage causes destruction far different from the largely collateral chaos created by the Brontosaurus in *The Lost World*. Kong goes out of his way to snatch people from their huts and hotel rooms, then purposefully crushes them beneath his foot or grinds them in his jaws. He destroys subway tracks and sticks around to peel open the crashed car, hammering on the luckless victims until they stop screaming. Such screaming dominates the soundtrack—not just Fay Wray's famous shrieks of horror, but the terrified screeching of doomed islanders and city-dwellers alike.

While the body count in *King Kong* might be less than those racked up in subsequent SF disaster films such as *War of the Worlds* (1953) or *Independence Day* (1996), the presence of death on the screen looms larger. George Pal's Martians thoughtfully employ heat rays that turn dead men to neat piles of ash or dark splotches on the landscape. Apart from a few survivors with neatly bandaged heads, or the fatally, if not visibly wounded first lady, who lingers long enough to deliver words of wisdom to her warrior president, the victims of Roland Emmerich's alien attack are largely invisible, too. Not so in *Kong*. When the Apatosaurus in the swamp spits out a body, it doesn't simply vanish. When Kong stomps on a hapless islander or New Yorker, we glimpse the pulped, writhing body when he moves on. The unfortunates who find their way to the Giant Terror Gorilla's mouth kick and thrash until he tosses them away. Their deaths serve no purpose, even for the monster. The innocents attacked by Dracula provide the vampire with blood, the thing he needs to survive. Frankenstein's Monster lashes out at those threatening him, and only accidentally drowns the young girl in the famous flower sequence. Kong's victims, on the other hand, include commuters blindly unaware of the monster's rampage. They've done nothing to deserve their fate.

In cinematic biblical epics, where mass destruction is a typical plot element, the root cause of a doomed man's destruction often resides within him. It's his pride or some other fatal sin that brings about his demise. In *Kong*, the annoying idle rich escape Carnegie Hall unscathed and the monster takes his rampage to the streets, where he savages innocent bystanders attempting to flee from him. Hiding will not spare you Kong's wrath, as demonstrated by the Skull Islander who tries unsuccessfully to cower in a hut, and heroism will likely just make your death more painful. The dozen brave crewmen from the *Venture* who set off through the jungle to rescue Ann perish in increasingly awful ways, culminating in the scene where Kong shakes men from a log bridge. In existing prints of the film, the crewmen plummet into the void, their screams cut short as one by one they strike the chasm floor. *Kong's* original cut purportedly depicted an even more terrible fate for these would-be heroes: giant spiders and lizards swarm over the still-living men in the chasm's depths, devouring them alive as a horrified Jack Driscoll looks on from his hiding place high above. Preview audiences in early 1933 were horrified, too, and Cooper promptly cut the scene.

As the Depression wore on, such vivid depictions of the arbitrary destruction of innocents would find their way into American popular culture more and more frequently. In the pulp tales featuring the vigilante hero known as the Spider, published from October 1933 to October 1943, citizens of New York found it all but impossible to stroll down Broadway without some mastermind's latest beam weapon melting their faces or boiling their brains. Crazed lepers sprang at them from behind every bush in Central Park. Major landmarks toppled around their ears with alarming regularity, often at midmorning, when the streets around them were packed with urchins on a field trip from the local orphanage. If it wasn't chunks of the Empire State Building raining down on New Yorkers from on high, it was poison-fanged bats or clouds of lung-searing death. The grimly paranoid *Operator 5* served up even more startling carnage as part of its infamous "Purple Invasion" sequence, with entire cities reduced to rubble and the populations of several Mid-Atlantic States slaughtered by toxic gas. For all their shock value and elevated body counts, such episodes were not groundbreaking. *Kong* had been there first.

Even without the infamous spider sequence, *King Kong* remains a disturbing film. Unlike typical disaster flicks, the chaos and carnage don't build toward a simple moral and the destruction doesn't serve as a harbinger of renewal. The New York of *Kong* is a divided city, with queues of starving women a short cab ride away from the bright lights of Broadway, where smartly dressed theater patrons complain about high ticket prices and poor manners. Kong's rampage and death don't create a hopeful bridge between these worlds, as the flood does in Fritz Lang's *Metropolis* (1926), leading as it does to the symbolic handshake between the leaders of the downtrodden workers and the privileged elite. The rich and the poor do not come together, as in *Frankenstein*, to destroy the monster through their communal action. Save for their fear and their ability to be victims, the rich and the poor New Yorkers remain separate and their problems unresolved, even Ann's—who is left atop the Empire State Building in a borrowed dress, exhausted from fear, in the arms of a working-class stiff in a similarly borrowed "open-front" suit. As romantic leads, Ann and Driscoll are united at the story's close, but their future is not Baron Frankenstein's life of entitlement or even the Harkers' less remarkable life of middle-class security. Like Denham, whose story is taken up in the disappointing *The Son of Kong* (1933), their prospects in the wake of the show's spectacular collapse are dismal.

Neither is the movie a paean to the marvels of technology. Gas bombs and biplanes may have brought Kong low, but technology was also the thing that first brought the Giant Terror Gorilla to the city. The weapons are not unconditionally positive, like the sunlight or the cross in *Dracula*. In fact Denham, with his famous final lines, dismisses the marvels of the age as useful against agents of fear. The real weapon that brought down the beast—love or lust, depending upon your inclination to romanticism—is beyond man's ability to control, and should be all the more frightening because of that.

Perhaps the lesson audiences are meant to take away after enduring the gruesome spectacle of *King Kong* is one Denham reveals during the screen test with Ann aboard the *Venture*. If death is meted out with equal fury to the cowardly and the heroic, the guilty and the innocent, the civilized and the savage, if technology cannot save anyone from the world's terrors, there's only one response possible. "There's no chance for you, Ann, no escape," Denham tells his actress, building her toward a proper reaction to the horrors she might face. "You're helpless, Ann, helpless. There's just one chance—if you can scream. Scream for your life!"

Ann's shriek during the test is the first of many, and so realistic that it alarms the watching Jack Driscoll and Captain Englehorn. Ann can fake fear for the camera because she's already experienced it in New York; she's looked up from the gutter and seen starvation and poverty crouching over her. And Denham's direction—that Ann's only chance against the horrors awaiting her is to scream—proves true. Ann's terrified screech brings aid from Kong against the various dinosaurs that try to steal her away, and from Jack and the *Venture* crewmen who hope to rescue her from her monstrous captor. For others, the scream is not so successful. The sound, with its sudden cessation, more often than not signals their death. In the context of *King Kong* as a horror film, though, the screams are vital. They indicate that the screamer recognizes the danger, can see at last the horrible thing in the jungle or the shadows. And out in the theater, maybe the audience is shrieking along, too.

Comprehending danger and escaping it are quite different matters, though, and the ultimate meaning of those screams, whether or not the recognition of peril implicit in them will help the screamer navigate their world's newly revealed dark corners, can never be divined. The hope is there, but it may well be false. For the horror tale is at its best, at its most profound and effective, when it refuses to acknowledge that safety can ever be guaranteed, or innocence restored, once the ordeal has been experienced. Such is the case with *King Kong*. As Denham promised, the battle against the beast provides a great show, but for the survivors in both the story and the audience, the real and fantastic terrors exploited for the performance linger uncomfortably, even as the final lines are delivered and the music swells. They loom in the dark, impossible to ignore or dismiss, like the immense and bloody corpse of Kong, foregrounded in the frame as the screen finally fades to black.

JAMES LOWDER creates fictional havoc in novels, short stories and comic books for a wide variety of publishers, and has written about film for such publications as *Amazing Stories* and *Sci-Fi Universe*. As an editor he's helmed ten anthologies, some of them not about zombies.

Divided Kingdom
King Kong Versus Godzilla

Robert Hood

I**T'S ONE OF THE GREAT,** unanswerable questions of our time: Cats or dogs? Coke or Pepsi? King Kong or Godzilla? Except, as Robert Hood shows, when you look a little closer, it isn't even a question.

For several decades following *King Kong*'s 1933 release, the great ape was top of the gargantuan heap—the unchallenged King of Celluloid Monsterdom. He was like nothing that had existed before and no challengers could put the slightest dent in his crown. But that clear title had become significantly less clear by the 1960s, Kong's direct simian descendants having proven remarkably impotent. From Japan, a genuine pretender arose, splitting the Kingdom down the middle. Even a confrontation between the two in 1962 failed to resolve the matter, so that today two very different giant monster superstars command their own hordes of loyal supporters. Kong or Godzilla? King of Skull Island or King of the Monsters? Where should our loyalties lie?

Given you're reading this in a book celebrating Kong, you might think the answer obvious. But I have to confess to some seriously divided loyalties. Yes, *King Kong* came first and is an unchallenged classic. But Godzilla's iconic presence has been huge and ongoing—and his first film, at least, is a world-cinema classic. Moreover, the Big G's birth in 1954 initiated a whole subgenre of films—known as *kaiju eiga* (or *daikaiju eiga*), Japanese (giant) monster films—that are distinctive in form, imaginatively fertile and long-running in popularity and influence. Their impact is still seen today: in the ongoing production of Japanese *kaiju eiga*, in proliferating anime and in U.S. products such as Tim Burton's demented *Mars Attacks!*, the CGI extravaganza *Sky Captain and the World of Tomorrow* and, arguably, Stephen Spielberg's recent *War of the Worlds* remake. Even the U.S. animated film *Rugrats in Paris* pays very distinct and extended homage to Godzilla and Co.!

I'm not old enough to have seen *King Kong* during its initial release, or even during its re-release in 1952. But as a kid, I certainly knew about Kong, and I knew he was King. All the monster magazines said so. I had the pictures. I had the Aurora model kit, which I carefully assembled and painted. Like most young boys I was fascinated by the very concept of dinosaurs (for which read "Really Big Monsters") and I knew that Kong had wrestled a Tyrannosaurus rex into submission. A T. rex! How impressive is that!

I must have seen the film at some point on late-night television, no doubt expurgated; I watched the creature features all the time—or at least whenever I could get Mum to let me stay up past my bedtime. However, in the mid-1970s there was a special showing at my local flea-pit cinema (part of an oddly inappropriate double with Andy Warhol's *Heat*, I recall)—and I went along in a lather of anticipation to see it. Needless to say, the sheer overwhelming power of the old film left me stunned. On that big screen, Kong was a towering menace and an inhuman tragic hero whose fate rivaled anything in Shakespeare. The film was mythic poetry. Seeing it like that, large and imposing, proved a turning point. From then on, Kong was confirmed in my mind as the King of Giant Monsters, and giant monsters were reinstated (if they'd ever been deposed) as primary inhabitants of my persistently monster-oriented imagination—along with all the zombies, vampires and bug-eyed greebies from outer space that have since proliferated in Hollywood and beyond.

All this time, however, I had been conscious of the other King through the same magazines and books, but his presence was more distant. It was only as an adult, edging past middle age, that I finally saw *Gojira*—subtitled, on ethnic television in Australia, completely bypassing the harshly re-edited and heavily Americanized version starring a displaced Raymond Burr that went under the more popular title *Godzilla, King of the Monsters*. I therefore knew the film as a serious piece of cinema, not just as another somewhat clunky '50s giant monster film. It was powerful and resonant and immediately ensnared me in its dark, and morally complex, anti-nuclear vision.

Since then I have seen all but the last of the twenty-eight Japanese Godzilla films in their original, undubbed and unre-edited formats. I am therefore familiar with Godzilla's varied history—ranging from powerful and entertaining to cheesy and childish. Everyone the world over knows Godzilla in some form, even if they haven't seen the films: as an icon of nuclear terror and simultaneously as a monstrous hero, or just as a sort of kitsch fire-breathing dinosaur. He is not merely recognizable as an historic artifact, but has a cultural presence as a continuing, viable franchise and a useful merchandising tool. On the surface, it seems that the *Kong* line stagnated, whereas Godzilla, the nuclear lizard, gave birth to a virile dynasty. Clearly his claim to being King of the Monsters is authentic.

KONG OR NOT KONG?

To many people the whole question could be considered a non-starter. It comes down to critical acceptance. *King Kong* is a film with deservedly immaculate credentials. Critics worldwide place it in their top twenty. *Godzilla*, in contrast, is often dismissed as cheap, poorly produced nonsense. Here isn't the place to argue about that at any length (though I do argue vociferously about it whenever the subject comes up at SF conventions, while lounging at bars or around the dinner table). Right now, I simply want to point out in passing that much of the scorn is based on badly re-edited U.S. versions of the G films, on the mistaken belief that suitmation and the attendant model work ("man-in-rubber-suit wrecking cardboard buildings") used by Godzilla's makers is cheapjack and lacking artistry, and on the worst, dullest and least effective of the series. To judge on this basis is rather like judging *King Kong* not on the original film itself, but on some poorly dubbed foreign re-edit, the *King Kong* cartoon series from 1966 or *King Kong Lives!,* sequel to the ill-conceived 1976 Dino De Laurentiis remake—or by adopting the nonsensical attitude that its once-advanced stop-motion techniques lack effectiveness in the face of the most recent CGI advances. The original unre-edited version of *Gojira* was not seen on American cinema screens until 2004, during celebrations of the film's fiftieth anniversary. The positive critical response that followed, amounting to a sort of collective gasp of amazement, speaks for itself.

My point here is that there are films in the Godzilla canon that are worthy of a King, especially the first—so the question of which contender should rightfully inherit the crown can't be decided through casual dismissal.

So, with two such heavyweight cultural icons as King Kong and Godzilla duking it out for the title of Supreme Monster Monarch, is it even possible to decide on a clear winner? If so, on what basis? In the remainder of this essay I want to examine a number of issues relating to *King Kong* and *Godzilla*, in particular tracing their origins and how the two films are related, both directly and as part of a tradition of giant monster films. Are these two Kings connected in any way, beyond their obvious monstrousness? What were their respective contributions to the giant monster subgenre of fantasy/horror films? What do they reflect of the respective social environments in which they were forged? In answering these questions, I hope it will become clear that while Godzilla might hold a strong ongoing claim on the crown, Kong is the patriarchal giant from which the whole monster subgenre (in both its U.S. and Japanese manifestations) was born, and hence the ultimate origin of the Big G himself.

KONG AS GIANT MONSTER

The template for giant monster films was forged from a novel, *The Lost World*, by Arthur Conan Doyle. In 1925, Willis O'Brien, who would go on to create Kong, was involved in filming Doyle's story of Professor Challenger and the historically backward Amazonian plateau to which he journeys. Several elements of the tale have become standards: the concept of a lost world and/or creature that is discovered, awakened or (sometimes) created by modern man; battles between monsters in which humans can be no more than victims or helpless observers; and the creature brought back to (or simply arriving in) civilization, where it then goes on a rampage. This last is not really part of Doyle's original book; though Challenger does bring back a prehistoric creature, it is only a smallish Pterodactyl that escapes from its cage and flies away. Its narrative purpose is to verify the professor's story; it does no menacing or rampaging. But the 1925 film turned the Pterodactyl into a Brontosaurus, which escapes from captivity and rampages through the streets of London for a bit, scaring the milling crowds and wrecking a few monuments and buildings. It finally plunges into the Thames when London Bridge collapses under its weight, and is last seen swimming out to sea.

It is easy to see how these elements could be developed into Kong's lost Skull Island where an ancient wall keeps back the denizens of a prehistoric wilderness; a god-beast who, lured into captivity by his fatal attraction to a diminutive blonde Beauty, is transported by commercial interests back to New York where he is put on show, escapes in a fury of possessive wrath and goes on a rampage; a last stand made atop the world's tallest building before the creature is brought down by the then high-tech weaponry of the "little people." *King Kong* took the template provided by the earlier *The Lost World* and reworked it, giving it a personality and a mythic quality that hasn't diminished to this day. So powerful is its imagery, and so superbly crafted its theme and central character, that its old-fashioned aspects and perceived technical limitations can be appreciated as a positive boon. Moreover, in thus creating a classic—and in becoming such a huge box office success at the time and on re-release two decades later—*King Kong* would inspire a whole new genre, both in its own country and more particularly in the East.

Oddly enough, however, given *King Kong's* success, that was pretty well it for giant monsters in the 1930s and 1940s, simian or otherwise. A few minor parodies of Kong appeared and there was the odd dinosaur, but no one really pursued the genre. A sequel, *The Son of Kong*, was produced on its predecessor's heels, but the film comes over as the rush job it was and didn't do particularly well, even though O'Brien's limited effects are excellent. It remains a minor offshoot of the Kong legend. What it lacked was the parent film's scope and emotional depth, its complex social and psychological subtext and its central character's awesome ferocity. *King Kong* created a myth, while his son was merely a more family-friendly franchise entertainment. Likewise, O'Brien's 1949 ape-on-the-loose film, *Mighty Joe Young*, though designed to replicate *Kong's* success, was too small-scale and benign to have had any influence on developing the genre to come.

King Kong's original popularity arose from the film's rich reflection of a society living with the threat of economic deprivation (the Depression), tapping into a desire for the exotic and playing upon a sense of innocent awesomeness that had not yet become jaded by the apocalyptic terrors of a second world war. Early scenes of Ann Darrow on the streets with other homeless and hungry vagrants, subsequently given a chance to go on an exotic adventure, set the story against a background of familiar social anxiety and desire for escape. On its initial release, indeed, *King Kong* was marketed as a jungle adventure movie, an escapist appeal that plays a strong role in the storyline itself, as Denham's intent to film the legendary Beast in its native habitat is motivated by the need to produce a jungle travelogue that would be a follow-up to his previous wildlife documentaries (thus reflecting the actual history of Cooper and Schoedsack, as a matter of fact). Even his cynical inclusion of a female/romantic interest makes ironic reference to the making of *King Kong* itself—"the public, bless 'em, must have a pretty face to look at," says Denham. It has always struck me that as a work of cinematic art *King Kong* is remarkably self-reflective. The first line spoken, by theatrical agent Charles Weston as he approaches the *Venture*, is: "Is this the motion picture ship?" Of course, that is exactly what it is: a *motion picture* ship—and the line places us in a very specific cinematic context. That the final tragedy is the result of a ruthless drive to entertain at any cost (bringing Kong from the prehistoric jungle into modern civilization in order to "attract an audience") in fact offers an ironic comment on Hollywood's own exploitative tendencies.

Then there's the scene in which Denham guides Ann through a screen test, anticipating what is to come:

> Look higher...still higher....Now you see it! You're amazed. You can't believe it. Your eyes open wider....It's horrible, Ann, but you can't look away....There's just one chance....If you can scream. But your throat's paralyzed. Try to scream, Ann, try....Perhaps if you didn't see it, you could scream. Throw your arms across your eyes and scream, Ann, scream for your life!

So Fay Wray, playing actress Ann Darrow, who is in turn playing at seeing something huge and frightening under the direction of filmmaker Denham, screams her now-legendary scream into empty space. Even though we know what she will eventually "see," we feel the thrill of anticipation tingle up our spines. The scene works in a complex, multilayered manner that perfectly captures the excitement of watching monster movies of any kind: knowledge of artistic separation and the correspondent fear that it will be breached, anticipation of the marvelous, the expectation of exquisite terror. That's the magic of cinema: we can be led to see the unreal, to be scared and thrilled by it, even when there's "nothing" there.

King Kong was, then, an effects-driven film that consciously referred to its own technical milieu—a work whose appeal was its exotic subject matter and use of a remarkable cinematic technique. These factors—along with the emotive strength of Kong as a personality (something hitherto unknown in large film monsters) and the film's effectively worked romantic theme—may be identified as the source of *King Kong*'s initial (and ongoing) success.

A NEW APPEAL

Though *King Kong* seen as exotic adventure and metaphor for Hollywood itself did not initially inspire a giant monster genre, this would change upon its later re-release. The film's new appeal would be to a society substantially changed by the specter of a terror even greater than the Depression—and this time its cinematic influence would be wide-ranging. The film would soon be seen not as an exotic jungle adventure, but as a rather more generic "monster film," first in a line of entertainments that at least pretended to offer a moral lesson as to the mortal dangers that can arise from human arrogance. In *King Kong*, it is unethical greed and ruthless exploitation that lies at the heart of the problem. Despite Denham's famous last line—"It wasn't the airplanes. 'Twas Beauty killed the Beast"—it is in fact Denham himself who is responsible. That he is still refusing to recognize the fact at the end is part of the tragedy. This "metaphorical quality"— the theme of responsibility, of the Beast brought into civilization through careless greed and allowed to run riot—could be adapted to reflect on larger problems, and the biggest problem in the 1950s was the recent War and what it implied for the future. The Bomb loomed large in 1952—and inevitably it was that fear that molded the "new" genre inspired by *Kong*.

The big change for giant monsterdom came with the release of a different giant monster film, one fuelled by the 1950s' nuclear, scientific and ideological anxieties. *The Beast From 20,000 Fathoms* (1953) was inspired by *King Kong*'s re-release success and its monster, like Kong, was created using stop-motion animation, the work of Ray Harryhausen—O'Brien's protégé. Unlike Kong, however, the Beast is a reptilian throwback, awakened by nuclear testing in the Arctic. It comes to New York and rampages through the streets, spreading radiation sickness as it goes, until it is destroyed by the very science that provoked it. The film was a significant hit, offering up a variant on the *King Kong* formula that over the following decade would be more or less replicated in films such as the giant ant epic *Them!* (1954), *It Came From Beneath the Sea* (featuring Harryhausen's giant five-tentacled octopus) and *Tarantula* (both 1955), *Behemoth the Sea Monster* (1958) and a host of others, most of them fuelled by concerns about what science and the War had wrought—nuclear paranoia and the fear of invasion by irresistible and inhuman (though human in origin) forces. The trend would continue into the 1960s, in particular with non-U.S. films such as *Gorgo* (1961) and *Reptilicus* (1962), before largely petering out in the 1970s and beyond (though examples sporadically re-emerge still, from time to time, usually without the nuclear subtext).

During its short life, then, the 1950s U.S. giant monster genre, though clearly borrowing elements from *King Kong*, quickly became something quite different from its ancestor. Thematically, however you read it, Kong's story, with its complex mythic overtones and humanistic emotional structure, is a far cry from the direct nuclear and social allegories of the postwar genre, however much it can be seen to reflect on these in retrospect. We remember Kong as a personality more than as a threat. His command of his prehistoric domain, his obsession with the diminutive blonde, his resentment and anger, his humiliation at the hands of modern technology: these give him character and psychological resonance. He has a name, unlike the majority of U.S. giant monsters, which are generally referred to by some generic tag such as Beast, It or Them.

Moreover, despite the possibility of various symbolic, sociological and psychological readings of the film (say, as an allegory of Depression-era economic problems, the battle between the *ego* and the *id*, the integration of the Shadow into the psyche or the development of sexual envy, whether adolescent or interracial), it is still closer to our actual experience of the film to see it as a well-structured adventure story with strong romantic, visual and emotive elements. The 1950s giant monster genre it spawned in the U.S. produced films that seem more directly sociological and much less humanistic in approach. In general their monsters remain "Other" and have not been taken to heart as individual personalities. They are the Enemy and that's all. There is little sympathy felt for them, and no guilt over their fate.

In the 1960s, however, this U.S. giant monster genre, left behind by the evolution of nuclear paranoia into a sort of cold-war hedonism, would be completely swamped by a unique Japanese version of the giant monster genre, one that also traces its origins back to *King Kong* and its 1952 re-release—and to nuclear fears. This genre is known as *kaiju eiga*, of which the Godzilla franchise provides the best-known example.

KAIJU EIGA

The Japanese version of the giant monster film offers a direct contrast to the nameless giant monsters of the 1950s. Like Kong, the monsters in these films tend to be less separated from humanity than the giant ants, reptiles and other mutated fauna of U.S. equivalents. They have names and personalities. They can be both monstrous villains and monstrous heroes—often at the same time. Simply killing them is rarely enough and is bedeviled by ethical and moral uncertainties. In short, while these monsters are totally "Other," their Otherness is accepted and owned. This approach—and the strange, colorfully absurd creations to which it gives birth—has been said to reflect differences in cultural constructions of Otherness and in approaches to visual realism. Whatever the dynamic, it produced a subgenre of film that is quite different from the short-lived giant monster genre that existed in the West.

The film that began the Japanese *kaiju eiga* genre was, of course, *Gojira* (1954). Godzilla's genesis has been much written about, but what seems certain is that producer Tomoyuki Tanaka, seeking a new film project, put together the box office success of the *Kong* re-release and the new *The Beast*

From 20,000 Fathoms with a then-current news item concerning a fishing boat crew that suffered radiation damage from secret U.S. H-bomb tests in the Pacific, and came up with his own idea for a giant monster film.

In *Gojira*, director Ishiro Honda wanted to, as he put it, "make radiation visual" (Galbraith, 1998, page 23, reporting an interview by James Bailey in Tokyo, c. 1991). But he has also stated that he was initially inspired by the original *King Kong*, which had performed well in Japan during its re-release. This inspiration is celebrated in the monster's name, "Gojira" being a combination of two words—the Japanese for "ape" and for "whale" (even though in appearance Godzilla looks like neither). At first Honda and SFX designer Eiji Tsuburaya had intended to create Godzilla using stop-motion techniques similar to those used by O'Brien to create Kong. Time constraints and lack of familiarity killed this aim—so they went with the use of a carefully designed suit and miniatures instead. The decision helped structure the genre, so that even now, when computer graphics have redefined SFX, *kaiju eiga* are still made using "suitmation" techniques.

Interestingly, *Gojira* wasn't actually the first Japanese attempt to make a giant monster film. An earlier foray into the field was even more directly inspired by *King Kong*. It was called *Edo ni arawareta Kingu Kongu* (*King Kong Appears in Edo*) and was released in 1938. Unfortunately the film has been lost, but existing stills show a giant ape (man-in-suit) running rampant in Edo with a doll-like female figure clutched in hand. The special effects were created by Fuminori Ohashi, who would have a part in designing the Godzilla suit sixteen years later (as well as undertaking uncredited work on Hollywood's *Planet of the Apes* in 1967).

This early film does not seem to have had much effect on the industry. *Gojira*, however, was so popular it spawned not just an immediate sequel (like *Kong*'s sequel, *Godzilla Raids Again* was rushed into production and remains a minor effort), but an ongoing sequence of (to date) twenty-eight Godzilla films. Unlike Kong, who was never effectively "resurrected" after his death in the first film, Godzilla as a monster has been notoriously hard to kill (both in the films themselves and at the box office). Moreover, other Japanese studios tried their hand at similar giant monster epics, particularly once the subgenre morphed into its more colorfully extreme, non-naturalistic form. They produced everything from the flying, jet-propelled turtle Gamera to the vengeful stone giant Majin, to Gilala, the giant space chicken. Other developments in the genre produced the long-running Ultraman series—in which a humanoid space giant comes to Earth to help humanity battle giant monsters of all shapes and permutations—as well as ever-popular *mecha* (giant robot) offshoots and such anime as the influential *Akira*, the gruesome and confronting *Urotsukidoji* (*Legend of the Over-*

fiend) and the hit TV series *Neon Genesis Evangelion*. Even the beautiful animated films of Hayao Miyazaki and Studio Ghibli, such as *Nausicaä of the Valley of the Winds* and *Princess Mononoke*, have been influenced by the subgenre to a large extent and feature giant monsters of their own—often giant monsters that are representations of the natural world reasserting itself against human destructiveness.

In short, *kaiju eiga*—which grew from the original *Gojira*—has been an incredibly prolific form. It came into its heyday in the 1960s, as the U.S. giant monster tradition was petering out, and offered a much more lively and varied set of tropes and possibilities for filmmakers to play with. Its metaphorical strength was obvious. In turn, it influenced U.S. fantasy films, which became slightly less concerned for documentary realism, at least among the exploitation filmmakers—though in the end *kaiju eiga* remained a distinctively Japanese form that provides imagery to U.S. filmmakers, but is rarely replicated in the West with any great success (as witnessed by the 1998 U.S. remake of *Godzilla*). Its underlying dynamic is a powerful sense of apocalyptic possibility; the impact of *Gojira*, remember, was driven by the fact that it was directed at a society that had actually experienced nuclear attack (most of its initial audience would have had immediate memory of the bombing of Hiroshima and Nagasaki or would have known people who had). Elsewhere in the world the fear was real, but less immediate. This metaphorical dynamic became a formative influence on *kaiju eiga* as a genre, drawing upon the images of destruction that were a strong part of *King Kong*'s appeal and making them thematically central. Even today that sense of apocalypse resonates within *kaiju eiga* in all its forms, though its meaning has been widened to include not just the Bomb but a general humanity-driven destructive potential. In such works as *Akira* and the *Neon Genesis Evangelion* series that potential includes the possibility of a monstrous evolutionary rebirth.

THE JAPANESE KONG

Interestingly, there are other connections between *King Kong* and the *kaiju eiga* subgenre. A quick glance at these shows the sort of changes wrought by Kong's translation into the new film tradition.

In 1960, Willis O'Brien tried to bring Kong back via a story he developed under the title "King Kong vs. Frankenstein." In this story, Dr Frankenstein creates a new, rather bigger monster that escapes and goes on a rampage. A group of U.S. promoters captures it to bring it back to San Francisco at the same time as another group sets out to fetch Kong from

Skull Island. Plans are made for a big stadium extravaganza but the monsters escape and fight through the city, causing more mayhem. O'Brien's idea met with some approval at RKO Studios (Kong copyright holders), who gave him permission to pursue the project, but in the end, via a series of rather tragic betrayals, producer John Beck took O'Brien's story (now called "King Kong vs. Prometheus") and sold it to Toho (Godzilla's production company), who had been trying to acquire the rights to use King Kong in a Godzilla film. Reportedly, when O'Brien heard the news, he was "heartbroken" (Ryfle, 1998, page 81).

Why was he so forlorn over this news? Well, on the surface it looked pretty bad. Toho, whose monster films were not considered highly in the U.S., took O'Brien's stop-motion ape, turned it into a man in a suit, replaced Prometheus with Godzilla, gave Kong a relative height that enabled him to stand up to Godzilla (Kong in *King Kong* was about fifty feet tall, Godzilla in *Gojira* was fifty meters or 164 feet tall—quite a difference), and transformed the story into a satire of Japanese corporate business—a comedy, in fact, featuring several prominent Japanese comedians.

King Kong vs. Godzilla premiered in Japan on August 11, 1962 (with no credit given to O'Brien). O'Brien died on November 8 that year; he may have seen the film, though it is unlikely (and the awful, hacked-about U.S. version didn't premiere until the following year—that *really* would have depressed him). At any rate, Toho's effort would not have come close to O'Brien's own concept for continuing the story of his most famous monster—which had thus been effectively removed from his control. Nevertheless the movie was a huge box office success, the first Japanese sci-fi film in color and widescreen, and it deliberately appealed to a wide audience, including kids. The film, the third in the Godzilla canon, was already pushing the newly developing subgenre toward its pure *kaiju eiga* form—colorful, spectacular and absurd—and it remains one of the highest grossing of all the G films.

Despite ongoing U.S. critical disdain (a disdain exacerbated by the fact that *King Kong vs. Godzilla* was vandalistically re-edited by distributors), the original *King Kong vs. Godzilla* is a unique and entertaining big-budget monster film. If the situation had not been so bedeviled by betrayal and deceit—and if he could have distanced himself from the idea of Kong as a stop-motion creature—O'Brien might even have enjoyed it as an eccentric reworking of his own story. Part of the ongoing scorn leveled at *King Kong vs. Godzilla* by Kong fans arises from the fact that, apart from the disappointing *The Son of Kong*, this film is the only extant sequel to the 1933 classic; yet it is so unlike that film in every way that the response of all those expectant multitudes could only have been one of tragic disillusionment, like O'Brien's. My advice to those who still resent the film, however, is to find a copy of the original Japanese version of *King Kong vs. Godzilla*, and enjoy it as a strange offshoot of Kong that has actually had greater continuity and influence than *King Kong's* own more direct descendents.

Interestingly, O'Brien's original "King Kong vs. Frankenstein" idea was at least partially reused by Toho a few years later, though this time they removed Kong altogether. Made in 1965, *Frankenstein vs. the Subterranean Monster Baragon* (otherwise known as *Frankenstein Conquers the World*) tells how the monster's brain is brought by Nazis to Hiroshima toward the end of the War, is irradiated in the bombing of that city and subsequently regenerates into a gigantic version of the monster. This film is pure *kaiju eiga* and an extremely odd legacy for Kong's creator to have left behind. In its non-naturalistic strangeness—and its use of underlying apocalyptic metaphors to address developmental and scientific concerns—it encapsulates the differences that exist between *King Kong* and the genre it inspired in the East.

ONCE AND FUTURE KING?

As of this writing, Peter Jackson's much anticipated new remake seems set to re-create Kong as the King rather than as the absurdist impostor that even the best of previous post-*Kong* Kong films have produced. Once again *Kong's* iconic power may be brought into the consciousness of a new generation.

Will that secure the Ape-God's claim to the Crown?

I would argue that the question is irrelevant. Whatever the outcome of Jackson's endeavors, *King Kong* was central to the creation of the new virile *kaiju eiga* subgenre and as such Kong will forever hold a unique place in the giant monster pantheon. It is valid to trace Godzilla's dynasty—as distinctive as it is—back to O'Brien's 1933 giant ape film; Godzilla, the iconic nuclear reptile, may have a strong claim to sovereignty as "King of the Monsters," but his evolutionary development from the Great Ape also allows us to see how strong *King Kong's* influence really was. In particular, its thematic undercurrents regarding responsibility and primeval threat gave the subgenre its metaphorical power, as nuclear paranoia offered up a new vision of apocalyptic destruction. Yet it also says a lot that the original *Kong's* humanistic aspects are what survived most strongly into the new subgenre, while the line of development from *Kong* that produced the 1950s giant monster films in the U.S.—based more on surface plot structures and cold realism, though also having a role in the creation of Godzilla and his clan—dwindled quickly and was largely abandoned.

Works Cited

Erb, Cynthia (1998), *Tracking King Kong: A Hollywood Icon in World Culture*, Wayne State University Press: Detroit.

Galbraith IV, Stuart (1998), *Monsters Are Attacking Tokyo! The Incredible World of Japanese Fantasy Films*, Feral House: Venice, CA.

Goldner, Orville, and George E. Turner (1975), *The Making of King Kong: The Story Behind a Film Classic*, Ballantine Books: New York.

Greenberg, Harvey Roy (1996), "*King Kong*: The Beast in the Boudoir—or, 'You Can't Marry That Girl, You're a Gorilla!'", in Barry Keith Grant (ed.), *The Dread of Difference: Gender and the Horror Film*, University of Texas Press: Austin, reprinted from *The Movies on Your Mind*, Saturday Review Press, 1975.

Hood, Robert (2005), "Man and Super-Monster: The Metaphorical Undercurrents of Daikaiju Eiga as an Expression of Sensory Apocalypse," paper delivered at Swancon 30, Perth, on 28 March 2005.

Internet Movie Database, <www.imdb.com>

Ryfle, Steve (1998), *Japan's Favorite Mon-Star: The Unauthorized Biography of "The Big G,"* ECW Press: Toronto, Canada.

ROBERT HOOD is a widely published writer of horror fiction, who also indulges his abiding passion for genre cinema through irregular critiquing. His articles "Nights of the Celluloid Dead: a History of Zombie Films" and "Killer Koalas: Australian and New Zealand Horror Films" are available, along with other film comment, via his Web site, www.roberthood.net. He recently co-edited (with Robin Pen) an international anthology of original stories entitled *Daikaiju! Giant Monster Tales* (Agog! Press, 2005) and won an Atheling Award for Genre Criticism for a piece on the film *The Weight of Water*.

He lives in Wollongong, which is a regional city south of Sydney on the east coast of NSW, Australia.

Queer Eye for the Ape Guy?
King Kong as Endangered Masculinity

Natasha Giardina

I T'S HARD TO IMAGINE King Kong as *insecure*. At fifty feet tall, what's to be insecure about? And he has no
trouble getting women. (Though keeping them....)

On the other hand, what's all the bellowing about,
hmm? Natasha Giardina thinks he doth protest too
much.

Pretty, young blonde seeks hyper-aggressive stalker/kidnapper for fun
times and exciting encounters. Must be monstrous, bestial and over-
protective, enjoy chest-beating and wholesale destruction. Conversation
optional, back hair mandatory.

Let's face it: in today's world, King Kong couldn't get a date. It's not
just his anger management issues, his psychopathic tendencies and,
well...his back hair (although that *is* a real turn-off for a girl). It's a bigger problem than that. King Kong represents a vision of heterosexual
masculinity that is, much like himself, an endangered species. That vision is of the "primal man": seemingly all-powerful, rough and untamed,
but at the same time both innocent and vulnerable. This construction of
manhood is at least as old as Gilgamesh and Enkidu, and has retained
its appeal over time. The story of *King Kong* is perhaps its most eloquent
twentieth-century example—the awesome power of unbridled manhood,
the nobility of the savage beast. But in this new century, is there anyplace
left for Kong, or do our current constructions of masculinity render him

inappropriate and obsolete? In short, is this now a question of "Queer Eye for the Ape Guy"?

The story of *King Kong* talks about heterosexual masculinity with a kind of anxious air. Of course, masculinity has always been a concept fraught with anxieties and tensions. Part of the fault must lie with the nature of language itself. Derrida argues that words establish their meanings by a process of exclusion; in this case, masculinity can only define itself by the absence of femininity. Historically, we have assumed that masculinity is a kind of universal, self-evident constant—that it is a concrete thing, a fact—but this assumption denies the ambiguous and mutable nature of gender and sexual identities.

Where facts and truths are scarce, myths and stories can step in to provide the illusion of certainty. *King Kong* is one such story: it reinscribes the mythologized essence of heterosexual masculinity in the form of the "primal man." The original version of the film, Cooper and Schoedsack's 1933 blockbuster, gives an almost frantically strident affirmation of this archetype: the uncorrupted, untamed man acting in a completely "masculine" way. It responds to the tensions of gender by whitewashing its ambiguities and creating a false binary of masculinity and femininity. Yet the film's exploration of masculinity does more than simply affirm a stereotype: it encompasses men's aspirations as well as their anxieties; it sounds a nostalgic lament for an imagined past, when manly men could do manly things; and it defiantly shouts its heterosexism in the face of an increasingly complicated world of gender relations.

Kong himself has always been the biggest drawcard of the film, which uses him to embody its construction of the primal man. This hunky essence of "real" manhood has a range of defining features. Firstly, the primal man is both unique and magnificent—he's the eighth wonder of the world, after all, at least according to his own opening credit! Then there's his appearance. Okay, so Kong is a gorilla, but he's also an exaggerated collection of traditionally masculine signifiers: deep voice, rippling muscles, towering height, shaggy pelt. There's not a single part of him that's soft, gentle or delicate—if he were a car, he'd be a Humvee. Or a Sherman tank.

There's also a strong element of the sacred and mystical to Kong and, by inference, to the primal man, as the initial descriptions of him foreshadow:

CARL DENHAM: Did you ever hear of "Kong"?

CAPT. ENGLEHORN: Why yes. Some native superstition, isn't it? A god or a spirit or something?

CARL DENHAM: Well, anyway, neither beast nor man. Something monstrous, all-powerful.

This mystical element reinforces the powerful position of masculinity in society: masculinity is numinous, it is associated with the gods and worthy of homage and worship. This exchange also taps into the ambiguity of masculinity: Denham is only able to define Kong in the way that masculinity is customarily defined—according to myths and values rather than facts.

The sacred element comes alive on Skull Island, as the native tribe indulges in an arcane, ritualistic frenzy, paying homage to Kong's manly greatness by giving him a nubile "bride." The film implies that the primal man is a god in his natural environment, awesome and omnipotent. Kong continues to prove his mastery over his world by butchering the other prehistoric creatures foolish enough to take him on: the Tyrannosaurus rex, the Pterodactyl and the snaky lizard thing all perish because Kong's manliness makes him supreme. This is a pointed consolatory fantasy, aimed at the modern man mired in the mediocrity of urban life. It says, "You may feel small and insignificant, but if you were in your natural state, in the primordial jungles of antiquity, you too would be great; you might even be a god."

The primal man is a man of action—feelings are for wimps and women!—so the bare minimum of emotional expression is generally sufficient. Kong has only three emotions: rage, joy and lust. Rage, signified by roaring, is his usual emotional state and is useful for smiting his many enemies in the forests of Skull Island. He is also enraged by the presence of men, especially white men; this is the primal man's alpha-male instincts coming to the fore. Joy comes from the successful smiting of his foes and from conquests in general. The primary evidence of Kong's joy is his rampant displays of chest beating, accompanied by more roaring. It's unlikely this roaring has a linguistic meaning: it's hard to imagine him saying, "Oh boy, what a grand time I've had. I'm feeling really chipper right now!" Words are for justifying yourself when you care what other people think; this is not a concern for the primal man.

Kong's lust is undoubtedly his most interesting emotion, as well as his most problematic one. Lust is a necessary feature of the primal man because it proves his sexual potency; it also signifies his bestial nature and in the film, the image of a huge beast despoiling a white woman works powerfully to titillate and horrify audiences. But how exactly does a giant gorilla consummate his "affections" with a woman smaller than his hand? The mechanics of the act are against him, so instead the film concentrates on the foreplay. Ann Darrow lies supine in his hairy paw and he peels her like a banana, stripping off her clothes and sniffing their intoxicating, feminine scent (reality check: given what she's gone through, she probably smells like his hand, wherever *that's* been).

This scene is all about power and control: the primal man takes what he wants without thought for others; if he's got an itch, he's going to scratch it. Normal human beings, male or female, generally have to ask for it when it comes to sex, and even then there's no guarantee of success; that's what makes this particular aspect of the fantasy so appealing. There is no sense in this film that Ann likes or empathizes with the monster in any way. She screams and faints a lot, but never acquiesces, and so Kong's lust for her is defined purely in terms of implied rape.

The most important idea in the film, as far as manhood is concerned, is the constructed paradox of masculinity: it is both motivated and endangered by feminine contact. The film says this explicitly in the "Old Arabian Proverb" that precedes the first scene and forms the rationale for the entire film: "And lo, the beast looked upon the face of beauty. And it stayed its hand from killing. And from that day, it was as one dead."

The same construction comes up again in the budding relationship between Ann Darrow and Jack Driscoll. When Jack first meets Ann, he's rather primal himself. He begins by accidentally punching her in the face and then complains that women on ships are "a nuisance." But after six weeks on board together, he definitely shows signs of mellowing, despite the fact that he still thinks "women just can't help being a bother—made that way, I guess." Luckily for Jack, Ann's too much a lady to be a woman, or else he would certainly have earned a slap for that little quip. Denham recognizes Ann's effect on Jack immediately: "Some big, hard-boiled egg gets a look at a pretty face, and bang: he cracks up and goes sappy," and Jack, methinks, doth protest too much.

But this episode is merely a prelude to Ann's effect on Kong. Kong is transformed by his contact with femininity and, like a drug, it enslaves and eventually destroys him (it's also possible that human estrogen is a kind of ape smack). Upon seeing Ann for the first time, Kong gives himself over to a massive attack of triumphant chest-beating. He grabs her, and stares at her limp form in his palm as if she were some kind of curiously animated doll. She may as well be a doll, because Kong treats her like a prized possession but never like a sentient being. The primal man is the center of his universe; women are objects to him.

Ann's escape from his clutches enrages Kong and eventually leads to his capture and death: he follows her out from behind his wall and falls victim to Carl Denham's gas bombs, then in New York he manages to hunt Ann down, steal her from her apartment and deposit her at the top of the Empire State Building. Yet his fate is to die on that Manhattan icon, toppling from his perch and rebounding quite satisfyingly off the walls on his way down.

The tragedy of *King Kong* is that Kong is eternally doomed: this beast cannot live without beauty, but he cannot survive her either. From the moment he falls to the gas bombs to his eventual demise, the film positions us to lament the destruction of the primal man and feel negative toward the cause of his destruction: not Ann Darrow specifically, but rather the entire scope of femininity as symbolized by "beauty."

This deeper message of "Beauty and the Beast" is deeply hostile toward women: the film uses femininity as a scapegoat for men's anxieties about their masculinity. Concerned you're not the man you should have been? Didn't manage to climb that corporate ladder? The world not treating you with the respect you know you deserve? It's not your fault: your contact with women has made you soft and weak; they've corrupted you with their feminizing influence. This is the vulnerable side of the primal man: he may be top ape in the jungle, but femininity is a disease against which he has no immunity. Paradoxically, though, primal man requires a feminine counterpart because, returning to Derrida, he can only be a man when there are not-males around to highlight his potent manliness.

The film may celebrate Kong's primal masculinity but it does not allow him hero status; that role goes to Ann's love interest, Jack Driscoll. Jack represents a different construction of masculinity that both overlaps and opposes the primal man: he is Prince Charming and while he initially appears savage like Kong, unlike Kong he is essentially domesticated. In many respects, Jack is the opposite of Kong: he treats Ann like a lady (eventually!), he's well groomed, he wears a uniform rather than a body-hair carpet and he's not much given to roaring or chest-beating.

Yet although the film positions Jack as the hero—rescuing Ann from the monster on Skull Island and hatching the plan to kill Kong by airplane—it's an idea the film has difficulty selling. The problem begins in the opposition between the hero and the monster. Usually in these types of monster stories, the monster is a two-dimensional antagonist, a secondary character existing merely to provide an opportunity for the hero to triumph. In *King Kong*, however, the monster is arguably more of a protagonist than the apparent hero is. Kong is certainly more powerful, especially because Jack is a rather limp kind of hero. He may rescue Ann on Skull Island, but in New York Jack is powerless to stop Kong from stealing her back. Furthermore, his arrival to save Ann on the Empire State Building is noticeably belated: he arrives precisely as Kong falls to his death. If we were very cynical, we might think our Prince Charming was hanging back behind the door, waiting for someone else to knock the monster off his perch.

The biggest problem with Jack's hero status arises from the film's endorsement of the primal man as the mythologized essence of manliness. If the monster is the "real" man, then there's no room and no reason for us to identify with the "other" man, the hero. So why is he there? Well, here's the paradox: monsters can't be heroes. The film may celebrate the magnificence of the primal man, but his behavior is completely inappropriate for the twentieth century. The same qualities that make Kong awesome also make him horrifying; we may fantasize about the primal man, but we couldn't cope with him in our living room.

Guillermin's 1976 remake of *King Kong* provides an intriguing contrast to the original production: it reflects the significant social changes that took place over the intervening forty years, especially in gender relations. By 1976, second-wave feminism was changing the social landscape: women were demanding to be treated as men's equals and along with this recognition of women's rights came a need to re-evaluate the social status of masculinity. This contemporary social context appears to have strongly influenced the remake's portrayal of Kong and his relationship with his feminine conquest Dwan, yet the basic storyline is still about masculinity and still endorses the primal man archetype.

One of the ways the film tries to negotiate this difficult path between staying true to the original story concept and espousing a socially appropriate ideology is by reconceptualizing the nature of the primal man. Initially, Kong II's physical appearance makes him look far more brutish than his ancestor: his eyes become bloodshot when he's angry or lustful, there are more rage lines on his face, his teeth are sharper, his pecs are larger and he's even hairier. But Kong's actions give the game away: this savage beast is neither as savage nor as bestial as his ancestor. Kong II is capable of a wider range of emotions: in addition to rage, joy and lust, the film also shows Kong's tenderness, despair and resolve. Moreover, Kong II reasons like a human being and, specifically, like a hero: at the climax of the film, Kong understands he will die on the World Trade Center and nobly shields Dwan from the helicopter gunship salvos. Of course, along the way he manages to cause widespread mayhem, death and destruction, which contrasts oddly with his gentle and noble last stand.

Kong II also displays that most problematic emotion—love. Indeed, in this film, there is more love and less lust than in the original production. More importantly, Kong's feelings are reciprocated in this version in a way that was impossible and inconceivable in the 1933 film. Sure, ditzy Dwan is initially freaked out at being kidnapped by a mega-monkey, but her fear quickly gives way to awe, anger and finally empathy. There is also an undercurrent of mutual sexual attraction. Early on in their "relationship," Kong picks Dwan out of the mud, washes her off under a waterfall and blows her dry. Dwan enjoys herself in an inexplicably erotic way...inexplicable particularly because the ape has probably never brushed his teeth.

These changes affect the film's construction of the primal man. In this version, the primal man is much less primal: he is in touch with his feelings, he forms a mutual emotional attachment with his feminine conquest and his relationship with her is not predominantly defined by masculine power and mastery. In contrast to the 1933 incarnation, this Kong is too pedestrian—too understandable—to work well as "a god or a spirit," "monstrous [or] all-powerful"; the special effects are better, but he just isn't scary. Instead, he's a cross between a big animal, a teddy bear and a sensitive new-age guy.

As Kong has become weaker, the woman in his life has become stronger, but the film remains ambivalent toward her. The film responds to its social context by portraying Dwan as more of an active agent than Ann Darrow was, but relies on old gender stereotypes to talk about its new, active woman. Dwan shows her agency primarily through sexual expression, intuition and emotion. Conversely, intelligence, rationalism and objectivity are not strong features of her character. She is, unfortunately, a classic "dumb blonde": a two-dimensional character defined by her sexual availability. This is a girl who proudly announces that her life has been "saved by *Deep Throat*" and seems to think that deliberately misspelling her own name makes it sound more exotic. Ultimately, she remains the cause of Kong's downfall because the "Beauty and the Beast" theme remains central to the plot. Primal man is still endangered by femininity; the difference now is that he's not just threatened by it in an abstract sense; he's threatened because he can't withstand the modern woman's assertive sexuality.

If the primal man had trouble adjusting to 1970s social mores, how will he cope in the twenty-first century? The differences between masculinity and femininity, which were once considered "natural" and "commonsense," are now blurred and indistinct. Constructions of masculinity are on the front lines in the battles over gender identity. Popular media is currently debating a perceived "crisis of masculinity." Apparently, we're concerned that boys will grow up without a clear sense of what it means to be a man. It's not that men have become invisible in contemporary culture, but rather that "good, old-fashioned manhood" is being supplanted by a range of new, unsettling and, according to some critics, "unnatural" constructions of masculinity, which are getting better press. Primal man, once endangered by the disease of femininity, may now be threatened by loss of habitat.

Right now, the new masculinity on everyone's lips is metrosexualism. It's not the only alternate form of heterosexual masculinity on the menu, but it is getting top billing on the daily specials list. We perceive metrosexuals as straight men who indulge in certain forms of behavior we have traditionally associated with women and homosexuals, like a strong interest in personal grooming and beauty regimes, skills in cookery and other "feminine" domestic tasks, and a predilection for designer-label clothing, accessories and housewares. Essentially, what defines metrosexualism and the other forms of new, straight masculinities is that they don't define themselves by the exclusion of femininity, but by their ability to incorporate aspects of it. In this way, they represent a radical departure from the "Me Tarzan, you Jane (insert manly grunt here)" style of primal manliness.

Primal man might be suffering from disease and loss of habitat, but he's not completely dead yet—he's still gamely hanging on to the skyscraper of popular media. One of the few primal men to remain hugely popular in this new era of masculinity is that lovable yellow guy, Homer Simpson. Homer is a true child of Kong raised in a world that does not suit his nature. He displays a range of primal man's features: he's gruff, inelegant, bearlike, uncivilized, prone to violence and emotionally stunted. In "Treehouse of Horror III" (5-4), Homer even plays Kong: he is King Homer the mighty, stealer of Marge and eater of Lenny, Smithers and Shirley Temple. Paradoxically, part of Homer's popularity comes from his unattractiveness to women: quite frankly, he's funny because he's repulsive. Marge may love him, but women in the real world want more than a hairy ape interested only in scratching himself and fulfilling his animal needs. Thus, Homer represents the survival of primal man—but only as an object of amusement and derision. We might as well put him in a traveling circus.

It's certainly not much of an encouragement for Kong himself, now undergoing a rebirth at the hands of the acclaimed director Peter Jackson. Can he hold his own against these new forms of masculinity? Specifically, will the masculinity he represents be attractive or repulsive to twenty-first-century audiences? Perhaps what Kong really needs is simply a makeover, a fresh new look to help him fit in more with popular masculinities. He might even benefit from a "queer eye for the ape guy." The whole purpose of the *Queer Eye* television franchise is to reconstruct old-fashioned straight blokes into new, hip metrosexuals; in essence, this show makes explicit and entertaining the same transitions taking place behind the closed doors of straight men's culture. We could give Kong a new lease on life: redecorate his mountain aerie in the colors of the season, teach him how to make pannacotta and impress his girlfriend and, yes, take him to a beautician and get rid of all that horrible back hair.

We can rebuild Kong—we have the technology. But do we want to? Like the woman's touch, if we cast a queer eye on this ape guy we risk destroying him. He may be irrelevant in his original incarnation, but a reconstructed ape is just another guy in designer-label underpants. Right now, those fellas are a dime a dozen and maybe what a single ape guy needs is just to stand out from the pack. In the end, species survive or die based on their ability to adapt to changing circumstances and fill ecological niches; maybe the time is ripe for a primal revival. He may never be top ape in the jungle again, but perhaps there's still a place for him on the fringes; after all, all he needs is one pretty, young blonde with an interesting set of fetishes.

Works Cited

Baeza, Carlos. 1992. "Treehouse of Horror III." In *The Simpsons*. United States of America: Fox Television.

Cooper, Merian C., and Ernest B. Schoedsack. 1933. *King Kong*. United States of America: Magna Pacific.

Guillermin, John. 1976. *King Kong*. United States of America: Studio Canal, Universal Studios.

Jagose, Annamarie Rustom. 1996. *Queer Theory*. Carlton (VIC): Melbourne University Press.

Middleton, Peter. 1992. *The Inward Gaze: Masculinity and Subjectivity in Modern Culture*. New York: Routledge.

Stephens, John, ed. 2002. *Ways of Being Male: Representing Masculinities in Children's Literature and Film*. New York: Routledge.

Wilchins, Riki. 2004. *Queer Theory, Gender Theory: An Instant Primer*. Los Angeles: Alyson Books.

NATASHA GIARDINA lectures in children's literature and young adult literature at the Queensland University of Technology, Brisbane (Australia). She also specializes in youth and popular culture, communication theory, fantasy literature and science fiction. She holds a Bachelor of Arts with first class honors and a Graduate Certificate of Education from James Cook University, and is currently completing a Doctorate of Philosophy in twentieth-century children's fantasy literature. In 2002, Natasha received the James Cook University Gluyas Prize for most outstanding postgraduate candidate in English literature.

'Twas Beauty Killed the Beast
King Kong and the American Character

John C. Wright

KING KONG MUST BE KILLED, yet we mourn his passing. Much of the power of Kong rests in the conflicts that he raises in the viewer. Conflicts that reflect our own ambiguous relationship to the civilization we've created, as John C. Wright explores here.

1. THE REMORSE OF THE VICTOR

Why do we pity the Monster?

Instead of skulking and hiding with his captive, or running away, the great shaggy beast, his lovely prize fainting in his savage grip, climbs the tallest tower in sight, the tallest in the world, so that his rage and defiance can be hurled abroad as far as can be. He roars a challenge to tormentors to do their worst.

The mighty Kong, greatest of all nature's beasts, staggers for a moment on his perch atop the Empire State Building, the greatest of all man's engineering works, while the technological marvel of the flying heavier-than-air machines of the Navy Air Corps pour machine-gun fire, efficiently and mercilessly, into the giant ape's breast.

The pilots are faceless, nameless, anonymous.

He clutches his throat in pain one last time, his massive head droops, he topples, he falls.

The audience does not cheer.

Strange. They cheered when the Death Star was blown up, didn't they?

Kong kills scores of people: he overturns a railway train; he tears a Boeing F4B out of midair, slaying the pilot; the women he mistakes for Ann he casually dashes to her grisly death from many stories high; there is no guessing how many natives of Skull Island lost their lives over the years, either when warriors defied him or maidens were sacrificed to him.

This monster who dared to overtop our proudest and tallest tower would provoke us to cheer to see him fall, if we had a simple loyalty to everything for which that building stands. If the engineering triumph of the heavier-than-air machines and the technological killing-efficiency of the machine gun won our undivided support, we would swell with unalloyed pride to see Mother Nature's proudest and hugest son fall doomed to Earth, unable to combat our mechanized civilization.

For better or worse (but probably for the worse), our loyalty to civilization is not simple, not undivided, not unalloyed.

Likewise, were we more callous, we would hoot with contempt when the mighty are lured by love to their destruction, great strength helpless before helpless beauty.

For better or worse (but probably for the better), we are not so callous toward the masculine weakness for the weaker sex.

Kong was killed, in effect, by Carl Denham, a side effect of his greedy sideshow barker's quest for gelt, and we would be dull creatures indeed to rejoice in such a victory. Both Denham's fictional audience and RKO Pictures' real audience come to see a spectacle more spectacular than any shown in the Colosseum of Rome.

For better or worse (but almost certainly for the worse) we love such spectacle; but there is a sinister side to such spectacles as well.

Illogical as it may sound, we are left with the lingering feeling that Kong was not beaten fair and square.

For better or worse (but almost certainly for the better), we are not so inert in our souls that we are smug when the stronger overcomes the weaker. Call it sportsmanship, or rooting for the underdog, or love of fair play, or chivalry, but we are not yet so far debased with our love of victory to be immune from the victor's remorse.

When the Roman conqueror in his triumphal car was carried through the cheering crowds, a slave stood by to whisper to him to remember his mortality, that he would not be so carried away by the thrill of triumph to think himself a god. To see the fall of any mighty creature is to hear in our ear the whisper of that slave: we, too, are mortal.

King Kong is not a great film. Lines like, "Gee, Ann, I kinda guess I love you!" are not Shakespeare. But this is a film that never will pass away from the American popular consciousness, not so long as the American character remains recognizably American, because it poses questions central to that character: the film questions our loyalty to civilization; it calls on our sympathies in a case where we can afford no real sympathy; it contrasts our hardheaded pragmatism with our softhearted romanticism; the film comments on our uneasy relationship with sensationalism, spectacle and showmanship; it reminds us of the impermanence of all things, including those we cherish.

2. LOYALTY TO CIVILIZATION

Imagine, if you will, the state of American society in 1933 A.D. The airplane was thirty years old, roughly the time from this writing since the birth of the Internet. The Empire State Building was but one year old, having been completed in 1931, roughly the time from this writing since Taipei 101 (currently the tallest building in the world) opened its doors.

The horror of the Great War had passed over Europe, from which a fragile peace was born. The aristocratic order of things was utterly passed away, both the fair and the foul of it, promising a more modern and scientific method to govern man and the free market. But the Great Depression mocked those promises and that fatal conceit.

So imagine, if you will, a state of mind which may seem utterly familiar to us, because we inherited it from those years, when that state of mind was fresh as a new wound: on the one hand, each dawn greeted with new marvels of engineering and progress; on the other, the true depravity of mechanized mass-warfare, the efficiency of the assembly line turned to the task of butchering men in anonymous masses. In other words, it was a time of the greatest hope and optimism for civilized men, but the time also of the greatest despair.

The genie was out of the bottle, and it was granting wishes, benevolent and malevolent alike.

Imagine, and now strain your imagination, a state of mind now unfamiliar to us. It was the time of the self-made man. It was a time when a man could take an axe, chop down a tree on his own land and put up a woodshed without leave or let asked of anyone. It was a land where no permits were needed. In half the states, to own an automobile required no license;

in none was there a test of competency to operate one. There were no identification papers. Social Security, and the degrading practice of numbering all citizens like cattle, lay in the future.

Americans, in that day, were bold. They did things without waiting for permission. They raised the Empire State Building in two years: less time than it would take, nowadays, merely to go through the permit process.

They also conquered. This was a time when all the great European powers maintained overseas colonies, and America was not immune from that ambition. The supremacy of the white man's civilization was nowhere questioned, though the ache of progress, the nostalgia for an inferior condition of life, was just beginning to be felt.

On to this stage steps Carl Denham.

Everyone in the audience recognized him from the first moment he opened his mouth to speak, or rather, to bark out his lines. He is P. T. Barnum.

Americans both love and hate such figures: we love them because they are successful, and because they can squeeze a hard-earned dime out of a yokel who came into town on the turnip truck. We hate them because we are sometimes the yokel who comes into town on the turnip truck, and that is our hard-earned dime.

The first thing we learn about Denham is that the police are on the lookout for him, to try to seize his shipload of weapons: poison gas and machine guns. The second thing we learn about him is that no actress in her right mind will accept a job from him, since he is such a shady character, and secretive about his plans. The third is that he lets nothing stop him: he says he will find a girl for his motion picture even if he has to marry one.

A modern audience is nearsighted to two things about this character, which the audience of the time would have seen far off, and understood at first glance.

First, they understood how outrageous Denham is.

He seems not so abnormal to us; his greed seems like the kind of motivation we read books by Business Gurus to learn. We want to unleash inner giants and study the leadership secrets of Attila the Hun, forgetting that giants are monsters, and Attila, a barbarian.

We have suffered from so many years of seeing folk reaching for success at any price that we are used to men of ambition trampling the norms of society. Before the days of Liz Taylor and Richard Burton, the adulteries and excesses of the Hollywood elite were quietly hushed up, out of a dignified loyalty to the norms of society. In 1933, those norms were not the subject of contempt: matrimony was sacred.

Second, they understood how welcome and cheering a figure Denham is. The poorer among them understood it with painful clarity.

The Great Depression has closed the doors of factories and banks all across the nation. A gray miasma of defeat and despair closes over all. Here is one man who is not going to starve. He is the kind of man who, come to think of it, would marry a girl to get a star for his motion picture. Matrimony is not sacred to him: winning is. In the midst of a defeated world, this type of can-do attitude is as uplifting to the heart as a blast from a trumpet.

The same mixture of good and bad we see in Denham's character is what we see in our mighty industrial civilization, so hopeful and so callous. We like him, but we don't exactly like him. The triumph over the beast is his triumph. And we don't exactly like his triumph. This is the first reason why we don't cheer when the monster falls.

3. OUR INNER APE

A more charming exemplar of the unconquerable American spirit is Ann Darrow.

Denham comes upon Ann Darrow stealing from an apple cart. She appears right after a brief scene where Denham surveys with disgust the weary and complaining figures standing in a soup line on the steps of a women's mission: Darrow is not there. She has not taken that final step of surrender one takes when one asks for charity. The audience of the time would have understood what that meant.

It meant that Ann Darrow is the "girl with a backbone" that Denham is looking for.

The strange thing for a modern audience is what is missing from the scene in the diner where Denham hires her. There is no paperwork. He hires her without filling out a tax form, asking for proof of citizenship or making arrangements for health benefits, maternity leave or occupational safety regulations.

It was a different world then. For good or ill (but probably for good), you were on your own.

Early on in the film, Denham admits that he has no use for women, and does not want one along on the expedition, "but the public, bless 'em, want a pretty face to look at!"

I doubt this line is an intentional irony on the part of the filmmakers: for pure plot purposes, the filmmakers needed to establish how deep the unknown danger into which Denham will lead the expedition is: namely, dangerous enough that no one in his right mind would lead a girl there. (If this seems condescending to a modern day where chivalry is dead, remember that it was a different world then. You were on your own, ladies, but the menfolk thought it their duty to look after you.)

Intentional or not, the irony is there. As I watch this film, bless me, I want a pretty face to look at, and Fay Wray, bless her, has one of the prettiest faces of the '30s.

I was struck by the strangeness of the scene where she flirts with the first mate. One thing you would never see these days is a grown woman acting so girlish. She chatters and pouts and tilts her head and rolls and flashes her eyes in a fashion even a twelve-year-old is too mature and too self-possessed to do these days. Since the guy is acting like a schoolyard tough-guy, maybe the whole scene was merely being played at an unsophisticated level. Or maybe women were protected from male predation in those days, and could afford to look vulnerable. Innocence was not scorned as weakness, and females were allowed to be feminine.

And Fay Wray can belt out a scream with the best of them. What a set of pipes that gal has got!

Maybe you, dear reader, have different tastes in damsels in distress: but, as for me, just about any time I see a sweet, young girl in a slinky dress tied to a post in a sweltering jungle with drums pounding in the background, it just brings out that protective, apelike urge in me that makes me want to knock over elevated trains and rip the jaws off giant dinosaurs to win her.

Of course, I cannot knock over an elevated train or rip the jaws off a giant dinosaur, but if other boys feel as I do, you have the second reason why we do not cheer when the ape falls to his death. Our inner ape is rooting for him.

4. A PRETTY FACE TO LOOK AT

For those of you who are puritans out there, who sniff and think it is demeaning to put a pretty girl in a monster film, all I can say is: Denham is right. Even though Ann Darrow spends more film time screaming than saying lines, without her, there would be no film: it would simply be a show about a big-game hunter who does not know how to keep his game caged up.

There is a famous anecdote that Robert Louis Stephenson's little boy was tired of the romance angle in the adventure books he was read, and so, when his father set out to write a pirate tale, he asked his dad to leave the girls out. True enough, there are no female characters in *Treasure Island*. Jules Verne did much the same thing, and so there is no romantic sub-plot in any of his *voyages extraordinaire*.

With all due respect to these great writers, I have to say, Oh, Come Now. Capturing a giant ape is a modest tale of modest interest, a Frank Buck story. Saving Fay Wray from a giant ape is a Spectacle! Thrills! Adventure!

The puritans may not like the fact that men feel protective toward girls, and want to save them from danger; but, if you feel this way, dear reader, take your complaint to Mother Nature.

So here are our exemplars of modern civilization at its best and worst: a man who wants fame and a gal who wants a meal, neither of them with anything to lose. Neither of them afraid of a place called Skull Island.

Skull Island! What horrors lurk behind the massive, ancient walls before whose frowning gates savage warriors cower!

5. THE CALLOUS AND THE ROMANTIC

En route to Skull Island, we meet the alleged love interest of this picture, a guy whose part is so forgettable that I have to leave off typing a moment to go look up his name. Excuse me.

(Later.) Sorry about that. His name is Jack Driscoll.

Carl Denham and Jack Driscoll represent the two opposing ideas of the American character: the callous and the romantic. Americans love a man who gets things done; but we also love a man who falls in love. Denham is the kind of man who, when Ann Darrow is being dragged at night by torchlight to her doom, looks out a porthole of the ship and regrets he does not have a camera which can photograph by torchlight. Driscoll, on the other hand, is the kind of man who (quite rightly) objects to putting a girl in danger, and wants her to stay on the boat.

Driscoll is at first manly and rugged, a "hard-boiled egg," but he "cracks up and goes sappy" when smitten with love.

In other words, he is the miniature, the human version, of Kong.

Now there is a reason why this film is called *King Kong* and not *The Adventures of Two-Fisted Jack Driscoll*. Driscoll, despite his obvious bravery, is about as unsuccessful at being a hero as can be.

He leads a group of men into the jungle to rescue Ann Darrow. Twelve men die. Some fall when toppled from a log; some are eaten by dinosaurs; some drown. There is a missing scene, thought too grotesque to make the final cut, when men are eaten alive by giant spiders.

Driscoll only manages to get the girl and spirit her away thanks to Kong's distraction.

Back in civilization, when Kong is climbing the skyscraper hunting for the girl, Driscoll has the unenviable role, when Ann is having her posttraumatic stress syndrome moment, of patting her hand and saying, "Aw—it's all right. Anyhow, you know they're bound to get 'em," while the audience can see the dark, titanic and savage visage of the killer ape, huge eyes ablaze, looming in the window just behind.

Driscoll's moment of heroism is to batter Kong's hand with a chair to protect his true love, and he is brushed aside. Kong does not even bother to kill him.

But, despite my mockery of poor Driscoll, let us note three things:

First, he gets the girl, and Ann Darrow is certainly easy on the eyes.

Second, he is the character in the film we need as a yardstick to show the stature of the other characters.

Driscoll, compared to Kong, is a pygmy compared to a giant. Driscoll is the man of action here, the man who thinks with his heart: the movie makes him a sad and forgettable figure, because the time and era of the man of action, the man who thinks with his heart, is passing away. There is nothing he can do with his muscles and his virile bravery that the great Kong, with his much large muscles, cannot do better.

Driscoll, compared to Denham, is the honest man compared to the rogue. Driscoll thinks with his heart, and Denham thinks without his heart.

The heart does not triumph over the head in this film.

Kong is not overcome by old-fashioned two-fisted action. The monsters in ancient myth, the Nemean Lion, the Dragon of Libya, were dispatched by Hercules and Saint George by strangulation or spear-blow. Kong, on the other hand, is hammered to death by machine-gun fire while he waves his mighty arms at planes that swoop (for the most part) just out of reach.

Had Kong been human and not a monster ape, we would cheer him. The crucial scene is his escape. Denham soothes Ann Darrow by saying, "We've taken some of the fight out of him," meaning, one assumes, that without the pretty face of the beauty present to tempt him, the big ape had no heart to fight his chains. Then the gentlemen of the press step forth: flashbulbs flare. Denham calls on the reporters to stop, saying, "Wait a minute! He thinks you're attacking the girl!" The newshounds bark back, "Aw, let 'em roar! It'll make a swell picture."

Compare this to a similar scene in something like, say, a Hercules film. The mighty hero is all chained up, the villains threaten the smoldering Italian beauty who is the film's love interest, he ripples his mighty pectorals and smashes the temple into flinders, sending throngs of heavily armed extras and spear carriers to Hades. The scene is pure derring-do: two-fisted action.

But Kong is the monster, not the hero. The era of romance is over: the technical age has begun. The beast stronger than Hercules, stronger than Samson, falls before the inventions of Hiram Maxim and the Wright Brothers.

As mentioned above, we root for the giant ape because there is no guy who does not turn himself into a big ape when he falls for a pretty face. But, even in Boston, marriages between apes and humans have not yet been voted into effect by the judiciary. We are men, a nobler form of life than any ape, no matter his size. Our sympathy simply cannot affix itself without hesitation to the monster, lest we become monsters ourselves, unable to see the difference between beast and man. In his heart, the lust of Kong for his Bride may not be any different from the love of Mr. Driscoll for the future Mrs. Driscoll. But in his brain, the big ape is not bright enough to see that such marriages never work out.

The heart cannot triumph if it is the monstrous heart of a beast.

Because to see the triumph of brain over brawn, modern over primitive or coolly cunning over straightforward, always carries a twinge of regret, of nostalgia for the romance of simpler days—the third reason why we don't cheer when the monster falls.

6. SPECTACLES AND SIMPLE PLEASURES

It is no coincidence that Denham, who represents this modern spirit of coldhearted brain at its best and worst, has the last line in the film; and no coincidence that that line is basically insincere: "'Twas Beauty killed the Beast!"

Insincere, in his mouth, it may be, but not untrue.

It is, in fact, the beauty of the fair damsel that tempts the monster: first, to pursue her to the native village, where Denham pelts him with a gas grenade and overcomes him; second, when Kong escapes from captivity, instead of running away from the crowded human city, to rampage through it, looking for his bride.

Were it not for her, he would have remained safe in his savage world where he was king.

But Denham himself does not believe this line. Or, to be precise, he does not care whether it is true one way or the other: it merely makes good copy. We know he merely means the line for effect because we see him practicing it, rehearsing it, when Ann Darrow is playing with the ship's pet monkey Iggy; he refers to it again when she is making a screen test; and again, it is the line he gives the newshounds swarming to his opening night; and again, he refers to it when making a speech to the opening night audience.

It is not really a line: it is a headline. A slogan. It is the promise of a spectacle: a gladiatorial battle where, for once, the virgin kills the lion.

What makes the line ironic, of course, is that the same idea is expressed

by the moviemakers of the real movie in the make-believe Arabian proverb that prefaces the picture. We, the real audience, are being promised the
same spectacle that the story-tale character Denham in the story promises
his story-tale audience.

I would say that this promise was kept. The film saved Radio Pictures
(later RKO Pictures) from bankruptcy; and we are still talking about this
spectacle half a dozen decades later.

If we feel both a sense of wonder at seeing this first of all giant monster
films, and a wry sense that the filmmakers are manipulating us to feel that
sense of awe, the filmmakers are also aware of that ambiguity. It is a different aspect of the same ambiguity we feel toward the promise and the cyni-
cism of civilization. The simple rural man is awed at the razzle-dazzle; the
sophisticated urban man is wryly aware of the effect, but willing to put his
sophistication on hold long enough to enjoy it.

The reason for this ambiguity is that spectacle is an urban pleasure.

To watch a stage filled with complex fireworks, illusions and trained
beasts, or to watch the complex technology of the motion-picture produce
sound and images of purely imaginary worlds, is not something the hermit can do in his mossy cave. Our hermit can enjoy the simple pleasures
of sunset clouds and singing birds, fresh bread and clear streams. All the
innocent pleasures of nature are open to him. That wry sense that someone is deliberately setting about to manipulate our emotions is simply not
present in a simple pleasure. That is what makes them simple.

Spectacles also do not have the redeeming characteristic of other urban
pleasures, such as plays or operas, where the poet introduces deep matter
to let the audience ponder the deep questions of life. Spectacles are meant
not to be profound.

There is an element of hokum, of sheer ridiculousness, in any spectacle
(which is why, by the way, science fiction actors must play their parts without any hint of insobriety; the merest smile or hint of tongue-in-cheek will
break the spell).

And there is also an element of dishonesty. The bearded lady is, after all,
just wearing false whiskers; the man shot from the cannon is not actually
propelled by gunpowder: the flash and bang and smoke are just for show.

There is also an element of decadence in spectacle. Watching motion
pictures of men getting eaten by dinosaurs is more akin to being a Roman
plebeian at the Amphitheatre, watching real men getting eaten by lions,
than it is to being a hermit enjoying the sight of dew on a rose petal. It
has a hint of something unsavory about it: I do not think, as a young boy,
it would have been right for me to watch this film, and say, "Oo! Look,
grandma! Kong threw the woman out der winder! Ain't it *cool*?" Cool it

might be, but it is also not the kind of thing a boy should say to his grandmother.

For all these reasons, spectacles appeal to the idle crowd.

Americans are slightly suspicious of idle crowds, even when we are in one. Americans are generally a hard-working lot. So we see a crowd and we think: why aren't those able-bodied men working? Don't they have something better to do than gawk at an ape? Aren't there chores that need doing?

At least, such was the American character back in the day.

In this case, the suspicions are amply rewarded. No noble purpose is served in bringing Kong back alive to New York: the risk was borne to line Denham's pocketbook. It ends in disaster. The only nobility of character is shown by the ape, who is unafraid, even at the end, of his killers.

The ape is the wrath of nature, like a divine judgment against the idle crowd and the panderer who services that crowd. They chained up the greatest creature on earth to titillate the pettiest of the appetites: the hunger for spectacle.

Here is the fourth reason we don't cheer when he falls: There is something sordid about dying to please an idle mob, even if it is a monster that dies.

7. REGRET FOR THE LOST WORLD

The core of the film, of course, is the sequence on Skull Island, when the rescue party following Ann Darrow is annihilated by prehistoric monsters.

The discovery, in the Victorian era, of the true age of the world, and of the antique monstrosities, enormous and reptilian, that ruled the earth for so many centuries in excess of the human span on Earth, had a thrilling effect on the imagination of the public.

It opened the gates of time. Vistas at which the mind's eye trembles were displayed.

Adventure tales for the next century would feature lost races of lost worlds in hidden valleys or remote plateaus, parallel dimensions or distant planets: in the popular imagination, every hero from Professor Challenger to Allan Quatermain, Tarzan to Steve Trevor, is forever stumbling across a secret valley or remote plateau where the Lost City of Ophir looms, or Atlantis, or Amazons, or ancient and hideous Cumae, stronghold and city of a deathless queen. In the world of pulps and comics, somewhere the Pharaoh still reigns, and somewhere the Tyrannosaurus rex still roars.

But in all these adventure tales, they are the last of their kind, a shrunken remnant, hidden exiles, forgotten: the orphans hiding in the cellar when the stormtroopers of time wiped out their way of life. Only their isolation from the world has spared them, and every adventure tale is about the breach of that isolation.

Any story of this kind, even in the hands of the shallowest author, carries a hint of a deeper meaning: they are all tales of the impermanence of our lives and our civilization.

Here is the final reason why we do not cheer when the giant ape falls: We have too much of the stature of giants ourselves to delight in the sight of greatness in ruins.

8. CONCLUSION: A FUTURE WITHOUT REMORSE

If we are persuaded of the central point of this essay, that several things in the American character make us respond with sympathy and remorse to the downfall of Kong, then this point leads us next to a melancholy question: What change in the character of our next generation would make the film seem to them incomprehensible, uninteresting or absurd?

The film may already seem absurd to some, for its dated special effects and its wooden acting. The audience of 2005 simply cannot be as shocked and thrilled by 1933 special effects technology as the 1933 audience who had never seen stop-motion animation before. As for the wooden acting, no fan of Star Wars will list acting range as something a memorable science fiction film requires. A myth has power because of its basic idea, not because of the elegance of the telling. So let us leave aside those who find the film absurd for these reasons, and ask instead what the character of the next generation would need be like if the very idea of Kong, the myth of the doomed giant ape, were no longer to appeal to them?

All the main points covered in this essay dwell on a tension between opposites, a happy medium between unhappy extremes.

For example, we are loyal to a civilization, but we have a sense of mistrust, a sense of nostalgia and loss for the things civilization sweeps away, that moderates that loyalty. A zealot of either extreme would have no taste for this film.

Imagine, on the one hand, an Ayn Rand–style Realist, whose love of industry and progress makes nostalgia for more primitive times distasteful to him. He would blink at the end of the film, and shrug, and say, "A big, brutal ape kills people and heroic pilots shoot him. How can you root for the beast?" For the Realist, who prizes human reason above all other things, there is no sympathy for the passions and courage of a beast.

Imagine, on the other hand, a Rousseau-style Romantic, who rejects the modern world and its works. To him, the ape is merely a victim, and the victims of the ape are ignored. Instead of a complex figure, Carl Denham is merely a villain, as black-hearted and one-dimensional as any mustachioed Snidely Whiplash tying pure Pauline to the railroad track. It is no coincidence that the Carl Denham figure in the 1976 remake of *King Kong* is an oil company executive who is just such a simplistic bad guy. The audiences demanded that he die in the film, and the exploitive capitalist white guy is trampled to death by the victimized-hero ape.

Our Romantic cannot see any reason why anyone would root for the humans. A film where the coldhearted head triumphs over the hotheaded heart is one the Romantic cannot care for.

In other words, a too-zealous loyalty to civilization will diminish the affect of the film, as will a too-zealous loyalty to primitivism. The tension between the characters of Denham and Driscoll falls along the same lines.

Again, the film becomes absurd or uninteresting to anyone with no sympathy for the delicate mystery that lies behind the war between the sexes. An Amazon from the mythic land, where women are equal and identical to men in all ways, would be nonplussed by the portrayal of Ann Darrow. The image of her golden beauty clenched in the hairy paw of overwhelming masculine strength would not reflect anything that ever appears in the Amazon's mental or emotional environment. The image would evoke neither tenderness nor horror, because the Amazon does not think of men as stronger than women. They do not see the ape in every lover's heart, that beast which makes the lover brave any peril or trample any law, either to scale the wall surrounding the Capulet's manse, or to betray the trust of friend and lord King Arthur, or to return across the peril of the sea pursued by Neptune's curse after ten years' odyssey, to reach his beloved. The Amazon does not hold with the romantic concept of love. The Amazon is not romantic enough to sympathize with the ape's doomed lust for Ann.

The opposite philosophy does not have a name, so let us merely call it the philosophy of the Lotos-eater. The Lotos-eater believes that love conquers all. No sexual drive, however base, should go without satisfaction. Adultery, polygamy, incest, sodomy, bestiality, necrophilia, pedophilia—all are fair to the Lotos-eater: he regards it as brave to seek any self-indulgence, howsoever monstrous. The Lotos-eater is too romantic, too supportive of love in all its incarnations, to see the point of the film, too dull to notice the central tragedy: he simply thinks the ape should have been allowed to keep Ann Darrow. He would dismiss the hero's defense of her as parochial xenophobia.

The Amazon is sure to be offended with the central conceit of the film, which is that beautiful women provoke men (apelike men, at least) to acts both destructive and self-destructive. As Driscoll says, "Women can't help it, I guess. They're just made that way." Whether true or not in real life, in the film Ann's beauty provokes the natives of Skull Island to kidnap her, and the ape to seize her. It is also her beauty, the pretty face for the public to look at, which makes Denham hire her in the first place. She causes all the troubles in the film. This is not through any fault of her own: she's just made that way.

Contrariwise, the Lotos-eater is sure to be offended with the central theme of the film, which is that the sexual passion unleashes a raging beast. It is destructive, not sweet and tender, and when it cannot be chained, it must be destroyed. The Lotos-eater regards sex merely as an entertaining pastime, whereas the film regards it as something like a force of primeval nature: gigantic, serious and beyond control.

Finally, and along those same lines, should we ever become a people so convinced of our manifest supremacy that we think our way of life will never end, or should we become a people so convinced of our manifest corruption that we pant and yearn for our own destruction, the sorrow and grandeur of the great ape's death will come to have no meaning for us. In the first case, we will be blind to the ways in which our mighty civilization is like the mighty ape; in the second case, our pity will be so much with the ape that we will not see his crimes, and not acknowledge the grim necessity of gunning him down.

The reason why we do not cheer when the monster falls is that, in the final word, *King Kong* is a tale about grim necessity. It is a theme the generation of the Great Depression understood better than our own. Should we ever become so coldhearted that necessities no longer seem grim or regrettable to us, or should we ever become so hotheaded that no necessity seems necessary to us, then, finally, we will have lost the romanticism and the realism of the American character, and finally, *King Kong* will pass from our memory.

Something great will perish in our souls should such a day as that arrive.

JOHN C. WRIGHT is a retired attorney, newspaperman and newspaper editor, who was only once on the lam and forced to hide from the police, who did not admire his newspaper. In 1984, he graduated from St. John's College in Annapolis, home of the "Great Books" program. In 1987, he graduated from the College and William and Mary's Law School (going from the third oldest to the second oldest school in continuous use in the United States), and was admitted to the practice of law in three jurisdictions (New York, May 1989; Maryland, December 1990; DC, January 1994). His law practice was unsuccessful enough to drive him into bankruptcy soon thereafter. His stint as a newspaperman for the *St. Mary's Today* was more rewarding spiritually, but, alas, also a failure financially. He presently works (successfully) as a writer in Virginia, where he lives in fairy-tale-like happiness with his wife, the authoress L. Jagi Lamplighter, and their three children: Orville, Wilbur and Just Wright.

King Kong "Sequels" and Inspired Films

Compiled by Bob Eggleton

The Son of Kong (1933)

Robert Armstrong, Helen Mack. Directed by Ernest P. Schoedsack. Written by Ruth Rose. RKO Pictures. Special Effects by Willis O'Brien. A "serio-comedy" sequel to the original film, featuring an albino "Little Kong" who steals the show, a guilt-ridden Carl Denham, a few more dinosaurs, a giant bear and the total destruction of Skull Island.

Edo Ni Arawareta Kingu Kongu (King Kong Appears In Edo) (1938)

Ryutaro Hibuki, Ginbei Inoue. Directed by S. Kamagai. Japanese version of *King Kong*; no known print exists save for still photos. Kong was apparently created with "man-in-a-suit" work, done by a technician who would later work on Toho Pictures' *Gojira* (1954).

Unknown Island (1948)

Richard Denning, Virginia Grey. Directed by Jack Bernhard. Adventurers go to a lost island and find dinosaurs (done with man-in-a-suit work) and a "giant sloth"—a stunt actor in an ape suit.

Mighty Joe Young (1949)

Terry Moore, Robert Armstrong. Directed by Ernest B. Schoedsack. Written by Merian C. Cooper and Ruth Rose. Considered to be a much superior follow-up to *The Son of Kong*. A large gorilla from Africa and his female friend are talked into coming to Hollywood to find fortune and fame only to encounter disaster. Note: while Willis O'Brien is credited with the stop-motion work, a good deal of it was actually done by his assistant—a young Ray Harryhausen—due to O'Brien's health problems.

213

Ju Jin Yoki Otoko (Half-human) (1955)

Momoko Kochi, Akira Takarada. Directed by Ishiro Honda. US version: Starring John Carradine. Directed by Kenneth Crane. Impressive film from Japan's Toho Studios portraying a father and son family of apelike creatures in a remote area of Japan who are worshiped by villagers. The 1959 US version was highly truncated, and the Japanese version is rarely seen due to having being banned for its portrayal of the Ainu people.

Konga (1961)

Michael Gough, Margo Johns. Directed by John Lemont. Written by Herman Cohen, Aben Kandel. A scientist creates a growth formula from strange, enormous African plants that he tests out on his chimpanzee—whom he uses to kill people. Eventually the ape becomes Kong-sized, rampages through London and turns on his master.

Kingukongu Tai Gojira (King Kong Vs. Godzilla) (1962)

Tadao Takashima, Mie Hama, Kenji Sahara. Directed by Ishiro Honda. Story by Shinichi Sekizawa. Toho Studios, Japan. US Version: Starring Michael Keith, James Yagi, Harry Holcombe. Additional scenes directed by Thomas Montgomery. Produced by John Beck. Written by Paul Mason and Bruce Howard. The giant ape, this time from Faro Island, is brought to Japan to battle the radioactive dinosaur, Godzilla. The story was originally conceived by Willis O'Brien, but didn't involve Godzilla. The Japanese film was a sort of oddly comical social commentary, but the co-producers at Universal International truncated and completely reframed the film, creating new footage, making, in effect, a totally different movie.

Tarzan and King Kong (1965)

Mumtaz, Bela Bose. Directed by A. Shamsheer. Obscure Indian-made production about...Tarzan and King Kong.

King Kong (1966/67) Animated Series

Billie Mae Richards, Carl Banas, Susan Conway. Produced by Arthur J. Rankin, Jr., Jules Bass. Toei Animation, Japan. This cartoon series had Kong on an island with dinosaurs, befriended and studied by Professor Bond and his son Billy. It used some characters later featured in the live-action *King Kong Escapes* (1968).

Eva La Venere Selvaggia (King Of Kong Island) (1968)

Brad Harris, Esmarelda Barros. Directed by Roberto Mauri. Written by Ralph Zucker. Mad scientists travel to an island and find a feral girl living with apes, one of whom is a descendant of the original King Kong. Some of the apes are captured, and the scientists perform experiments on them to create gorilla soldiers.

Kingukongu No Gyakushu (King Kong Escapes) (1968)

Rhodes Reason, Mie Hama, Akira Takarada, Linda Miller. Directed by Ishiro Honda. Written by Arthur Rankin, Jr., Jules Bass. Special Effects by Eiji Tsuburaya. Toho/Rankin Bass/Universal co-production. Kong is discovered on a remote island battling dinosaurs, kidnapped by the evil Dr. Who (not the time-traveling British Sci-Fi hero) and winds up battling his robotic "Mecha-Kong" double in Tokyo.

Queen Kong (1976)

Rula Lenska, Robin Askwith, Valerie Leon. Directed by Frank Agrama. Written by Frank Agrama and Robin Dobria. Tongue-in-cheek British film has a chesty female "Kong" that falls for a blonde male named Ray Fay and rampages through London. Compete with Busby-Berkleyesque musical numbers and a giant-sized bra-burning scene.

King Kong (1976)

Jessica Lange, Jeff Bridges, Charles Grodin. Directed by John Guillermin. Produced by Dino De Laurentiis. Written by Lorenzo Semple, Jr., based on the original screenplay. This remake updates the classic film to 1976, where Kong meets his end on the World Trade Center towers in NYC. Kong is played by Rick Baker in a well-done ape suit.

A*p*e (a.k.a. Super Kong, the New King Kong) (1976)

Rod Arrant, Joanna Kerns, Nak-hun Lee. Directed by Paul Leder. Low-budget South Korean–made spoof has a giant thirty-six-foot ape wandering around the outskirts of Seoul, battling a giant shark and capturing an American actress.

King Hsing Hsing (Mighty Peking Man; Us Title: Goliathon) (1977)

Evelyne Kraft, Danny Lee, Feng Ku. Directed by Meng Hwa-Ho. Written by Kuang Ni. Shaw Brothers Studios, Hong Kong. A giant apelike creature and the feral woman he raised from childhood are captured on the China/India border and brought to Hong Kong. They wind up as a stadium show, and when the creature gets loose he rampages through Hong Kong, eventually climbing to the highest building to be attacked by helicopters.

King Kong Lives (1986)

Linda Hamilton, Brian Kerwin. Directed by John Guillermin. Produced by Dino De Laurentiis. Written by Steven Pressfield, Ron Shusett. This sequel to the 1976 *Kong* gives a barely alive Kong an artificial heart at an army base in North Carolina after his fall from the World Trade Center towers. A female, red-haired "Lady Kong" is discovered in Africa and brought to the US to provide Kong with a blood transfusion and, in the end, after some destruction, Baby Kong is born.

Mighty Joe Young (1998)

Charlize Theron, Bill Paxton. Directed by Ron Underwood. Written by Mark Rosenthal and Lawrence Konner, based on the original script. Disney/RKO Pictures. Rick Baker's giant ape FX are the highlight of this remake of the 1948 original.

King Kong (2005)

Naomi Watts, Jack Black, Adrien Brody, Andy Serkis. Directed by Peter Jackson. Written by Peter Jackson, Fran Walsh, Philippa Boyens, based on the original story. Universal Studios. Big-budget remake of the original. Director Jackson takes the story back to mid-1930s setting, filming it entirely in New Zealand and using special digital effects by Weta Ltd.